Holiday Isle: the Golden Era of the Manx Boarding House

Holiday Isle:
the Golden Era of the
Manx Boarding House

from the **1870s** to the **1970s**

John Beckerson

Manx Heritage Foundation

First published by the Manx Heritage Foundation 2007
Reprinted 2008
PO Box 1986, Douglas, Isle of Man IM99 1SR

Designed and typeset in Parisine by Keystroke
28 High Street, Tettenhall, Wolverhampton WV6 8QT

Printed and bound in Wales by Gomer Press Limited, Ceredigion

Cover design: Ruth Sutherland
Graphic art: David Livesey

British Library Cataloguing in Publication Data
A catalogue record for this book is available from the British Library

ISBN 978-0-9554043-1-3

To all the contributors whose memories made this book come alive.

With gratitude to the Manx Heritage Foundation for the research grant which made it possible to write the book.

To the Beckerson family for their unwavering support.

And in fond and loving memory of Harry Watterson, one-time proprietor of the souvenir shop, Peel Promenade, a friend to the author and to all who knew him.

Contents

Preface

The Island's tourist industry was once the mainstay of its economy, and in the early years of the last century hundreds of thousands of people regularly came to the Isle of Man for their annual holiday. The Island geared its entire way of life to catering for these happy holiday makers, and entrepreneurs built hundreds of boarding houses as well as dance halls, theatres and any number of amusements.

Since the advent of the package holiday and more affordable air travel, the traditional market for the Isle of Man has changed, and the huge numbers of visitors that were once the essential feature of a Manx summer are no more.

The Manx Heritage Foundation has been keenly aware that this important part of the Island's history was fast being forgotten. To try and record as much of what remained as possible, especially by means of oral history interviews with those who were involved, we were delighted that John Beckerson accepted our invitation to create as complete a record as possible of the industry over the past century. In undertaking this task he has interviewed many people from all sectors of the industry: chambermaids, cooks, landladies, grocers,

politicians and some of the visitors themselves. Many of the interviewees had personal memories which went back as far as the 1920s or '30s. The resulting interviews and archive photographs have been placed in the Manx National Heritage Library and can be accessed by anyone interested in the Island's history.

This extensive oral history project, combined with research into newspapers, Tynwald debates and other relevant documents has produced a book which gives a remarkable overview of an industry which once defined the Isle of Man.

There are many fascinating stories in this book as well as a wealth of photographs that have never before been published and anyone reading *Holiday Isle* cannot help but get close to the trials and tribulations and the joys and sorrows of being a Douglas landlady in the Golden Era of Manx tourism. Apart from being a valuable record of an important part of the Island's history, it is a highly enjoyable read.

Hon. Anne Craine MHK
Chairman, Manx Heritage Foundation

Acknowledgements

The author wishes to thank for their kind assistance:

Charles Guard, project administrator; Muriel McVaney, project audio typist and contributing local historian; Sandra Caley, Alan Franklin, Pat Griffiths, Andrea Roberts, Roger Sims and Wendy Thirkettle of the Manx National Heritage Library; Vivien Allen; John Cottier; Frank Cowin; Martin Faragher; Yvonne Cresswell; Valerie Cottle; Professor John Belchem (Liverpool University); Peter Kelly; Kit Gawne; Ray Moore; Robert 'Bob' Foster; Ruth Jeavons; Carola Rush; Hazel Bell; Professor Roy Church (University of East Anglia); Martin Caley; Derek Winterbottom and many others without whose help this book could not have been produced.

He also wishes to thank the following for their contributions to the book:

John, Phillip and Doreen Allen; Reny Ashton; Mona Atkinson; Sheilagh Barlow; Linda Barron; Jeanne Bell; Shirley Birch; Gordon and Joy Birnie; Rosalia Black; Violet Bridson; Vince Buckingham; Raina Chatel; Stuart and John Clague; Pamela Clark; Vincent and Gertie Clarke; Mary Clinton; Muriel Cottier; Megan Creer; Stella Crellin; Terry Cringle; Dave and Annette Curtis; Betty Deans; Deidre Doherty; Vanda Dudley; Alf Duggan; Letty Edgar; Brian and Carole Evans; Peter Farrant; Kathleen Gore; Sue Gowing; Hilary Guard; Margaret Hodson; Bert and June Hope; Marjorie Inman; Brian Jarvis; Audrey Jarvis; Deidre Joyce; Ivy Kaneen; Brian Keenan; Betty Kelly; Dollin Kelly; Brian King; Arthur King; Jennifer Leece; Breesha Maddrell; Olive McFee; Cyril Mulhern; Ron Needham; Frank and Christina Newbould; Beatrice, Bert and Maureen Quirk; Ronnie and Mary Rigby; Godfrey and Margaret Saxon; John and Carmel Sherlock; Dursley Stott; Julian Sullivan; Thomas Sweeney; Frank Swinnerton; Muffet Tarrant; Keith Teare; Bill Watson; Harry Watterson and Elsie Wegener.

Introduction

The Isle of Man is a small and proudly independent island in the middle of the Irish Sea. A place with many ancient traditions and a history all its own, it has also been a part of the great historical changes which affected life throughout the British Isles. During the nineteenth century, the greatest of these changes was the industrial revolution. It created a radically new way of living and working as new technologies made Britain the workshop of the world. Alongside new ways of working came new ways of enjoying leisure. Time off for workers was at first very limited but it gradually grew sufficient to sustain another great Victorian invention: the seaside holiday.[1]

Holidaymakers supported a major industry which came to employ thousands of Manx women and men and dominated the Isle of Man for a hundred years from the 1870s to the 1970s. It was a remarkable period in the Island's history and created a way of life which was very different from anything seen before or since.

Before the eighteenth century very few people visited the seaside. The sea was thought to be a miserable and dangerous place. The rich travelled for health and pleasure to inland spas, such as Harrogate and Bath, to take the waters. However, a new fashion for sea-bathing began in the 1750s and as the habit spread it benefited many seaside places. By the end of the eighteenth century resort visiting was de rigueur for the well-to-do. As Britain became richer and the number of middle-class people increased, they too started to take holidays. It was the middling classes in large numbers who created the real boom for resorts. The Isle of Man developed a little later than some English areas because it was rather inaccessible, but once a reliable steam packet company was established in the 1830s visitors came in increasing numbers. Cheap steam

Children paddling on Douglas beach, c.1895.

power made travel easier than ever before. By the 1860s there was a definite summer visiting season (often just called 'the season').

Over time the better-off working classes in certain trades and areas of the country began to win the right to holidays of their own. In the cotton districts of Lancashire this was particularly noticeable by the 1870s. This area was one of the first to establish factory work and time-keeping habits for large numbers of people. Time off was channelled into official holidays, many of which took the dates of much older festivals called 'the Wakes'. Employers accepted the Wakes because their predictable dates made workforces easier to manage. It was also easier for workers to save up when they had a definite holiday date in mind. Time off was unpaid, but rising living standards and a fall in the cost of living allowed a week away for many by the late nineteenth century. For seaside towns within reach of Lancashire this brought rapid growth.

As going away for the Wakes became the norm in the cotton districts, communities such as Douglas, Blackpool, Rhyl and Scarborough reaped the benefit. By the 1880s many Lancastrians were able to take a full week off. Visitors flowed in their thousands and a new holiday industry grew up to cater for all their wants, from entertainments to accommodation. The Isle of Man underwent a great boom as it caught up with much older resorts in a rapid space of time. A new tourist infrastructure was built to cater for the mass market. The creation of the Victoria Pier for steamers in 1872 marked the start of a building boom of promenades, boarding houses, dance-halls, theatres and rail systems, all to serve the season.

Thousands of visitors needed hundreds of boarding houses. Speculative builders were happy to play their part and there was no shortage of people keen to buy, let and run houses once they were built. In Douglas, the newly constructed Loch Promenade of 1877 and its sister project, Victoria Street, were lined with elegant terraces of hotels and boarding houses. A few landmark hotels such as the Villiers and Sefton were grand and costly to visit. Most buildings, however, were boarding houses which catered for the tastes and pockets of the middle and working classes. They employed huge numbers of people and covered street after street, rising into the upper part of town by the

View of the Victoria pier from a bedroom at the Villiers Hotel, c.1898.

1880s. Douglas alone had around 1,800 boarding houses in its heyday and there were many more in Ramsey, Port Erin, and Peel.[2] In 1873 the Island's Governor, H.B. Loch, wrote to the Home Secretary in London explaining that:

> There has been a very general progressive prosperity . . . since last season I have been informed that 100 additional lodging-houses have been either built or otherwise opened in the town of Douglas alone, each capable of containing, on average, 40 persons. These are in addition to 800 lodging-houses which existed, exclusive of hotels, previous to this year.[3]

A lot of the buildings Loch described were in the upper part of Douglas which grew extensively to meet the requirements of the summer trade.[4] The streets were closely terraced but generally attractive in appearance.[5] There was, however, a shortage of green space, a sad fact which was ignored because parks and gardens made little money for the developers.

By 1894, Manx commercial life was thoroughly suffused by tourism. One third of the Island's limited companies were directly connected to the industry which had spread into all the towns.[6] It had resulted in the capital being transferred from Castletown to Douglas. The small fishing village of Port Erin found that when it was linked to the port facilities of Douglas by rail in 1874 the developers set to work at once to build hotels and boarding houses all around the bay.[7] By the 1890s, Ramsey boasted 89 lodging houses and 9 hotels, Peel offered 53 places of accommodation, Port Erin 52 and Port St Mary 40.[8]

The local economy benefited a lot from the new prosperity. The building and provision trades flourished and employed many men. There were also a large number of jobs for women. This was unusual at the time. Boarding house keeping and catering were among the few areas where Victorian women could make a

Postcard showing Ellerslie Private Hotel and Boarding Establishment.

Postcard showing Earle Boarding House.

respectable living of their own, and many seized the opportunity that seaside resorts offered to do just that. Most boarding houses were held in women's names and a leading historian of the seaside has explained that the real substance of the industry was 'in the pockets of the women'.[9]

The heady days of the 1870s and 1880s gradually settled down as tourism was confirmed as the leading industry and employer on the Isle of Man. The years up to the outbreak of the First World War were prosperous ones. The building boom and investment in new facilities slowed down, but visitor numbers were buoyant. The best ever season was in 1913 when 634,512 people were recorded at the landing piers.[10] The demand for holidays in high season seemed almost limitless and the boarding houses were full every summer. This period would later be remembered as a golden age.

The First World War brought disaster. The industry was starved of visitors, and many landladies

1920s view of Loch Promenade from a commercial souvenir brochure.

faced financial ruin. When the government failed to look after them at all they launched a political campaign for relief and political reform which made headlines in England. Recovery came quickly after the war, but it is significant that apart from one half-finished square, not one new hotel or boarding house was built in Douglas between 1918 and 1967.[11] Nor was the once-innovative fleet of electric tramcars replaced. The Great Depression was also a struggle but despite all these worries the inter-war seasons were generally satisfactory. Local authorities spent money on improvements, and most boarding house keepers found that hard work during the summer ensured a more than adequate living. The increasing number of workers able to take paid holidays underpinned their businesses and the demand for rooms in August ran far ahead of capacity, though the season was still rather short. It was a time when the culture of holidaymaking flourished with a new emphasis on fun and freedom that made resorts lively places to live and work. Out went bathing-machines and saggy woollen costumes; in came 'mackintosh bathing' and exciting new swimwear. Suntans became fashionable and resorts seemed as busy as ever. The Island benefited from an enterprising shipping company, a tourist industry which was cheap to run (most of the debts incurred in creating it having been paid off) and a high level of support from its Tourist Board. The sort of holidays on offer changed only a little from year to year. Two of the biggest innovations were the spread of motor travel in coaches and cars – which made exploring the countryside part of the holiday experience – and cinema. The picture houses boomed, with Douglas boasting several of the latest design and new releases at the same time as London.

The outbreak of war in 1939 again wrecked business. Restrictions on movement, the requisitioning of holiday steamers and the threat of enemy submarines turned the Island into a forlorn place. However, salvation of a sort came for Manx landladies in the form of civilian internees, labelled 'enemy aliens'. These were people with connections to Axis nations, living in Britain at the outbreak of war, who were perceived as security risks and interned without trial. History has judged this policy as controversial. Although some were Fascists, many others were German Jews with pro-British sympathies who had fled the coming Holocaust. The Isle of Man became the largest internment camp in the British Isles. Whole streets of hotels and boarding houses became billets for internees or troops, many at short notice. Some proprietors were able to remain but many had to move out in haste and distress. Their premises were often damaged by careless treatment, but at least the government paid rent and there was no bombing. By the last year of conflict most innocent internees were released, and a season of sorts returned.

1930s bathing belles advertising the Alexandra Hotel, noted for its marketing.

With the coming of peace, the demand for holidays from war-weary Britons ran high. Wartime wages were good, prices were controlled and many had lots of savings but nothing to spend them on because there were almost no durable goods to buy in the shops. Holiday-making was one of the few ways to spend money for fun and to feel good. Beaches, promenades and boarding houses were once again thronged and returned to something like their former state. Nevertheless, the virtual bankruptcy caused to tourism during two wars in quick succession had taken its toll on the Isle of Man. Facilities which might have been replaced had to struggle on, looking increasingly out-dated. Demand for holidays still ran high in the 1950s but there was a growing sense that improvements had to be made. By the 1950s many of the Island's boarding houses were criticised as uncomfortable and old-fashioned. Proprietors fought back with new facilities, including interior-sprung mattresses instead of flock ones and running water instead of jugs and basins. Fortunately for domestic resorts, holidays abroad were still out of the reach of most citizens who had very few alternatives to a week or two in a boarding house.

The 1950s were the last decade when this holiday habit was the norm. In the following years, the Isle of Man, like many traditional resorts, began a long, slow decline. By the 1970s boarding houses were being converted to self-catering holiday flats, homes or offices. Those which remained had to work hard for business. Some modernised to become small hotels, others simplified their tariffs to become bed and breakfast establishments, or closed and were converted to other uses.

The world we have lost

Several excellent histories of the Isle of Man contain chapters on the visiting industry. They tell of the railways, the steamers, the dance-halls and the glens, the amusements and the crowds. However, few have anything to say about the thousands of boarding houses which were almost taken for granted. In recent years many of these fine old structures have been knocked down, leaving ugly gaps in the Island's promenades. This is a sure sign that the world they were built for no longer exists. It has gone from the Isle of Man just as the coal industry has gone from the valleys of south Wales and the cotton factories from Lancashire. Yet in its heyday the boarding houses employed huge numbers of people whose lives and stories should not be forgotten. Who were the people who lived and worked in them? What was their world like? What went on below stairs out of sight of the visitors? What did everyone do in the winter months? This book tries to answer some of these questions and is full of the memories of those who were there and who saw it happen with their own eyes.

This book studies the visitors whose arrival turned the Isle of Man from a little-known place into the playground of the north-west, changing life for ever. The challenges, joys and sorrows of working in a boarding house live again, as staff and proprietors tell their stories and reflect on a lifetime in the industry. The secrets of kitchens and dining-rooms are revealed and the menus of the past tempt the palate in a tantalising history of food. Nor is drink forgotten, for the scandal over alcohol in boarding houses which brought down a government and caused a general election is remembered, along with the hard times of both world wars. The challenge of making a living in high and low season is told by proprietors who did it. The fascinating story of the seaside architecture of the Isle of Man is illustrated with unique plans and photographs of boarding houses which have never been published before. Finally, the painful years of decline are remembered in a chapter which brings the story right up to date.

Victoria Pier, Douglas, late nineteenth century.

I ENJOYED PACKING TO COME—I'M ENJOYING PACKING WHILE I'M HERE—BUT I DON'T WANT TO PACK UP TO COME HOME

A good *holiday* and good *food*

For proprietors and visitors alike, food lay at the heart of boarding house life. Landladies knew that to keep a good table was the essence of success, and beautifully laid out dining-rooms were often used in advertising to whet the appetite for a seaside holiday.[1] Until the early 1960s, most houses served three hot meals a day and their kitchens were constantly active, so cooking dominated landladies' lives. When visitors stayed for a week and met so often in the dining-room, mealtimes were very sociable affairs. Moreover, the changing tastes of visitors regarding how and when food was served, and what dishes were offered, creates a fascinating and intimate history-within-a-history. The way in which food was consumed and in what situations was a reflection of the wider world. From the heyday of 'full board' to the invention of fast food, the story of mealtimes has a lot to say about how we once lived and how society has changed.

The 'apartment system'

It was the serving and preparation of food that distinguished boarding houses from their predecessors and gave them their name. They were preceded by the 'apartment system', as it was known on the Isle of Man. This resembled a compromise between self-catering and full board. It involved buying one's own food but giving it to the landlady to cook and serve at her table. Its origins lay in the early nineteenth century, when seaside visiting was in its infancy. At this time, well-to-do seaside visitors rented furnished suites of rooms in a house (termed apartments), purchased their own food, and had it cooked by the owner or her servants. In later years, when middle- and working-class visitors could afford to travel, the term 'apartment' survived, and the habit of giving food to the landlady to cook continued. Visitors even had their own compartments in the dining-room sideboard. This caused problems at busy times and only worked in fairly small houses because it was not easy to prepare so many different meals at the same time. It was no coincidence that the really large boarding houses on the Isle of Man were not built until all cooking was placed in the hands of the proprietor. It also helps explain why there were so many cheap restaurants and dining-rooms in Douglas in the 1870s and 1880s, many of which even opened for breakfast. They were not just for day trippers, but also for those staying on the Island whose meals were not yet included in the cost of their accommodation because full board was not then the norm.

Mrs Vanda Dudley ran the system with her mother and her sisters in a boarding house called Cornbrook in the 1920s. This was on the upper floors of a large building in the wide and centrally located Victoria Street in Douglas with a shop underneath. The house later became the Isle of Man Tourist Board offices. In the Cornbrook dining-room there stood a large wooden sideboard for the use of visitors. Within it were several compartments, each family having one to themselves to store sugar, butter, bread, jam and anything else they required. The visitors also bought their own bread and meat, and would go out at eight o'clock in the morning to Duke Street and the local grocer's shop to buy fresh bacon and eggs for the landlady to cook. Just before breakfast, the women would come to the kitchen door carrying their choice of food from the cubby-holes, a few slices of bacon and perhaps three eggs, two for their husband and one for themselves. Bacon and eggs were always served in the morning; breakfast cereals other than porridge were rare in the 1920s.[2] If bacon and eggs were insufficient, there was always bread and jam. White bread was a staple part of the working-class diet. Being cheap, filling

and portable, every family kept plenty in the sideboard. On the Isle of Man, bread with kippers and jam was an unusual breakfast favourite for some.

Mrs Dudley's family had to cope with many different meals. One person would bring chops, somebody else would bring stewing meat, somebody else would bring fish – it was difficult for her mother to manage.[3] To make it work at all most landladies simplified the system, so that only the most expensive part of the meal, such as meat or fish, was bought by the visitors.[4] Some houses then began to offer cheap and filling puddings at the end of meals, whilst still remaining partially on the apartment system. Visitors paid for their vegetables and puddings at the end of the week, and any food left behind in the cupboards when they departed was used up by the landlady.

Visitors were particular about their eggs and many would write their names on them. But Vanda Dudley remembers:

They put their names on the eggs thinking they were going to get those eggs. I was only the young one, and I said to Mum one day, 'Why do they put their names on the eggs?', and she said, 'They think they get the same eggs – but they don't. Everybody gets any eggs that happen to be there!'[5]

Gradually the old system was replaced by full board as the economics which lay behind it changed. When it began, foods such as meat, eggs, tea and jam were expensive for workers and had to be treasured.

This joke about mean landladies showed how sensitive visitors could be to any suggestion of stinting in the kitchen!

But as food became cheaper and more plentiful and living standards improved, the balance changed, the system made less sense and it was continued only out of habit. This habit did take a long time to die, and in many of Britain's northern resorts, the apartment system was in fairly common use up to the 1920s. It clung on into the 1930s in some smaller or more old-fashioned houses. But by the 1930s most new-comers to the industry were not in favour of it.[6]

The apartment system as it used to exist has almost passed out of living memory. The broadcaster Terry Cringle remembers the apartment system in operation at his parents' establishment, Studley House,

in Douglas in the 1950s. His father had trained as a ship's cook with the Steam Packet Company, and gained experience at cooking in all situations, which stood him in good stead on the promenade. Mr Cringle explained:

> The system in boarding houses in those days was that you didn't always give people full board, you didn't give them set meals which they paid for in advance. They used to bring their own food and they would give it to my mother and father, and when they wanted a meal or at mealtimes they would say 'Can you give me two of my sausages please?' or 'Can you give me one of my pork chops with some chips?'[7]

Full board

The logistics of running such a system meant that Mr and Mrs Cringle did not take very kindly to it; they thought it was a lot of work for little gain and in their second season they changed to offering full board. When full board was first offered, prices appeared to leap upwards by comparison to the old system because of the food costs involved. So, to keep the advertised price of accommodation down, landladies started to charge for 'extras'. One such habit was to charge guests for the cruet, a move which was very unpopular. In Douglas in the 1920s the charge for the cruet could be as much as 1s 6d a week.[8] A careful if more cheerful landlady even made sure that her kitchen helpers did not eat the peas they were supposed to be shelling by making them sing as they did the work, a vivid memory for those who were there.[9]

Sunday lunch

Perhaps the most popular part of the full board system was a lavish Sunday lunch. Large joints of meat were cooked and served with all the favourite trimmings including roast potatoes in place of the 'baked and boiled' of weekday fare. Sunday lunch was the heaviest meal of the week and, as one landlady remarked, 'it was heavy going' in the kitchen.[10] The heat of large coal-fired

ovens in the basement, where many seafront boarding houses had their kitchens, was stifling.

Keeping up the appearance of plenty was an important part of creating a happy holiday atmosphere. Yet to make a profit, proprietors had to be careful not to waste food or to have many leftovers. It needed a certain skill and when this was well done visitors never knew how close to the wind their landlady was sailing. One waitress recalled her work in the 1920s:

> Cook used to send me back after the visitors had finished with their main course (we didn't have a first course then). She used to send me back and she told me to go and ask them if they would like some more. I knew that there was no more in the saucepans or in the big dishes in the kitchen. I used to say 'But what if they did want more?'. But it was 'Just go and ask them!' I was scared stiff, in case they would say 'yes', they would like some more, when there was no more left for them to have.[11]

Fortunately for that young waitress her cook was generous, and always put enough on the plates so that nobody ever asked for more. However, if extra visitors turned up for Sunday lunch, cook had to send her girl at a run over to Brew's the butcher's in Castle Street, to buy a little more because meat was too expensive and perishable a commodity to waste through over-ordering.

MENU

Bass

for men

DINNER

Grapefruit Segments
Spring Vegetable Soup

Roast Manx Lamb Mint sauce
Braized Celery Carrot fingers
Roast and Boiled Potatoes

Cold Buffett
Ham, Pork with Green Salad

Pineapple sponge
Ice Cream

Cheese Board

Coffee.

A rare survival – a Belvedere Hotel dinner menu from the 1950s.

Sunday tea

Once the ritual of Sunday lunch was over, there was only a short rest for staff before Sunday tea had to be prepared. This was usually a cold collation of ham, salmon, salad and sandwiches. Salmon was popular because it gave a classy tone to the Sunday tea. Violet Bridson remembers Sunday teas at Manchester House on Empress Drive:

> I had a menu set for a week, and we never varied from it . . . so we went right through the summer and I knew

we would have a salmon salad on Sunday. You'd get the fish from Frank Curphey at the fish market, you see, and he used to come over for the order. It was always a fresh salmon bought for a Sunday and we cooked it and skinned it and cut it up and that was on a salad for the Sunday tea. Then there was a trifle or a fruit salad or something like that [for dessert].[12]

After Sunday tea there might even be a light supper later in the evening. Visitors were keen to get value for money and they usually scoffed whatever was offered to them. Those who felt they were not getting their fair share were quick to complain, as one proprietor discovered – but both parties got a surprise into the bargain, as the inspector who dealt with the case said:

> THE ATHOL HOTEL, DOUGLAS, ISLE OF MAN
>
> DOUGLAS ALLOTMENTS ASSOCIATION
>
> Wednesday, 2nd March, 1955
>
> ## HIGH TEA
>
> ### Menu
>
> Kidney Soup
> • • •
> Steamed Smoked Haddock
> • • •
> Casserole of Beef
> • • •
> Creme Potatoes
> • • •
> Cold Roast Home-Fed Turkey
> Cold Roast Manx-Fed Beef
> Cold Roast Manx Pork
> Cold Roast Manx Lamb
> Cold Boiled Home-Cured Ham
> Cold Pressed Ox Tongue
> • • •
> Salad
> • • •
> Rich Fruit Pudding and Rum Sauce
> Wine Jellies
> Ices
> • • •
> Biscuits   Cheese
> Tea

A special Athol Hotel high tea menu, 1955. Note the date in March: function catering was a useful source of income during the winter.

> For years, Mr C– gave his visitors salmon sandwiches. But one night he ran out, and this woman complained to the Tourist Board that there was no salmon sandwiches laid on. So they came to see C– and said 'Excuse me, C–, how long have you been doing these salmon sandwiches?' So he said 'Since we've been in, about ten years.' They said 'You don't have to give them those', and the woman's face dropped like a clog.[13]

Labour and the working day

Preparing huge amounts of food was hard work. The proprietress Mrs Muriel Cottier remembered that 'I never panicked, but I would certainly be everywhere'. Staff had little time to enjoy their own food before starting on the preparation of the next meal.[14] Many cooks worked straight through the season with almost no time off, relying on the winter time to recuperate. Their working day would begin at half past six. In the large promenade boarding houses, cooks sometimes had a basement bedroom near the kitchen so that they could start work early without disturbing the people asleep upstairs. Once breakfast was done, preparations for lunch began, and so the day went on, cooking almost non-stop as Mrs Elsie Wegener says:

> People, when I started, now they'd come in for all four big meals. I don't know how they could eat it. But they were coming in for afternoon

The staff of the Savoy hotel in the 1930s, showing how the proprietors, Mr and Mrs Rigby (seated), created a family atmosphere.

tea, they'd have sandwiches and scones, cakes and things and then at night it was a full dinner, seven o'clock. There was soup and grapefruits and roasts and puddings and oh, it was a long day but as I say, you weren't expecting to get time off.[15]

Staff of the Savoy hotel take a break in the kitchen in 1980. A happy family atmosphere continues, with proprietors Mary and Ronnie Rigby (right hand side) alongside staff Violet, [?] Sue Lucas and Mary Clinton.

Mrs Wegener found that she enjoyed satisfying the visitors with good food and good service. She was happy to let the younger staff go out dancing of an evening, whilst she experimented with new dishes. A cheerful kitchen was an advantage for the cook, but even in a well run large establishment there was a clear hierarchy to be obeyed. Jennifer Leece, working as a waitress in the 1950s, found herself at the bottom of the pile. Above her in rank were the two ladies who ran the still-room, 'a really high place to be . . . the rest of us couldn't go there'. Young women provided the bulk of the labour force in boarding house kitchens and worked long hours for rather low pay. Male chefs were found in larger establishments and were also important in small husband-and-wife boarding houses. Here, husbands often ran kitchens whilst wives did front-of-house work. At the Hannah family's boarding house on Bucks Road in Douglas, just after the Second World War, it was the newly demobilised Mr Hannah who kept the kitchen. His daughter recalls:

My father did the cooking and mother did the bedrooms and the tables. The kids helped out wherever they could. At that time, in that house, we took about twenty–five people, so it was hard going. I remember my father sitting every evening peeling the potatoes for the next day, and then some enterprising body started up a service delivering peeled potatoes which seemed to do very well – I remember my father being very pleased about that one.[16]

The Hannahs were still a young couple, with the energy essential to make a business thrive without hiring extra hands. The difficulty of getting staff after the war led one promenade landlady to decide almost as soon as she entered the business in the late 1950s that cooking three hot meals a day was no longer possible.[17] After taking over from her husband's mother, she was one of the first on Douglas promenade to stop offering lunches.[18]

The post-war years were also a time when a lot of new 'labour-saving' machinery arrived in the kitchen. Electric mixers were a boon, as were slicers for bacon and bread. Potato-peeling machines were also highly prized because they did away with a long and boring daily chore. After a refrigerator, a peeler was one of the most useful devices for the busy cook.[19] The Imperial Machine Company advertised that one only had to 'tip a sack of assorted potatoes into the Imperial Machine Company's model . . . and with hardly a murmur it will discharge a shiny bunch of spotless spuds'.[20] Before the coming of such machines, the Island's largest boarding house even employed a man who simply peeled potatoes all day.[21] But it was not until the 1960s that kitchen machines became cheap enough for all the small boarding houses to buy them.[22] Some machines, such as dishwashers, were so expensive that they were rarely seen in smaller houses until the 1970s.

Some of the gadget manufacturers advertised on the basis that purchasing their machines would allow proprietors to use fewer staff. One Hobart advertisement of the 1930s contrasts a sweating, elderly, dishwashing maid with a gleaming and smug Pledge dishwasher.[23] The hidden appeal of this machine, whispers the advert, is that it will not only save you money but also get rid of a person you do not want in your kitchen. In the picture, the machine stood alone,

suggesting that it somehow operated itself without any need for labour. Of course, this was not so.[24]

The real saving in the kitchen was made by combining the time-saving properties of these machines with the advantages of processed food. Refrigeration, freezing, dehydration and canning allowed sweeping changes to the way food was cooked in the 1960s as changes which had swept America ten years earlier hit the British Isles. Early processed food such as instant mash, frozen peas and tinned soup were enthusiastically bought by boarding house keepers just as housewives did the same. They were later joined by almost every ready-prepared food imaginable. All promised to save time and allow more flexible cooking. This was in complete contrast with the era up to around

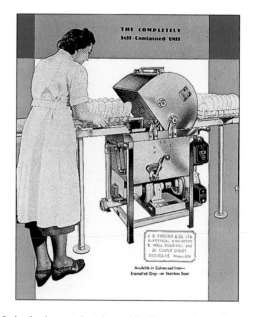

Only the largest hotels could afford costly equipment such as this dishwasher, available from J.C. Fargher & Co Ltd in the 1950s.

An immaculate corner of the Hydro kitchen, photographed for its proud proprietor Hilary Guard in 1965. It was unusual to take these sorts of photographs and this is a rare insight into the period. Note the combination of the modern oven and improved Victorian table, topped with Formica.

1960, which was a time of long hours in the kitchen making home-made meals for guests on full board.[25] Only lately has the move towards processed food begun to be questioned, as its nutritional value and broader side-effects come under scrutiny. It has also allowed kitchens to be run with fewer people.[26] The change was accompanied by cutting the number of mealtimes served each day; from three in the 1930s to two in the 1960s to (often) one in the 1980s; as boarding houses turned into guest houses and then bed and breakfast establishments.

Mealtimes

Before these changes took hold, the typical boarding house served breakfast between eight and nine; lunch (usually called dinner) about one; afternoon tea at four o'clock; and an early dinner (tea) between five and six. This was in contrast to hotels, which served the evening meal between six and eight.[27] Preparations for breakfast in an average boarding house of the 1960s started early. Mr Brian King remembers that in his parent's house in Port Erin:

> Mother would get up at six o'clock at the latest in the morning, and would have to cook a breakfast for twenty–eight people plus all the toast and everything. My brother's job, before he started on the washing–up, was to do the toast — he used to sit in front of the big toaster, which took about ten pieces of bread, and he did all the toast for the house. My mother would be alongside, cooking all the eggs and bacon and putting them on the hot plate for twenty–eight people and that was one of the jobs she would do first thing in the morning. My sister would do all the waiting–on. And it was the same at teatime: my father would be home at 5 o'clock, we'd all be home and we'd fit our meals in between the visitors'

courses or after. We used to have more or less the same as them. We'd have the egg and bacon or whatever, though it would always be the bits that were left over, but my mother would make enough for all of us and we would usually have it after them.[28]

Early dinner times were kept on the Island, and especially in Douglas, for two reasons. Firstly, they were what many visitors from the north liked at home. Secondly, they allowed visitors to begin an evening's entertainment in plenty of time. 'The rule in Douglas,' wrote an Edwardian boarding house keeper, 'is to dine when the day's outdoor pleasures are over'. Once dinner was done, dancing and the theatre would follow, to meet 'that zest for entertainment that a good dinner invariably creates'.[29] At the end of the evening many houses offered a light supper. The fixed times of these meals meant everything else had to give way to them, as Mrs Joy Birnie remembers:

> We'd see people going out of the theatre at 10 o'clock: everything had to finish at ten so they could go back and get their supper because it was included in the tariff. I remember telling my daughter this when she was in one of the shows at the Gaiety. I said, 'You know what will happen if you're after ten o'clock:

you'll see people getting up and leaving, because if they don't get to their hotel by ten or just after, they don't get their tea and biscuits.' She thought I was joking. But apparently a quarter of the people got up at about five to ten and walked out![30]

Routine

The reason that mealtimes were so rigidly fixed was to enable houses to be run as efficiently as possible. 'There was only one thing I was strict on', said a Peel landlady of the 1950s, 'and that was to be on time for meals.'[31] Nearly every boarding house displayed a card in the hallway showing mealtimes until the 1970s, and local printing companies such as the Norris Modern Press printed such cards by the thousand because everyone used them.[32] So fixed was boarding house routine that when a Scotch Week pageant was put on in the grounds of the Nunnery estate in Douglas in 1930, its organisers had to make a special appeal to all the hotel and boarding house proprietors to serve lunch on the day at 12.30, in order that visitors could arrive at the Nunnery in good time.[33] As a young man, Mr Terry Cringle had to sound the dinner gong in his parents' establishment, and remembers the ritual well.

Mealtimes [at Studley House] were always notified by a gong, a genuine Burmese gong . . . you'd start hitting it in the middle, then you'd slowly work out in concentric circles, rather

as if you'd dropped a pebble in a pool, and doing it louder and louder so the volume would build up so the thing would be echoing right through the house. It was something which really characterised those days, because everybody had the same mealtimes, unless there was a late dinner which was probably about half past seven.

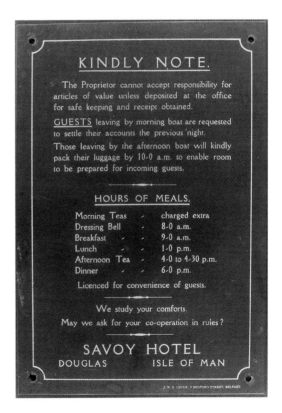

With a meal every four hours, guests at the Savoy had no chance of going hungry in this late 1950s notice. As long as they kept to the rules!

Hours of meals at the Hydro in the 1970s. Note how afternoon tea has been cancelled – the world of the boarding house was changing fast.

Hours of Meals	Varied **Table d'Hôte** Menu	
BREAKFAST	9 a.m. - 9.30 a.m.	
LUNCHEON	1 p.m. - 1.30 p.m.	
~~AFTERNOON TEA~~	~~4 p.m. - 4.45 p.m.~~	
DINNER	6 p.m. - 6.30 p.m.	
SUPPER	9.30 p.m. - 10.30 p.m.	
Wednesdays—Dinner 1 p.m.	High Tea 5.30 p.m.	
Sundays—Dinner 1 p.m.	High Tea 5.30 p.m.	

Dining Room closed 10.30 p.m.

Packed Lunches available upon request

Telephone : Douglas 6870 (STD Code 0624)   **Guests : Douglas 4167**

Telegrams : Hydro, Douglas, Man

Tea was always at 5.30, so the 5.30 tea people, they'd all be there at the same time. Dinner at one o'clock . . . right along the Promenade you could hear the gongs going.[34]

Even at the up-market Empress Hotel, where Mr Gordon Birnie worked in the early 1960s, many still kept to the traditional ways. He saw how this affected the way guests could spend their time in between.

An awful lot in those days were booking dinner, bed and breakfast or full board, so they literally would take their kids out on the prom, have breakfast, take the kids out on the prom for three or four hours, come back, have lunch, go out onto the prom again with the kids, bring the kids back . . . the dinners don't go on like they do now. It was more regimented.[35]

As Mr Birnie implied, it was no longer obligatory to take full board. During the 1960s an increasing number of visitors became enthusiasts for flexible mealtimes and the freedom to take lunch elsewhere. Some seafront houses introduced beach-trays, provided by the cook, which for a time were very popular.[36] Packed lunches also became common.[37] It also became easier to invite friends to one's boarding house for a meal or a drink.

There has been a great change over the years in the availability of alcohol. Very few Victorian boarding houses on the Island were permitted to serve their own beer with meals. (Wine with meals was only for the wealthy at this time.) Some were even run on temperance principles. Others wanted to sell liquor, but the temperance movement and many members of the Manx government strongly opposed any such move. The battle for and against booze was a tumultuous and long-running one which pitched many boarding house keepers into the centre of political debate. It was not until after the Second World War that licensing became widespread, but even in the 1960s there were many establishments which were still 'dry'. By this point the

Wartime tea coupons – guests had to bring their own and give them to the proprietor.

decision not to serve was rarely made from temperance principles but because it was not worthwhile to run an expensive bar for only a few people.

War and rationing

Both world wars were traumatic times for the Manx holiday industry and there were food shortages in both conflicts. Grainger's Café in Peel stayed open throughout the Second World War and was one of the few places to do so; it served visitors to the internment camps and the soldiers who worked there as well as locals. Mrs Bea Quirk, who worked in the kitchen, had to make sure that only one in three of its main meals was allowed to contain pork, beef or lamb. The remainder had to contain either fish or poultry, which weren't rationed. The government also demanded that a pound of precious tea had to serve 240 people and the café had to send returns of what it had served to the food control office to prove that it was running correctly.[38] If a food inspector turned up unexpectedly and found that portions were too big then a harsh fine could be imposed.

Even with the return of peace after the Second World War, rationing went on for years and post-war holidaymakers had to bring ration books with them. The 1948 official ration for perishable foods per adult was two pints of milk, two ounces of cheese, seven ounces of fat, one ounce of bacon, one egg and around one shilling's worth of meat.[39] The Isle of Man Publicity Board explained that the import and export of food into the Island was controlled; but told visitors that they could bring food for their own use as long as they didn't come with the intention of selling it.[40] It was a far cry from Edwardian abundance. Nevertheless, the black

Girls from 99 Squadron Royal Signals outside the Rutland Hotel, 1944. A change from the pre-war happy holiday gang, but there is still something of the old spirit in the air, despite wartime worries.

market seems to have been remarkably effective in making a Manx holiday just a little more tasty! Boarding house keepers eagerly sought out hard-to-obtain commodities on the black market whenever they could.[41] One hotelier's post-war pride was to have a big bowl of sugar on every table.[42] At £9 a hundredweight it cost him a lot, but guests loved it.

A side-effect of the conflict was that it made seaside property very cheap. As a result, Mrs Muriel Cottier was able to buy a boarding house at a very reasonable sum, but making it work under food rationing was not easy. She remembers:

When we first started in 1946, the rationing was still on and we couldn't give a dinner every day, because you didn't have enough meat rations. So it used to be that on Sunday, Tuesday and Thursday we did dinner, full board, and the other days we did tea, bed and breakfast. You couldn't serve meat every day because everything was still rationed. You couldn't have bacon every day, and butter was rationed too, so we used to put their own rations of butter on the tables for them and say 'that's your butter ration for the week,' and 'when that's gone, you'll have to have marge'. But we had to do that, because otherwise we would never have had enough. I remember we used to hold the visitors' ration books. The inspectors used to come round every so often and they'd do you and count up your coupons and all that sort of thing.[43]

Shortage of meat caused the most problems because the traditional British meal of meat and two veg. made little sense without it.[44] Whale-meat companies advertised to hoteliers but nobody liked the stuff much.[45] What little could be found of the normal meats had to go a long way. Ted Pullen at Westlake's Sea Level was known for his carving skills and 'he had a butcher's knife that looked about three foot long', remembers an old colleague. 'He would be cutting haunches of beef so thin that you could read the newspaper through them!'[46] Another boarding house keeper remembers how his neighbour was

. . . 'in' with a local farmer. He used to buy a cow every so often, or half a cow, and I got half a cow one day too. It was on the back kitchen floor which was a stone floor and I'd got three or four boarding house

people there having some of it because there was too much for me. Fortunately, my brother-in-law happened to be a butcher, and we had the big scales going. Suddenly the real butcher came in with a week's supply of meat, which was only a few pounds of cuts and a round of beef — he came down the back kitchen steps — he saw this babble going on and all this meat on the floor. So he took his meat and he threw it down and swore at us. But you had to do your best back then. I found that if I spent a few quid a week extra on [black market] food, I'd more than get a return in the number of visitors, so it paid off.[47]

For the black market to work, one had to have good local connections. For those new to the Island, such as Margaret Hodson who settled in Peel just after the war, the butcher was the sole source of supply. After years of munitions work in cities, Mrs Hodson had a pleasant surprise from the kindly Manx tradesmen in her first week as a boarding house keeper:

I ran down Christian Road and down Well Road Hill with the ration books to the butcher's [to place an order]. Now, coming from England, our ration for meat was 1s 2d per person per week. When the butcher said to me 'Would you like something now?', well, had there been a lottery, I would have thought I'd won it! I came back home with sausages and braising-steak and liver. I just could not believe it when he said what would I like for the weekend? We really thought we were in paradise![48]

With all sorts of food in short supply, some ingenuity was called for to make meals look appetising. Muriel Cottier, at Ferndale on Central Promenade, couldn't get her usual fresh salmon, but she managed to find a supply of the tinned sort.

You used to get tinned salmon, as you couldn't get the red salmon. So you got the pink salmon and you reddened it up by adding a bit of cochineal or something like that and it made it look better. Then of course you could serve that for tea with salad. Food was scarce then . . . it certainly wouldn't satisfy a person, especially a man or a youngster.[49]

There were all sorts of austerity meals, from the famous Woolton Pie (named after the English Minister

of Food) to recipes for 'cream' made from semolina, or gelatine, sugar, vanilla and milk.[50] Another tactic was to buy eggs in winter time when they were more plentiful and preserve them in water-glass until the summer.[51] But there was no complete way around the ration; people accepted this and did the best they could. Boarding house keepers had to juggle thirty or more ration books for even a modest establishment. It was a relief when at long last the ration books could be thrown away in the 1950s and holiday food was once again plentiful.

Quality

In the ideal boarding house, portions were big, food was fresh and it tasted home-cooked. When the seventeen-year-old Lancashire lad Thomas Thurman took his first ever holiday away from home in the 1890s, he wrote to his parents with all the relish of a hungry teenager about the food he had eaten in Douglas.

We have thirty-five boarders in this house, and we all sit down at the same table, at the same time, to meals. Breakfast, at 9.30: fish, turkey, duck, fried eggs and ham etc, with butter, bread and jam to finish off with, and tea. Dinner, 1.30, has four or five courses. Specimen: tomato soup, fish, peas, potatoes and game, pudding, stewed fruit and custard. For tea: tongue, eggs, ham, other cold meats, butter, bread and jam. Supper is a grand assortment . . . I am enjoying myself immensely.[52]

The illustrations below show the sort of rooms in which Thomas Thurman and his friends might have dined. They were always set with the best glass and silver plate that a proprietor could afford and often looked remarkably fine. The well-known firm of Mappin and Webb offered 'thoroughly reliable silver plate and cutlery for boarding houses' of the sort which can be seen on these tables.[53] The dining-rooms, like the rest

of the houses, were at their best until the beginning of the First World War. In the 1930s, a few proprietors modernised and went with the new styles but many did not. The boarding house market was a very cautious and traditional one and the art deco age virtually passed it by. 'Just recently,' noted an hoteliers' newspaper in those years, 'some "ultra-modern" crockery designs have been introduced. These may be very novel, but an hotelier should carefully consider if he could live with them.'[54] It seemed that both plates and the food that went on them were best kept traditional and plain.

When new boarding houses of ever-larger size were being built in the 1880s and 1890s, the problem

Crookall's Imperial Restaurant interior in the late nineteenth century. The table settings and room decorations reflect the Victorian love of ornament and decoration. The table here is set at its best and would not be like this every day.

The (Douglas) Hydro dining room, photographed around 1900. A long exposure with a glass plate camera gives this fairly dark room backing onto a cliff a charming luminous quality, and the photo was used for many years. A close look will show the art deco lights added to the photo by hand in the 1930s, to make the hotel appear more up-to-date without the cost of taking a new photograph.

Ramsey Hydro's dining room, c.1900. With the latest in gas lighting and classical decoration, this high-class dining room photograph was designed to tempt guests to this new and, at the time, slightly isolated hotel.

STILL ROOM "GRASMERE"

The still-room (plating-up, washing up and china storage area) at the Grasmere Hotel in the 1950s. An evocative and very rare photo. Note the Edwardian salt cellars and silverplated toast racks and teapots, combined with modern facilities such as stainless steel table tops and dishwashers.

of serving in their large dining-rooms became pressing. New inventions such as gas-fired bains-marie and hot cupboards were bought to keep food warm. Dumb waiters were also used and many large boarding houses had a pair installed to link basement kitchens with still-rooms above. The still-room became an important adjunct to the kitchen. Here, soup, sauces, meat and plates could be prepared ahead of mealtimes and kept hot until required whilst the kitchen worked on more delicate foods such as vegetables which were sent up at the last minute. Some places plated up entire meals and kept them in the hot cupboards until serving, though this was not good for flavour and the best cooks frowned on it as it was bad for quality.[55]

Whether or not the food on offer in a Manx boarding house was well spoken of had a real impact on the success or failure of the business. Multiplied by hundreds of houses, it was an important issue for the Island as a whole and this was well known by the Victorians. As the *Isle of Man Examiner* pointed out in 1899,

Our reputation is much dependent on the reputation of the guest-houses, and at present the latter is phenomenally high. English visitors grumble at many things in Douglas, but one almost never hears a grumble about the catering in Douglas hotels and boarding-houses.[56]

The ID card of Tourist Board Inspector, Frank Swinnerton.

Sadly, this was not always true. Visitors have complained about the food for as long as the Isle of Man has boasted a tourist industry. In the height of the season it was hard to keep food fresh before refrigeration became common. Local food suppliers were flooded with orders and there were always some unscrupulous tradesmen prepared to take advantage. As late as 1933, a Douglas butcher was severely fined for selling meat unfit for human consumption. The High Bailiff, passing sentence, reminded the court that in a seaside resort 'only the best' food should be given to visitors.[57] Nor did the increasing availability of cheap processed food solve the problem, because not all proprietors used it well. One unhappy visitor told a government researcher in 1951 that the vegetables in his boarding house seemed to consist of nothing but tinned peas, day after day.[58] The Tourist Board began to concern itself with the quality of establishments after the Second World War and by the 1970s it employed visiting officers to look into complaints. One officer was Mr Frank Swinnerton, who early in his career planned to eat incognito at an hotel which had been the subject of several complaints. Casually, he mentioned the idea to a colleague, only to receive the unnerving reply, 'I don't think you should take unnecessary risks

like having lunch there'. Some time later, recalls Mr Swinnerton, 'when I came to inspect the kitchens I began to see what he was talking about . . . there were awful things'.[59] Even when cooking was not actually done under unhygienic conditions, the result was often a little dull. 'Is it any wonder,' asked one newspaper critic, 'that English cooking has the reputation for being the worst in the world?'[60] She went on to say:

There are a great number of women keeping boarding-houses, small hotels and inns, who take little or no trouble about the details of their [food] buying and catering, and know less than they ought to about cooking, leaving it entirely in the hands of a so-called good plain cook, with emphasis on the plain; often a woman of no imagination or skill, who knows but one way of cooking any one thing.[61]

Fortunately, such broadsides were fairly rare. The official enquiries of the 1950s found that, 'generally speaking, the standard of food . . . offered by hotels and boarding-houses in the various resorts of the Isle of Man is satisfactory having regard to the low tariff charged'.[62] In other words, it was okay for the cheap price. Low tariffs did make it hard to keep up the quality, especially in a small house where only one or two people did all the work. Growing up in a boarding house in one of the lower-priced parts of Douglas in those years, June Hope remembers how her hard-working parents had to cram in the cooking between everything else.

There was breakfast, a hot lunch and high tea, so it was a round of dishes, peeling potatoes, making beds, and of course later on you'd come home from school and it would be, 'I'm sorry your bedroom has gone again,' because it was just so crowded.[63]

The whole Hope family would be pressed into service at busy times. During the TT, hot lunches were replaced by packed lunches for visitors who were keen to stay at the racecourse all day. To prepare all these lunches was a job in itself. The night before every race the whole family made up a sandwich production line in the kitchen; one person buttering, one slapping on ham and cheese, one putting the sandwiches in a bag and another one adding apples and biscuits. This way, the Hopes were able to satisfy their visitors. On the Isle of Man, where almost everyone had an interest in tourism, the quality of boarding house food became a matter of public pride. No less a person than the Speaker of the House of Keys went on record in 1951 to claim that, 'there is no other resort in the British Isles where the visitor gets such good service and such good food – at such low prices – as he does in the Isle of Man'.[64] Places such as the Hydro on Queen's Promenade even printed testimonials from visitors in their advertising, emphasising that it kept a 'first rate table' with 'everything of the best'.[65] Many landladies vividly remember the pleasure that their visitors took in good food and enjoyed doing their best for them.[66] The Compton, on Clarence Terrace, even offered guests honey from its own hives.[67]

Homemade

The love of homemade food was strong in many of the Island's small boarding houses, and retired cooks often mourn the end of homemade food and the coming of ready made dishes. Many took great pride in making almost everything themselves, however long it took.[68] Mrs Muffett Tarrant of Peel remembers that, in the 1970s, 'for my first two years when we had tea I used to make all the cakes, I don't know now how I did it, but I did it. Do you know, I enjoyed it'.[69] To offer homemade cakes when bought ones were cheaper was a way of showing pride in one's skills and they were popular with visitors. Homemade cakes also represented an *idea* – of homeliness and friendliness. They were a potent symbol that for the landlady the boarding house was more than just a business; it was something of them- selves. Keeping up this high standard could take a lot of time and worry, as Mrs Ivy Kaneen experienced in her Peel boarding house in the 1960s. 'The cooking took a long time to do because again everything was fresh', she found. 'People in the larger houses then were starting to get tins of everything; but I always felt I was failing somehow if I did that.'[70] The attraction of homemade food continued to be a pillar of some successful hotels on the Island. At the Imperial in Douglas, Shirley Birch and Jeanne Bell kept up the old ways for the old reasons and their customers loved it. As Shirley noted:

> It's all homemade. I cook like my Mum did, and make my own tarts and my own steak pie. When you do the homemade things, people know. I think they go down very well. I make as many things as I possibly can. Going right through it [the menu], a lot is very homemade. I cook all the meats, it's all with nice gravy and it's all proper food, it's proper, old-fashioned, good, wholesome food. People like the plain cooking really, to be honest. I think nowadays that families come who are usually all out at work and they all live on frozen stuff; so they come here and get a proper meal.[71]

Quantity and price

Generous portions and a 'proper meal' were always vital to the 'food culture' of the boarding house. In the past, food was much more expensive relative to income than it is today. The rapid growth of the tourist industry in the late nineteenth century created new problems for the Island's food supply system and made summer prices even higher. Yet winter demand was tiny by comparison. A commentator of the 1870s reported:

> With the great influx of visitors — they now number more than a hundred thousand each season — has come a greater demand for many articles which the Island is unable to produce in sufficient quantity, and this has naturally led to increased imports, and to increased prices . . . but even yet Douglas may compare favourably with most watering places. Beef and mutton may generally be had at about 10d per lb; potatoes 8d per stone; cod fish are seldom more than 3d per lb; and that greatest blessing to Manxmen, the herring, from a halfpenny each to any number for a shilling, according to the success of the fishings.[72]

The Isle of Man government's commission of enquiry into local industries in 1878 reported the difficulties which the Island's small farmers experienced in supplying the new large boarding houses during the season. Dairy farmers were faced with a particular dilemma, because if they expanded to meet August levels of demand, milk would go to waste for the rest of the year.[73] The commissioners also mused on whether tourism contributed to food supply problems in another way, by drawing labour away from fishing and farming.[74] Some farmers tried to smooth out fluctuations in demand by forging alliances with particular boarding houses and bypassing wholesalers altogether. There were even a few entrepreneurial landowners who bought boarding houses, supplying them with produce from their own farms.[75] Despite all these moves there was, ultimately, no alternative to importing food in the summer, much of it from Ireland.[76]

The reason food had to be imported was so that boarding houses could offer generous portions at a low price. It was an essential part of the holiday formula and generous portions made visitors feel that they were getting value for money. Proprietors knew that this was an attraction and made much of it in their advertising. The St Elmo went straight for the stomach with its advertising slogan in the hungry Great Depression era when it claimed: 'Good food, and plenty of it!'[77] Milne's Waverley also boasted 'good food, well cooked, and plentiful helpings'.[78] Standard phrases such as 'ample catering' and 'generous table' were nearly always found in boarding house publicity from the 1880s to the 1970s. Advertisements targeted at proprietors by the Shredded Wheat company even claimed that serving the food would 'satisfy those holiday appetites'.[79] When competing with the boarding houses, Cunningham's Holiday Camp advertised 'unlimited' helpings of food as a unique attraction.[80]

Visitors were quick to complain when portions seemed mean. Jokes about boarding house food were never very far from the lips of comics, but they infuriated seaside hotel and boarding house keepers to the point of red-hot rage. It is true that the 1955 Isle of Man Visiting Industry Commission found instances of insufficient portions in a few cases.[81] But this would have horrified most who worked in boarding houses, who maintained a sense of pride in their generous portions, and in the fact that their visitors were never stinted.[82] Remembering generous late suppers in the late 1950s, one remarked wryly of his visitors: 'They never missed that supper at all, I've got memories of that and I sometimes thought, 'My God they're like pigs at a trough some of them'. That's the way they were.'[83]

Another put it more gently, saying 'I don't know how they could eat it all!'[84]

Food fads

Human nature being what it is, some visitors were inevitably faddish about their food. Their odd requests still live in the memory of those who had to cope with them. One retired hotelier who accommodated over two hundred guests at a time has always treasured an eye-popping letter which arrived from a concerned mother in Eccles one morning in the 1950s. It ran:

My son Stanley is coming to stay at your hotel for his holiday, he is coming with Mr Ellard, 23rd July to Aug. 6th. I hope you won't be offended by what I am about to ask you. You see, Stanley is not really funny over meals, but he does not like best butter, he would rather starve than eat it, and he will only have one kind of margarine and that is Echo. Believe me, I have done my utmost to give him other kinds, but he knows before he eats it and then he won't have it. If you can't get it for him, would you please let me know, as I would willingly send some along with Mr Ellard when they come for their holidays. I daren't let Stanley know I have written to you, he would have a shock. He would say I was insulting you, but I am very far from trying to do that. You see, last year they had very good digs in Blackpool, but he

"Good Board Here!"
"Yes, tastes like Sawdust!"

Although most landladies were on the best of terms with their guests, those who were stern were the butt of many a joke, such as this card of the 1930s.

was hungry all the time because he wouldn't tell his landlady, he had no bread all week.[85]

Tourist Board complaints officer Frank Swinnerton had to deal with another visitor for whom potatoes seemed to be the paramount concern:

One chap fell out with quite a reputable hotel because he couldn't get the potatoes cooked the way his little child wanted them. We had a five-page letter on these blasted boiled potatoes and it went through every permutation. First, what happened the first day when they complained about the boiled potatoes and his child would only eat mashed potatoes. Then the second day, when the chef produced mashed potatoes, was all right. But on the third day they went back to boiled potatoes again. When he sent for the chef, the chef said 'Oh well, the kid didn't eat the bloody mashed potatoes the first time'. We had five pages on those potatoes. Then at the bottom of the letter came the magic paragraph, 'and by the way they're running the place as a brothel. We occupied a room on the upper floor and we were disturbed all night by men tramping up and down'![86]

Local and familiar food

Fortunately, most holidaymakers were not faddy nor so hard to please. However, many visitors preferred to eat the familiar meals which they knew at home, and this longstanding social trend is still seen in the 'British pubs' of modern Mediterranean resorts. A group of young men visiting the Island for Oldham Wakes in the summer of 1881 were no different. Being of moderate means, they stayed in the upper town at 5 Circular Road and were catered for under the apartments system. One night they decided to feast as far as their money would permit. One of the party recorded the evening in his diary:

After dinner we decided to have a good old Oldham potato pie, so we sent out for five lbs of beef between the twelve of us, and directed the landlady how to cook it. Presently we were seated round the table, ready for the 'feed'. The door flew open and in came the pie, and the landlady at the back of course. But alas! It was only half cooked! Our disappointment was terrible; and every mouth that had watered about five minutes before now dried up as if it had a red hot cinder in it.[87]

After this disaster the party took most of their meals at supper-rooms or a nearby pigs-trotter shop.[88] They also ventured out early in the morning to Douglas fish market for their breakfast kippers or mackerel which were sent to the kitchen for their landlady to cook. Kippers, oysters, tripe, trotters and haslet were popular among many hard-up Edwardian visitors, because they offered bulk and flavour for a very low price. Oysters on the Isle of Man were a treat for many, as *Brown's Holiday Guide* of 1878 remarked: 'Oysters, though not wholesome during the summer months, are so plentiful as to become a nuisance, and the quantity of these bivalves which daily disappear must be something astounding.'[89]

Oysters as they were served on the street in Douglas were a working-class fast food. The Isle of Man was essentially a working-class resort by the 1880s and it remained so for many years. A landlady of the early 1960s knew how social background affected the kind of food which her guests liked, and admitted straight-forwardly:

It's not a high-cuisine place, it's ordinary working-class people that come. Now, if I did turkey, there were always cheese and biscuits and condiments on the table, and afterwards one visitor might say to me 'that was nice jam you put with the crackers'. You know, they didn't know that was the cranberry for the turkey. You couldn't put all fancy food down, because they wouldn't

know what the heck it was. I'm not
being funny.⁹⁰

Another, reflecting on a long career, said, 'I don't
remember my food becoming any more sophisticated
. . . it was just home cooking and I think that was the
way it was in all the boarding houses. Just good home
cooking. It seemed to go down well'.⁹¹

Deliveries

Before refrigerated and frozen foods, deliveries had
to be made to boarding houses almost daily. In the
1880s a multitude of small traders made the rounds of
boarding houses. A memorable figure was the tiny 'Aunt
Anne' McAleary, who sold Irish eggs at Douglas market
on Saturdays and during the week carried her basket of
eggs around the boarding houses, and who collected
leftovers from the kitchens to help the very poor.⁹²
Gradually small street traders such as McAleary were
driven out of business by shops which could deliver
larger quantities of food at lower prices. Many shops
opened long hours in the season and served the
boarding houses well into the evening. Many farmers
also delivered direct to boarding houses because they
were such large purchasers. In the years before the
Second World War, the food delivery system was highly
developed. Landlady Violet Bridson found she hardly
had to go out for food at all.

I didn't need to go out shopping very
much those days. Quirk the bakers,
they used to come for the orders, and

Quirk the butcher in the Esplanade
too. They used to come every teatime
for the order of meat for the next
day. The grocer came once a week,
as well, so you seldom went out at
all for anything. The farm produce,
potatoes, cabbage and so forth, we
got from Clague's, Ballagawne . . .
a hamper full of peas and sacks of
potatoes which were all stacked in the
little shed in the yard.⁹³

When working as a grocer in the late 1940s, Mr
Harry Watterson used to make urgent deliveries to the
Loch Promenade boarding houses as late as 11pm on a
Saturday night.⁹⁴ Before refrigeration, food went off
very fast and so there was a need for a constant stream
of deliveries as only a little amount of perishable stuff
could be kept in stock:

Before the fridge, the whole thing
was organised on a daily basis
because you couldn't [keep] anything
. . . so it was a daily cycle. Fresh
bread every day, fresh fish on
fish days, fresh meat on whichever
day it came . . . the volume and
the activity were enormous. The
place was always full of bustle
and people were forever passing
through.⁹⁵

Smaller establishments might not need daily deliveries, so it was up to the proprietor to shop for food. The landlady of one of Peel's Marine Parade houses would go out on her bicycle in the evening to get the next day's food because the shops stayed open late in summer. 'It was,' remembers another, 'like shopping for a large family. We never had any supermarkets to go to. We used to have to buy locally . . . we didn't have anything pre-packed.'[96] Ivy Kaneen remembers how she kept food fresh before the fridge:

> You had to have deliveries every day because you just didn't keep things. We all along the Promenade had what we called a food–safe in the back yard, against the wall where the sun never hit. We kept food in there, but it wasn't like a fridge, and you had to be very, very careful. Milk was another problem, and I thought it was wonderful when I got a fridge in, it made everything so much easier. Mind you, I think there is more food poisoning today with fridges than there was then. I think people must have taken more care with food.[97]

Hidden horrors

The Isle of Man holiday industry suffered many bad patches through the twentieth century. Two world wars ruined many proprietors and many seasons were only just long enough for the resort to be viable. As a result, there was not much money to spend on repairs and renewals to buildings. That which was spent usually went on rooms which guests could see. Staff quarters and kitchens tended to be left until last and a maintenance backlog had built up on the Victorian buildings even by the 1930s. Many kitchens in particular became out of date. Modifications to massive coal-hungry ranges began to be made after the First World War and the coal strikes of the 1920s. Efficient stoves by Rayburn or the Ideal company were a popular choice. But the need to spend as little as possible was often a stumbling block. When Ideal stoves were installed, they were often placed in front of the old cast iron ranges which were too costly to rip out. Gas stoves were often fitted without a flue and this could make an unpleasant smell of town gas and cooking rise to floors above. Only vigorous daily cleaning could keep basement kitchens sweet. The 1950s picture on the next page of the kitchen of the Grasmere hotel, though spotless, reveals how a less perfectionist proprietor than Hilary Guard could have been overcome by the 'pipes, old and new, both gas and water, wending their dusty, grease-collecting progress through space' in the gloomy basement.[98] The problem remained that most proprietors either did not want to spend money on modernising kitchens or could not afford to do so.[99] Not until the 1970s did the pace of improvement speed up as modern equipment became a little more affordable and new hygiene regulations forced hoteliers to meet ever-stricter standards.

SECTION OF "GRASMERE" KITCHENS

The Grasmere Hotel kitchens in the 1950s. Two basement rooms have been knocked into one and fitted with the latest gas cookers, electric food mixers and refrigerators.

Change in perspective

The type of meals served in most British seaside boarding houses remained unchanged for almost a hundred years from the 1870s to the 1970s. But by the end of that period, even small establishments began to sense two distinct changes. The first was customer desire for more variety in food. The second was a demand for greater flexibility of mealtimes. To stop serving lunches was easy enough, but flexible mealtimes and more varied menus posed greater difficulties. It was the drive to make these changes that lies behind many of the histories told in this chapter. Until about the 1970s, guests were content to have roasts, pies and stews, thought tinned grapefruit was sophisticated and placed a premium on big portions. Now, new standards of choice and quality are more important than ever.[100]

When the long-term decline of the Manx holiday industry became obvious, a great deal of the blame was levelled at some seaside hotels which had failed to modernise. No doubt a few establishments served poor food, but in most it was probably no different from the diet that many visitors ate at home. Many places tried hard to serve the very best they could. The food improvement problem was most cruelly felt by small establishments, where kitchen facilities made it hard to cook many different menus at the same time. The need to control staff costs meant that it was also hard to draft in more labour to prepare food of higher quality or greater variety.

Other changes have been driven by new technology. Refrigeration changed menus as well as buying habits and was technically possible by the 1910s, but not until the 1950s did fridges become small and cheap enough for smaller businesses to afford them. Just after the war it was a major business decision to get a fridge.[101] Fridges and freezers revolutionised cooking for boarding house proprietors.[102] Frozen vegetables were welcomed despite nostalgia for the old ways. Frozen meat was also accepted quickly. Many who worked during the 1960s remember the enthusiasm with which they first embraced the novelty of convenience and frozen foods. For a time there was a tangible enthusiasm for whatever the processed food industry had to offer. In 1967 a convention of the Island's landladies gathered at the Villa Marina to learn of the latest marvels which science had brought to the boarding house kitchen. A Nestlé demonstrator, the appropriately named Mr Tester, gave a demonstration of how to cook for only 8s 6d per head per day. Dried foods of every kind, including powdered potato, egg, and dehydrated cabbage – which would keep for over nine months – were on offer. Mr Tester reminded his audience that 'many people say you can't beat the old ways in cooking, but this is an age when time is money'.[103]

Having revealed the speed by which his dehydrated horrors could be prepared, he went on to reveal his pièce de résistance: monosodium glutamate. Under the trade name Fondor, this wonder additive was especially designed, he said, for those such as smokers who had ruined their palates and complained that food had no taste. Flavour enhancers had arrived, and many more chemicals followed. Preservatives, colours, thickeners, stabilisers and chemical food scents flooded into all kinds of foods. There were still many who were keen on home cooking, but time shortages in the kitchen were enough to tempt even the unwilling away from the old ways. As Mr Tester pointed out: 'The company . . . is trying to show the small boarding house keeper that it is possible to whip up some excellent meals for their guests and also have some time off for themselves.'[104]

Now, it seems that the pendulum has begun to swing back once more to an emphasis on wholesomeness and freshness, and home-style cooking commands a premium price.[105] However, guest houses face a lot of competition and guests are more likely to eat out than ever. The changes are told by Mr John and Mrs Carmel Sherlock, who traded on Christian Road in Douglas during the 1980s:

In the early days when we came in, first it was all evening meal, very few people ate out. But through the years now it has changed. People will tend to eat out more, and with that there's a lot more restaurants and a lot more choice. People didn't have the choice ten years ago, and you had to do an evening meal to get the business. This year we are just doing B&B. For the past three years we did evening meal on an optional basis and we found it varied: some days we might have only two or three people for dinner. It's not very profitable just having two people for dinner, so with the choice of restaurants now, we think we will be all right just to do B&B.[106]

The invention of variety

The 'invention of variety' was one of the key movements that turned yesterday's boarding house into today's small hotel or 'B&B'. Some have become small hotels by retaining dining-rooms, bars and function rooms and catering for the demanding modern market. Others have returned to the core business of straightforward bed and breakfast from which the boarding houses evolved. Maureen Quirk recalls that when she first came into the business:

There would be fifty—four breakfasts just slammed out, and fifty—four dinners slammed out . . . well you know, not slammed out, but wham, bam, thank you ma'am, until half—past—five, and by six o'clock the dining—room had gone. Everything that you would normally serve on a breakfast plate would go out in those days, and people took it, and if they didn't want it they just left it on the plate, because it was all plated up

apart from eggs which were the last thing to go on. But now because you do a choice, the range of variations on breakfast is incredible. And we often laugh and say whatever happened to the days when you just served bacon, egg, sausage, tomatoes, mushrooms and fried bread, and nobody changed it.[107]

As Mrs Quirk explained, multiple choices did not fit the way things were once run in busy establishments, where the ideal was routine, efficient and predictable catering with as little waste as possible. She went on to explain that in the 1960s:

A lot of people when they first came in would ask you every day what [the food] was — although you had a paper on the wall to say, and if they didn't look at that you had to say what you were serving that day. If they didn't like it they'd say 'Oh I don't like that', and the alternative then was a salad. That was it.[108]

Up to this point many boarding houses operated a fixed menu which went round once a week and stayed the same almost all the season. When more people began to take a fortnight's holiday hoteliers had to introduce more variety. Young entrants to the business were among the first to bring in changes. When Ronnie Rigby took over the Savoy from his parents, he introduced a fortnightly menu in place of his mother's weekly one.[109] The increased popularity of breakfast cereals also made for more variety at breakfast-time. Manufacturers such as Weetabix promoted their products by claiming that proprietors could offer variety at almost no trouble.[110]

The boarding house is now a memory, and in its place are bed and breakfast establishments, hotels and self-catering flats. All three types of holiday accommodation are defined in large measure by the type and price of food they offer. This is no accident. The history of food at Britain's seaside holiday resorts is completely interwoven with the larger history of the towns and their inhabitants, permanent and seasonal. During the later period of this history, changes in boarding house food were driven by three interlocking forces which came from society at large. First, a changing British palate; second, the invention of new food preparation and preservation technologies; and third, the price and availability of labour in the kitchen. But some things remained sacred, and perhaps the last word should go to the son of one successful hotelier, who remembers how:

> They never actually got round however to having breakfast, lunch and dinner. It was always, breakfast, dinner and tea.[111]

Edwardian afternoon tea as it would have been set at the Savoy Hotel, c.1900.

YOU CAN'T DO THAT THERE 'ERE !

2

The importance of good staff

Staffing has always been a burning issue for the hospitality industry, because without the right staff the industry cannot do its job. This means that wage levels, working hours, staff morale and the problems of recruiting, retaining and dismissing people have always preoccupied those in charge. Similarly, working conditions and wages have always been of great concern to employees. Some aspects of this relationship between employers and employees have changed noticeably over the last hundred years. For example, full employment after the Second World War meant that wages went up. This was a shock to seaside businesses, which had always relied on cheap labour. Another change was that during the later twentieth century employers had to meet increasing costs for the welfare of their employees. This was true even on the Isle of Man, despite the Manx Government's traditional hesitation to protect workers' rights with legislation.[1] But in other respects, the problems faced by Manx hotel and boarding house keepers and their staff remained remarkably unchanged. As the editor of *Hotel* magazine commented in 1936, 'staff is a real pet question in the trade'.[2]

To understand the 'staff problem' (on both sides) we have to consider how the boarding house business was originally structured, what its staffing needs were, and how these changed over time. In the late nineteenth century, many new businesses – including hundreds of boarding houses – were created on the Isle of Man especially to cater for holidaymakers. An important part of the holiday pleasures enjoyed by visitors was the leisure gained by paying others to do jobs they normally undertook themselves. Therefore visitors didn't just take time off work, they also employed other people to do the cooking, cleaning, laundry and chores which they normally did themselves. A small army was needed to undertake this domestic labour so the visiting industry linked the entire job market in resort towns towards the service sector. Think of the needs of any group of holiday-makers coming to the Isle of Man – perhaps from Bolton – for ten days in the 1890s, and staying at one of the big new boarding houses on Douglas's Queen's Promenade. To sail to the Island, they needed the work of sailors, porters and stewards. At the sea terminal, more porters and tram or cab-drivers were required to move them and their heavy luggage to the boarding house. Alternatively, tram drivers and conductors served them if they travelled by rail. On arrival at their holiday home, their bags would have been carried by the boot-boy in a large establishment, or the landlady's husband in a smaller one. When they went up to their room, it had been cleaned and swept by a maid earlier in the day. There would have been no plumbed-in basin, just a washstand; so if they wanted to wash, someone had to heat water in the kitchen and carry it upstairs in a jug. The dirty water then had to be taken away again. If the evening was chilly, a fire could be laid and lit, needing more labour to haul coal upstairs and take the ashes back down. When the party went to dinner, the food they ate could have been prepared by up to half a dozen people. Two or three waitresses would serve in the dining-room, with another two or three people assisting them in the still-room, plating up food and then washing dirty dishes. After the meal the holi-daymakers probably went out dancing – so the work of an orchestra of musicians, a bevy of refreshment-room staff and transport workers was needed to make their evening a success. If they enjoyed the brilliance of the new electric light, a team of men worked to operate the generating plant which made Douglas sparkle. When the revellers returned to their boarding house, a light

supper would be laid on by the kitchen staff before the evening ended. It was no coincidence, then, that the popular Silvercraigs boarding house on Queen's Promenade advertised its 'attentive employees' to attract visitors in these years.[3]

To keep the Isle of Man operating so smoothly that visitors gave little thought to the lives of the thou-sands who served them was a challenge. The seasonal holiday industry was difficult to staff because it rarely offered a good year-round job. Most of the people serving our typical party only worked in the summer time. Boarding house proprietors retained only one or two important staff members in the winter – perhaps a cook and a housekeeper if the house was a large one. Other employees would be laid off. This hardly attracted those in search of a permanent career. Most jobs were poorly paid, and so they fell to young working-class women more than any other group in society. Many of these women, however clever or able, were given few opportunities for education or training. Social custom even up to the Second World War dictated a narrow range of jobs for women. On their marriage, most were expected to give up work. This meant that most boarding house employees tended to be young single girls. They had to work hard, and had few rights, but thankfully life was not always grim. If there were lots of jobs and not enough people to fill them, as in the 1950s, then the casual nature of seaside employment was in their favour. A girl could walk out of a job she disliked at one hotel and start another that same day.

Boarding house jobs

Over the hundred years covered by this book, there were changes in the nature of boarding house work, but

Letty Edgar and friends outside the Alma Hotel, 1947. Although staff worked long hours in the season, in the happier establishments there was always time for fun.

Accommodating guests has traditionally taken up a lot of time. By the standards of a modern bed and breakfast establishment, Victorian boarding houses employed a lot of staff. The Isle of Man was one of the earlier resorts to depart from the 'apartments' system to provide full board and lodging for all its visitors. This is how the term 'boarding house' came about. An efficient and well-staffed kitchen was needed to provide three hot meals a day, which began with a cooked breakfast and ended with a substantial dinner. In large establishments, a full-time kitchen staff was needed; in smaller places, the proprietress had to devote nearly all her time to the making and serving of food. In a large boarding house on the Central or Queen's Promenade, the size of the business meant that at least ten, maybe a dozen, staff were required. Cook had to co-ordinate the work of a couple of assistants, helped out by the proprietor at busy times. Above the kitchen, in the pantry or still-room, another two or three people would be required. Working with the still-room staff would be the waitresses, three in high season and two when things were quieter. A food preparation and serving staff of at least nine people was normal in the larger boarding houses in the 1890s. A number of full- and part-time chambermaids and cleaners were also required. Some cleaners doubled up as waitresses.

Service levels began to change after the Second World War. Visitors desired more flexible holidays, including the freedom to eat lunch elsewhere rather than being tied to a set meal time in their boarding houses. As a result, lunch gradually stopped being served and by the 1960s the change was complete. By the 1970s, dinner was also becoming optional as restaurants became more popular and diners grew more adventurous. Dinner menus in the remaining

the pace of change was not constant. The most steady period was between 1890 and 1939. The time of most rapid change came after the Second World War. The main changes were different levels of service to visitors and the use of fewer staff, and the introduction of new 'labour saving' technology.

For those living through the period 1890 – 1939, the pace of change was slow enough to be almost imperceptible. However, over the long view we can trace these changes in turn, starting with a look at the question of levels of service.

A refurbished bedroom at the Alexandra Hotel, showing how the Victorian building was updated to new styles, with its artificial silk bedspread, Lloyd-loom style chairs and hot and cold running water.

A bedroom, possibly at the Avondale in Palace Terrace, photographed in the 1930s, but showing an essentially unchanged Victorian interior, except for its electric light. Note the wash-stand recently converted to a wash basin with fitted plumbing.

A refurbished bedroom at the Metropole Hotel in the 1930s with a consciously modern decorative scheme on the walls giving a lighter, brighter interior and fitted sink in place of a washstand. The arm chair is probably a re-upholstered original piece.

boarding houses also had to offer greater choice. This meant kitchens had to be run more flexibly than before, but for fewer diners and for fewer meals overall. When guests started to arrive and depart all through the week rather than all changing over at the weekend, chambermaids had to clean rooms more often and change beds more frequently. However, this labour was spread throughout the week, so it was often possible to turn jobs which had once been full-time into part-time ones. With the introduction of bed and breakfast, very great economies in staffing could be made. A few owners even made a complete change and converted their premises to self-catering flats in the 1970s and 1980s, thus requiring little more than a weekly clean between lets. So, reducing service levels was one way of cutting staff costs.

The ways in which boarding house staff used their time also changed with the introduction of new technologies. Chambermaids who had once scrubbed wooden floors on their knees later turned to vacuuming newly fitted carpets. The vacuum cleaners they used were sold as being 'labour saving'. But was this really the case? The idea of labour saving was a big selling point for many of the devices which were introduced to homes and hotels during the twentieth century. They certainly made many heavy jobs easier. However, there is evidence to suggest that they didn't much reduce the overall time spent on cleaning. They merely allowed people to clean to a higher standard than before in the same space of time. Similarly, in the kitchen, new food technologies such as frozen foods and electric choppers and mixers permitted kitchens to offer a more varied menu with the same number of staff. More recently, computers have made administration more efficient and (allegedly) easier. But, unlike many other industries, there is a limit to what can be mechanised in tourism. So much of the job relies on personal service, provided face-to-face. Recognising the value of the personal touch, many customers are once again prepared to pay a little extra for the results of work which is labour intensive, such as the serving of genuine home-made food. By and large, the impact of machines on the work of accommodating tourists has been modest and has been felt indirectly, for example, through the purchase of processed food, prepared off-site.

One of the changes which we can say for sure reduced working hours was the introduction of washbasins and central heating. Washbasins came first, arriving in the 1920s at progressive boarding houses. Hours of hauling hot water and slops were done away with. Later, central heating (which was by no means universal until the 1960s) saved a lot of work in tending fires. The combined effect of these changes in a large boarding house was noticeable and all the proprietors who saw basins installed remember well the difference that the new fittings made to their lives.

Recruiting and retaining staff

Winter gave proprietors time to think about their staff for the following year and to plan changes or improvements. To the novice landlady this could be a great worry; for old hands, no other subject brought forth such a store of reminiscences. The small family-run houses which made up most of the Manx industry often handled their staff differently to the large establishments. Small places not only needed fewer employees, they needed them to be more versatile, and there were usually informal relationships between employers and employees which could generate a happy atmosphere which helped them retain staff. However, a small landlady could also feel vulnerable and alone if things started to go wrong. There was clearly enough of a problem to support advice columns in the boarding press and books on the subject. One manual from 1935 firmly allied itself with the embattled proprietor, stating that 'the staff problem, like the poor, is always with us'.[4] Some writers advised hotel and boarding house proprietors to turn their thoughts to 'efficiency', that cornerstone of much early twentieth-century management thinking. The first step – choosing the right employee – was crucial. Proprietors were advised not to take on staff who had come down in the world, however sorry for them they might feel. This hard-headed attitude was allegedly needed because:

Such people always live in the past, dream of the future, and are absolutely discontented with the present. To them the whole environment and routine are infra dig . . . to the average female of this type, one way to escape is that of marriage . . . so business is transcended by perpetual day-dreaming of the latest male attraction . . . such appointments to the staff cannot possibly make for efficiency.[5]

The same writer warned new proprietors that they might easily find themselves having constant clashes with their staff. It was considered inadvisable to be on 'familiar terms' with employees, in case this led to them 'taking advantage' or becoming jealous of each other. Also interesting was the unequal treatment of men and women. Today, the perspective of the 1930s seems extraordinarily biased, with its talk of 'average females' dreaming only of men. There was certainly a greater division between male and female jobs before the Second World War, but the belligerent approach of the male management writer above contrasts with the memories of many of the women who ran boarding houses in these years. They knew how to roar when necessary, but most women managers preferred to try to work by consensus and in a friendly way whenever possible.

Management by paternalism – or more often, maternalism – and by building a consensus among staff and not using force unless necessary was the most common approach to managing staff. But how to recruit? Some people emphasised the freedoms and interest of boarding-house work, but this could not entirely disguise its rather low social status.[6] This problem was unavoidable because the industry needed cheap labour which could easily be hired and fired – it was in the nature of seasonal work. This problem led to a long-standing gripe by employers that they could not find the quality of staff which they desired. During the Great Depression, when horrifying numbers were on the dole, one boarding house keeper wrote:

The unemployed . . . cheer themselves in their futile search for work by regarding this [industry] as a certain source of economic security if everything else fails, saying, 'If the worst comes to the worst, I can always get a job in a boarding-house or hotel'.[7]

The trouble was that poor pay and conditions were unlikely to attract those in search of a permanent career. The only people who really made a decent living out of small seaside businesses were the proprietors. In a larger boarding house or hotel, the higher grades of staff could do somewhat better. Women such as housekeepers and cooks could rise to positions that were seen as respectable and which earned a fair wage because of their skills and experience. Alternatively, many girls entered the business at a low level with the intention of working their way to a boarding house of their own and many managed to do so. Another part of the picture was the large numbers of respectable married women who were happy to top up the family

income with a little bit of summer work in local boarding houses. Such women were a godsend to proprietors. They often returned to the same house year after year, forming the backbone of the staff. They often trained new employees such as girls who had come over from Ireland for their first job. They held a store of skills and knowledge which was essential for the business to re-start successfully after the winter closure. This mixture was the norm until the 1970s, when hoteliers found that the formula was failing because there were no longer enough youngsters available at a price they could afford. Ambitious young people were leaving the Island to work elsewhere. A few establishments became part of youth training schemes. Others began to bring in labour from abroad. It also made the work of relatives much more useful.

There was a clear hierarchy in the ways of staff recruitment for boarding house proprietors. Members of the extended family were always first choice. Blood ties made the likelihood of sudden walk-outs or theft much lower, and relatives were generally prepared to work for less. In fact, employing family members was not just desirable, but often essential. Much of the British seaside accommodation sector has always operated at the margins of profitability, and needed family labour to keep afloat.[8] Terry Cringle's account of his mother's recruitment strategy in the late 1940s reveals how this approach worked:

My father was a Manxman, but my mother came from Liverpool, so she would try as hard as she could either to get local Manx girls to come and work, or else family members from Liverpool. At least when you had family members there you felt better about it. So that, to a large extent, was what we did. We had quite a lot of cousins and second cousins and third cousins from Liverpool coming over to do jobs. When my father died in 1964, it left my mother in something of a dilemma. It was a problem for her to keep running the boarding house and doing the cooking as well. So what she did was to find staff who would come regularly . . . always family from Liverpool, so she was able to carry on.[9]

If family members were not available, then the second best choice was generally thought to be local girls. If a girl was personally known to a landlady she was often thought to be steadier and more reliable than a stranger. Girls could be informally recruited through networks of friendship or mutual interests, such as clubs or churches. This knowledge also gave the bonus of providing a free and detailed character reference. A third choice, especially useful to a landlady who had moved to the Isle of Man from elsewhere, was to take staff from her old home town. Friends and family back home could provide the informal vetting and recruitment process on her behalf. For landladies who had come to the Isle of Man from the towns that formed its core market – Lancashire and the West Riding – pickings were fairly slim. The textile towns absorbed labour all year round and a good deal of work for young women was to be had, except during times of depression. Girls had to be recruited young and they were generally only available for a summer or two in between school and serious work or marriage.

Sometimes when landladies formed a strong friendship with their girls this was kept up through marriage and the birth of children so that once children had grown up a few came back to work again. Mature married or widowed women were much sought-after by boarding house keepers, for they were experienced domestics, with little desire for dancing, night life and unwanted gentleman callers, any one of which could easily result in the loss of a staff member after an argument. If these strategies were not enough then many short-staffed proprietors would seek out country girls in preference to their city counterparts. It was thought that their expectations – both in terms of wages and comforts – were more modest, and their moral character was supposedly superior to that of high living city girls. There were other advantages. Violet Bridson recruited most of her staff in the 1930s and '40s from Maryport in Cumberland and realised that because it was such a small place, most of the staff were either relatives or friends.[10] Her staff became almost self-renewing, as girls recommended their friends when they left.

Occasionally, a family would come on holiday and a landlady would be approached by their daughter wanting work, after her parents had vetted her potential workplace for themselves.[11] Only when all other avenues had been exhausted would staff be recruited from the totally open market. Advertising in Irish newspapers was a well tried method. Some businesses also used employment agencies. When Muriel Cottier set up in business just after the Second World War, she had few contacts to draw upon. At this time, labour was

particularly scarce. Through necessity she went to an agency, but did everything she could to build up personal connections, having found that 'if you had to rely on the agency staff, it was a nightmare'.[12] With wages low and jobs plentiful, agency staff just didn't care.

When deciding whom to employ, a landlady's first step was to examine the candidate's 'character' reference. Formal qualifications were rarely important. A school leaving certificate was enough and vocational qualifications were few and far between in tourism until the 1970s. So the testimonial was crucial, and the problem of being dismissed 'without a character' before the 1920s and during subsequent times of high unemployment was a very real one. Landladies looked for girls who would be reliable and hard working, and if they were smart, bright and friendly, then this was the ideal.

Many young women worked very hard and gave of their best to their boarding house jobs. Most were treated well by their bosses. A few employers were undoubtedly harsh, for it was all too easy to let hard work tip over into exploitation, or rudeness and lack of respect. If staff were treated with antagonism, the result was an unhappy house where guests felt uncomfortable, or might even leave. This is why one Douglas boarding house advertised its 'permanent staff . . . throughout the season' before the First World War as a means of reassuring potential visitors that it was steady and respectable.[13] The fact that such a statement was unusual reveals that the same staff all season was uncommon. A further reason why proprietors had so much trouble in keeping staff was that moving between businesses was the main way for workers to improve their lot.

Tourist businessmen and women in the early twenty-first century Isle of Man find that recruiting and retaining staff is a more pressing issue than ever. With a new prosperity in the local economy, the problem has become hard to solve as potential employees are lured away from the traditional jobs by cleaner and often better paid office work. One well established local hotel in Port Erin has converted part of its premises into self-catering apartments almost solely because of the difficulty in finding the number and quality of staff that the traditional business requires.[14]

Learning the business

As with any job, people coming into the boarding house business had to learn their trade and conform to its rules and customs, which were once very strict. Personal appearance was important, and staff starting work at a larger boarding house in the early twentieth century would first be issued with their uniform and shown how to wear it. A style laid down in the Victorian era was still the norm, but this was beginning to change. Violet Bridson describes how at Manchester House, on Empress Drive, Douglas, the waitresses of the 1920s had to wear:

> Black dresses and caps and big aprons that crossed at the back. The upstairs girls (as we used to call them) had their overalls, or goodness knows what they would have worn, because they didn't have any money. After a little while, as it got towards the end of the '30s, things were beginning to get a bit more modern. The girls

> started 'forgetting' to put them on, or they would have a tape off or something. Towards the end of my time, the last two or three years before the war broke out, they were getting to dislike the uniform as being old-fashioned.[15]

Apart from a smart uniform and the need for good manners, training in the modern sense was provided neither for guest house proprietors nor their staff until comparatively recently. To be brought up in the trade was the best and often the only good training on offer.[16] Anyone else entering the business had to rely on their native wit and the advice of other proprietors, though there were a few self-help manuals which offered advice on how to buy, equip, and staff a boarding house. One such writer thundered in the 1930s that:

> Fully sixty per cent of the troubles which arise in the hotel and boarding-house industry have, as their root cause, an alarming state of inefficiency. It permeates proprietors, administrative staffs and the general staffs alike. Still more alarming is the fact that this inefficiency does not arise out of bad training or a failure to make the best of a good training, but is due, in the main, to a lack of any training at all.[17]

"Smart, bright and friendly . . . ideal!" Early twentieth-century waitress at the Villa Marina, Douglas.

It was not until several decades later, in the 1970s, that formal training became widespread in seaside hotels and guest houses as a worried response to falling visitor numbers. But even after institutions such as the Isle of Man College opened their doors to caterers, many smaller businesses were unwilling to pay for training. What was the use of training a chef or a waitress at one's own expense, asked many landladies, only to see them leave the following year? Equally, from many workers' point of view, what was the point of training for a poorly paid job which was, for many, only a stepping stone to better prospects?

The problem has long roots which go down to the basic economic rules governing the tourist industry, and these were recognised as early as the 1930s. During the war, the British Government set up a Catering Wages Commission to study the problem, not just of wages but of catering staff in general. Its recommendations for training and regulation were not generally welcomed by the trade. The idea of quality was tantalising, but who was to pay? Even today, the British Hospitality Association is still complaining about 'the poor perception of the industry as an employer', whilst it simultaneously fights welfare provisions such as the minimum wage and working hours regulations which might make staff more contented and loyal.[18] It cannot have it both ways.

Such problems didn't greatly concern the average landlady of the 1930s and '40s when staff were cheap and easy to get. She would have been an expert

in pricing food, booking rooms, and exercising close personal control over her establishment, all in a manner learned from experience. This led to a pride in the job. When a proprietress could rise up the social scale to employ and train staff she knew she had arrived. The daughter of Mrs Grainger who ran the Carrick Bay in Port St Mary before the war, remembers her mother's pride in the staff she had created:

> She had a receptionist and proper waitresses, chambermaids, hall porter and — well — what they have in hotels, everything. My husband became the Bars Manager, he ran the bars and the cellars, and my mother and I did the catering. We had . . . professional waitresses and chambermaids and receptionists, whatever: everything was run properly, as a proper residential hotel.[19]

It was not until the summer of 1955 that the first scheme for training cooks for the Manx holiday industry was set up, and there were plans to follow it with training for other staff. A grant of £500 was made by Tynwald for the cooks scheme.[20] This was a time of inflation, with strong upward pressure on wages. The Government had just completed its first big enquiry into the tourist trade, the bold new Visiting Industry Commission report, and was beginning to think that the inner workings of small businesses mattered to the general prosperity. The catering department of

the Isle of Man College later came about as a result of this concern. Sadly, relations between trade and college were not always trouble-free. In the mid-1980s, the College complained that it lacked both students and support from hoteliers. The Hotel & Guest House Association claimed in return that the College did not offer the courses which it needed.[21] Matters were smoothed over when the college proved keen to listen to Association members, who suggested courses on menu planning, cost control and practical cookery. In addition to the good work of the College, new technology made training videos available for in-house use by the 1980s. Hoteliers could choose from titles including *The Fine Art of Keeping Your Cool* (on refrigerating food safely) and advice on *Portion Control* and *Simmering and Poaching*. There was even the amusingly entitled *Suggestive Selling for Waiters and Waitresses*, which sounds a lot more fun than *Dish Machine Operator*.[22] Nowadays, the Island's larger hotels combine formal courses with in-house training to achieve their staffing goals. Some even work with the Irish Government's tourism training arm, and NVQs and other formal qualifications in tourism are becoming the norm for those looking for a career in the business.[23]

Staff shortages

There have always been periodic staff shortages in certain years on the Isle of Man. However, from the late nineteenth century there was also the annual problem of summer crisis followed by winter unemployment. It caused much distress to local workers and a Commission on Local Industries tried as early as 1900 to discover whether new kinds of industry could be set up on the Island to smooth out the demand for labour. Sadly, it could find no way round the problem. Tourism always sucked in all the available workers in the summer, so however much surplus there was in the winter, this was no use to manufacturers. Nor were English industrialists likely to come to a place so far offshore with no coal and few raw materials.[24] The Government therefore continued to ease the situation of the most destitute by creating winter works schemes for local men, one of which was the building of the Loch Promenade Gardens. The Isle of Man was not the only resort to suffer the seasonal work problem. Even in the 'hungry thirties', with unemployment running high, the British Hotels Association claimed that its members' staffing problems were still acute in high season.[25] The difficulty was that although many men were unemployed in the heavy industries, they were not suited to working as waiters or cooks and many would have refused to do so – they wanted full-time skilled jobs. The ongoing shortage meant landladies often had to take anyone they could get, which led to frustrations and unhappiness on both sides.[26] On Central Promenade in Douglas, Muriel Cottier found that,

> If you had good staff, you were all right. You could enjoy life. But we had so many scruffy people come over, it was dreadful, they'd think nothing of saying before a meal, 'Well, we're going, we're not staying here, we're going', and they would go and that would be your staff gone![27]

A grocer who delivered to boarding houses in the 1950s remembers that some staff 'were rough, dead rough sometimes, and some of the boarding house keepers used to be pretty rough too in their way, but it was all part of life's rich pattern'.[28]

The good manners of staff were not a landlady's only worry. By the 1930s, the Victorian boarding houses of the Isle of Man were, as in many UK resorts, becoming rather old-fashioned. They had been constructed at a time when staff were cheap and plentiful. Their many floors, inconvenient 'outlets' and basement kitchens had been thrown up with little thought to saving time. The coal ranges and coke boilers fitted to their kitchens also took hours of stoking, cleaning and maintenance. This was all a problem as the cost of staff slowly rose. The 1930s were also the decade in which some of the first convenience foods began to make their way onto the market (such as Weetabix and Ribena) and their makers specifically advertised the products to the trade as being quick and easy to prepare with fewer staff.[29] By 1960, one short-staffed Peel landlady found herself telling guests that if they wanted early morning tea they would have to fetch it themselves, because there was no one to carry trays upstairs. Fortunately, most visitors saw the funny side, and there were a lot of early morning tea-parties in the kitchen that summer![30]

The places with the fewest staff worries were the smallest ones, such as Ivy Kaneen's Rock View on Marine Parade in Peel. Nearly all the work was done by Ivy herself, and her background in farming had trained her well to cope with hard work and unexpected troubles. Mrs Kaneen needed only a couple of people to help at busy times of the day and here, as was so often the case, family members were first choice. Later in her career, Ivy regularly employed an experienced older woman who ran the kitchen at mealtimes whilst the proprietress served in the dining room. Mrs Kaneen saw the advantages of running a small business, and said:

> You could always improvise in a small place like Rockview. But I think staff got to be a problem in some of the bigger houses — a real problem. I don't know how they managed . . . I never had to cope with that.[31]

The small boarding houses provided ideal light jobs for local schoolchildren during the summer holidays. In the little resort of Port Erin in the 1950s and '60s, Brian King and his siblings helped their parents in the business, with the aid of a couple of local teenagers who waited at table and washed up. In these

A quick snapshot of new recruits to the Savoy kitchen, from Madeira, taken in the 1970s by proprietor Ron Rigby.

years, there was a large amount of summer work for youngsters in the Island. As well as boarding houses, deckchair hire, rowing-boat hire and tram conducting were all favourite opportunities, especially with young men who preferred outdoor work.

By the middle of the 1960s, a few bold hoteliers began to experiment by bringing cheaper labour from abroad to run their establishments because they were dissatisfied with either the price or quality of British seasonal workers. In 1965 Ronnie and Mary Rigby, who ran the large Savoy guest house in Douglas, began to import staff from Portugal to help run their business each summer.[32] As an employer, Mr Rigby liked the approach which his Portuguese employees took to their work. He explained:

> I would bank their money for them every week, though whenever they wanted their wages they could have them. But they never did, until they went home, apart from buying souvenirs. For every one of them, the idea was to come and earn money for those three months. They had their own rooms, husbands and wives together, with a television and their own shower facilities and of course all their food. How they saved. Now some of the English staff we had, you'd pay them on a Friday, and it would be gone. They'd be wanting subs off us. Not all of them of course, but some of the youngsters we used to

have; they'd go out to the Casino and it would be gone — that was their attitude. But not with any of the Portuguese.[33]

For Mr and Mrs Rigby, this arrangement seemed to work well, probably because it was backed up by the proprietors' own regular visits to Portugal and personal contacts in the town from which they recruited. Some other employers found that foreign staff could introduce new kinds of tension into the workplace. Differences of age, gender and culture could be explosive, as John Clague found when he ran the Ramsey Hydro in the 1960s:

We had two Spanish boys came over and they came over to learn English. Now the head of the dining-room, the head waitress, was a Scots woman and she spoke with a very broad Glasgow accent. Even I had trouble understanding what she said, and these Spanish boys hadn't a clue what she was talking about. She had a row with them . . . and these Spanish boys went round and put their fists on all the butter pats. There was a hell of a row.[34]

Because the cost of living in the Mediterranean countries was low by comparison to Britain, foreign staff

were able to make a respectable amount of money to take home. There were also other advantages to working in Britain that were not merely financial – such as the chance to learn English, as Mr Clague pointed out.

Friendship and trust

The value of a trusted and reliable employee was immense and when an inexperienced landlady had a good 'right hand woman' for her first few seasons it made all the difference in the world. One of the advantages of buying a business from a person who was retiring was that staff contacts came ready-made with the house. Old hands, too, greatly valued colleagues whom they could trust and who returned year after year.[35] In many cases, landladies and their staff became friends, as one Douglas landlady found out. Recalling two Irish girls who worked for her one summer, she said:

I feel it was my pleasure to have known them. They were marvellous, they were, really wonderful. They went back after the summer and in January the following year I got a letter from another sister of the girl who had worked for us the previous year. It said, 'I would like to come and work for you. I must tell you that I am deformed, but it would not stop me from working.' I read the letter, then I passed it over to my husband, and he said 'Well, she's got the job, hasn't she?' I said 'Yes.' So I wrote back and I said I would be pleased for her to come and work for us. So we arranged that she would come on a certain boat, and I would be down at the boat with a flower in my coat, so she would know who I was. This person got off the boat and I stood waiting and, as she said, I saw she was deformed, very much so. You don't see an awful lot of this today — where children had quite a hump on their back on account of a disease of their spine which made one of their legs quite short — but that's how Theresa was. If ever anybody was sent to me to help me, it was Theresa. At one period she worked for us for four years and after we'd retired and [my husband] Fred was in Noble's Hospital she came to see him. What more could anybody else want than that?[36]

The Melrose staff in the 1960s, showing a smaller boarding house with a traditional local staff. The old couple are visitors.

Such loyalty was every landlady's dream – no wonder that Sheilagh Barlow, on Peel's Marine Parade, sighed in the 1960s when she contemplated the preference of her maids for a little light dusting over getting down to cleaning the toilets.[37] The trouble was, had she pressed them too hard over the issue, they might have walked out. This was the dilemma faced by a successful hotelier in Douglas during the 1950s. To keep his staff happy he could not overwork them. So he began to close his dining-room at 10 p.m. sharp, instead of letting guests stay as long as they wanted. When the angry visitors complained, he explained to them:

> We can get any amount of visitors, it's the easiest thing in the world. But do you know what is the hardest thing to do? It's to get staff, and staff that will put up with the visitors drinking and eating at 1 o'clock in the morning when they want to get off to bed. You expect the staff to be down there at 9 o'clock sharp in their uniforms and everything, going flat-out to give you service, and yet you keep them and you won't let them get to bed![38]

This sort of behaviour could only have happened in the years when staff were hard to come by and visitors were plentiful. It now seems rather dated, with a real ring of the 1950s about it. Another way of life now gone was the job of live-in cook in the big boarding houses. Mr Bert Quirk, whose mother was a cook in the 1950s remembers:

> We were just treated as family by the owners in those days, because the cook was an essential part of the business, especially in the bigger places. They were more reliable than chefs who invariably left. So Mum and Dad and me had a room to ourselves, certainly in the Westlakes and the Doric . . . when she was in the Regent, latterly, she had her own bed within the staff-room, so if she wanted a lie down she could go and have one during the day, once breakfast was over and preparation was done for dinner. That was one of the cook's privileges.[39]

Poor staff conditions

Mrs Quirk was fortunate to cook for some of the Island's most respected and prosperous boarding houses. Lower down the scale, conditions could be less salubrious and not all proprietors had the scruples to accommodate staff as they should have done. One enquiry in the 1930s revealed that:

> Some of the staff quarters in hotels and boarding-houses would not be tolerated as stokers' quarters of a ship at sea. The Board of Trade would never permit such conditions and

The Crescent Hotel, 1967, then as now a popular nightspot, though night-clubbing as it exists today was still unknown.

Cocktail waiters at the Crescent Hotel, 1960s. A total of 44 staff gave full table service.

Crescent Hotel Proprietor Jack Quirk behind the Toby Jug bar.

Crescent Hotel Proprietor Jack Quirk caught by a friend on his way to the bank with a night's takings in about 1960.

overcrowding in the sleeping-quarters on a cargo boat . . . the writer has seen staff quarters in hotels and boarding-houses which were unholy as well as uneconomic. Such conditions are not economic because they do not give the necessary physical and mental rest to the staff, upon whom proprietors and guests alike are dependent. They are the cause of much discontent and unrest . . . the staff should have quarters which afford them comfort and ease.[40]

Because so many resorts, including the Isle of Man, operated such a short season, there was little incentive to tackle overcrowding or to make pleasant those parts of buildings which visitors never saw. Even in the 1960s, when Mr Jack and Mrs Beatrice Quirk took up the tenancy of the Crescent Hotel (which was one of Douglas's largest tourist pubs and employed forty-four staff in the season), overcrowding was still the norm.[41] Mrs Quirk was horrified to find that staff slept in bunk-beds, six to a room. Improvements were quickly made and numbers cut to two per room. The dispossessed people could find rooms elsewhere in the town because the Crescent, being a pub, did not need staff to make the early start necessary in boarding houses and hotels.

For hoteliers who tried to squeeze the maximum occupancy out of Victorian buildings there was a real temptation to overcrowd staff quarters long after the overcrowding of visitors became unacceptable. By the 1970s, however, declining occupancy rates and a concentration on quality rather than quantity for guests reduced these pressures. The need for employers to offer better conditions to keep their staff also made a difference.

The pleasures of the job

Work in a boarding house was not always an endless chore. Although it was often tiring and hectic, it also offered staff many opportunities for fun, making friends and even for romance. The houses were busy, bustling places with new faces forever passing through.[42] For the more sociable type of person, it was ideal. As one Tourist Board inspector joked, many of the Irish girls who took jobs on the Island just after the war mostly came to escape their mothers and the boring, quiet countryside![43] Nor was it only country girls who enjoyed a summer by the sea. Some young women from industrial areas also liked to spend a season in the resort towns. One who did this was Letitia (Letty) Edgar, who left the shipyards of Clydebank for the Isle of Man. A friend at the yard told her that work was to be had in Douglas and the enterprising young woman made the journey alone to take up a job she obtained by letter.

Letty was fortunate for she was able to come and go to the Island several times and still return to winter shipyard work. As she remembered: 'I wouldn't have gone back year after year if I hadn't liked it'.[44] In the depressed areas, not all girls were so fortunate in their employment. Some Manx landladies were horrified when they found out how badly nourished their new recruits were from slump-hit industrial cities between the wars. The pleasures of good food were an unexpected bonus for these workers.[45]

Letty Edgar, aged 16.

We had a standard in the kitchen which we carried on to everything that went into the dining-room . . . it wasn't a matter of one thing for the guests and one for the family. It was the same with the staff, everybody had what was cooked, that was how we ran the business.[46]

Even when jobs were easy to come by, a lot of young women liked to come to the Isle of Man for a summer's work and a change of scene. When times were prosperous, as in the 1960s, they could do this even more easily because there was no trouble in getting a job back when they returned home. Boarding houses were friendly and cheerful places most of the time, and in a good house, employees were well cared for. If a house lacked a happy atmosphere, staff didn't stay long, but when proprietors sat down with staff to meals, and made an effort to be fair, this was appreciated. At the Savoy in Douglas, in the late 1940s, Ronnie Rigby remembers how his parents behaved towards their staff:

When Ronnie Rigby took over his father's business, which had been in the family for three generations, he knew people who had worked for his grandparents and who loved to keep in touch with the family.[47] This was often the way amongst small Manx businesses and the Island's size also kept a family closer. Only a few of the largest establishments were run on more formal lines. In the massive hotel Alexandra (now demolished), which had been created out of a whole row of former boarding houses, the Raineri family employed more than fifty staff before the war. The cosy feeling found in a small boarding house was clearly impossible, so staff socialised in their own way, without mixing with the owners.[48]

The smaller the house, the more likely it was for proprietors to get involved in the personal lives of their staff. A perennial anxiety for landladies was the likelihood of their girls having too much 'fun', entering into romances and having flings with holidaymakers. Not only was such behaviour frowned upon for many years, it could also make a house unhappy or inefficient from the landlady's point of view. For example, one Douglas chambermaid in the 1970s kept her most recent boyfriend secretly stowed away in what the proprietor thought was an empty room, a deception which was only uncovered when the girl failed to turn up for duty after a particularly exhausting night.[49] At the Hydro in Douglas, Hilary Guard employed some fifteen young Irish girls each summer, and such a large concentration of feminine beauty was sometimes too much for visiting groups of young men to bear. Mr Guard did not enjoy having to deal with the complaints of guests disturbed by roaming lads in search of chambermaids at night.[50] But beneath flirtation sometimes lay a serious purpose: many girls were in search of a husband. Changing attitudes by the 1960s saw landladies become less concerned about staff romances. Only if love interfered with work did they step in. Muffett Tarrant, running Peel's Waldick House in the 1960s, saw no fewer than seven of her girls marry local boys – as she laughingly recalls, 'It was like a matrimonial agency!'[51] This relaxed atmosphere was appreciated:

> They all used to call me 'Auntie Muffett' and they used to call Ralph 'Uncle Ralph' – he always used to bring them sweets on a Saturday. We treated them like our daughters, you know, and are still friendly now. I went to their weddings . . . and if you were to ask any of the girls that were up there, I guarantee not one of them will tell you they were unhappy. We had a lovely time.[52]

The intermingling of work, romance and family life was one of the appeals of boarding house work. A girl could use her family contacts to enter the business, train herself, work her way up, and perhaps even take on a boarding house of her own. With a husband or relatives to help her, times could be truly pleasant when everyone got along. Many workers enjoyed socialising with visitors, and though this was thought of as most unsuitable for young ladies until the 1920s, it was easy for girls to avoid the eye of a busy employer as long as they were off the premises. Places with bars, such as the Douglas Hydro, were reluctant to let staff drink with guests, preferring each group to keep to their own quarters.[53] Staff today have more freedom than in the past. In the average 1950s guest house, workers had to be in by midnight. In the 1990s, a hotelier on Queen's Promenade admitted that his staff:

> Know more about the Douglas night-spots than I do. A lot of the staff go out at 11 or 12 o'clock and go to Toffs or Studebakers [night-clubs] or somewhere like that, and don't come back until 3 a.m. The good ones are up at 7 o'clock anyway in the morning and they're still working; the other ones we don't know about, because we lose them when they're no use.[54]

It was unsurprising that young staff liked to party because they often worked long hours and wanted to make the most of their free time.

Hard work, long hours

In the early twentieth century, staff began work about half-past six, or sometimes earlier on a changeover day.[55] At Douglas's largest boarding house in the 1930s, one chambermaid looked after as many as around fifteen rooms, and on Saturday she would work from half-past six to three in the afternoon.[56] In the summer of 1936, the popular magazine *Tit Bits* ran a scandalous exposé of the conditions which some seaside workers suffered in an article called 'Slaves of the Seaside'. Readers learned that many girls from the economically depressed areas had moved to resort towns in search of work. But, it went on:

> Poor pay, long hours, stoppages from wages, bad food, wretched living– accommodation — these are common conditions of domestic service on the coast during the season. . . . Numerous girls, indeed, soon leave their employment with only a few coppers in their pockets.[57]

When staff worked long hours, those who supplied them worked late too. Grocery deliveries in Douglas in the 1940s sometimes carried on until eleven o'clock on a Saturday night, resulting in fifteen- or sixteen-hour days for the delivery-men. When changeover day was on Saturday, it was the most hectic time of the week. There was rarely a good time to deliver to a hot and hectic kitchen, and tempers occasionally became frayed or worse. Harry Watterson made a call

to deliver groceries to one sea-front boarding house in the early 1950s only to find the police were there in force. Standing on the steps with the groceries, he began to realise that matters had got rather out of hand:

> I said to the copper on the door, 'What's going on here?' 'Oh,' he replied, 'there's a fellow in there with an axe . . . he's threatening the proprietor' . . . eventually it calmed down a bit so I went inside and there was the proprietor. I said 'What's happened?' and he said, 'Oh, the cook has gone berserk. He's had too much to drink and he's threatening everybody with an axe.'[58]

Even when drink was not the problem, a mixture of sleep-deprivation, long hours, and the pressure to get everything done on time all mounted up. In the 1920s and '30s, when three meals a day were cooked for boarders, there was sometimes no night off for kitchen staff. The landlady Violet Bridson remembered that her girls 'weren't allowed out at all those nights: they had to be shelling all the peas, chopping the cabbage and peeling the potatoes'.[59]

Before the advent of affordable small washing machines in the late 1940s, those landladies who economised by laundering at home had to reserve a whole day for the job. Washday started at six and the fire under the copper boiler was lit before starting breakfast. A mountain of sheets would be waiting from the last week's guests. Violet Bridson remembers it well:

We used to wash the sheets in the boiler, boil them up, then we used to lift them out. That was always my job, because if anything happened to the staff you were responsible, so you couldn't let them do things where there was a bit of danger about. And we used to lift the sheets out of the boiler, put them through the rinse with the dolly–stick, through the mangle, then into the blue dip. When they came out of that you had to mangle them again and fold them all up damp. Then we used to take them down onto the beach, and lay them out on the stones. We'd peg them down with the stones, you see, and then during the afternoon (before the tea–rush started) we had to go down and gather them in and bring them home and fold them up. Then they were all mangled again. There was no ironing for things like that, but they all had to be perfectly folded and done and put on the racks in the kitchen to air.[60]

Proprietors used all the means in their power to keep staff working hard. In the 1940s the proprietor of the Ramsey Hydro made sure that:

The Catholic priest used to come up at the beginning of the season and he'd have a scotch or two and he would discipline them [the girls] as long as we made sure they would go to church on Sunday mornings, you see. Well, we had a minibus at Ramsey, and we used to send them down to church. The way they disciplined them was of course that they got on to their priests in Ireland and so to their mothers . . . The priest would look after them if we had any trouble, as long as we sent them to church.[61]

Even tender-hearted employers, such as Sheilagh Barlow in Peel, had to ask their staff to make sacrifices from time to time. When she accidentally overbooked one summer, her assistants had to move out of their bedrooms and sleep elsewhere.[62] When such incidents occurred, some grumbling was inevitable. Boarding house work was, for many staff, only for the season after all. If they got too upset, they could always walk out, and many did, so many that threatening to walk out was something of a tradition.

Walking out

Walking out and telling the boss where to stuff her job was the ultimate option for the discontented employee. Oddly enough, some aspects of the holiday industry made the habit more, rather than less, likely. Because boarding house proprietors liked to recruit staff through informal networks of relatives or friends, many staff already knew each other and felt a strong common loyalty. This could add to the community spirit of a house when times were good, but it also made conflicts between landlady and staff worse when things went sour and it was more likely to result in the loss of several people at a time as Muriel Cottier found out:

> I had three girls who came together and they were from Lancashire. I was busy stirring the porridge, and I said 'Come on girls, it's late, it's time you were bringing the toast and stuff up', and they said 'We're not doing anything, we're going.' So I said, 'All right then, go!' and I let them go. Then I thought 'Oh no, what have you done?' but we managed. They'd just got another place, that was all, they just did that in those days.[63]

Violet Bridson, who recruited for years from a small town in Cumberland, was well aware of the dangers of putting all her eggs in one basket. She found that it was important to treat the girls carefully. As she said, 'if you fell out with one, you fell out with the lot, and they were all liable to walk out, you know. And they would, too!'[64] Another landlady, Olive McFee, found that friends or relatives were often happy to share rooms, which was handy, but the old problem was never

far from her mind. 'If one went,' she remembers, 'two went, and you were left high and dry.'[65] Proprietors tried various means to stop staff walking out, from cajoling to contracts. At the Belvedere Hotel in 1955, the owners drew up a contract which stipulated that their chef's end-of-season bonus would be lost if he left before 9th September.[66] But there was always a way round such problems for people who really wanted to leave. One old trick was to claim that a relative had died, or was at death's door back home. A landlady might be persuaded to pay the return fare of a 'distraught' girl, never to hear from her again. Mrs McFee did just this in the 1960s to a girl who swore to return as soon as she could. Forty years later, she ruefully remarked, 'Well, we're still waiting for her!'

The practice of walking out reminds us that trouble at work was just as real on the promenades of the Isle of Man as it was in the factories of the Midlands or the mills of Lancashire. With no unions and few rights, walking out was one of the few ways that boarding house workers could show unhappiness with their jobs, with working hours, conditions, or wages.

Wages

During the first Isle of Man tourist boom in the 1870s, the energetic new industry offered such a contrast to the rest of the slumping Manx economy that its pay-levels, though modest, seemed splendid. An unskilled or semi-skilled worker could do comparatively well in the season. But this euphoria did not last long. The very prosperity that tourism created gave Manxmen and women higher expectations and modernised the Island, but realists who knew about the nature of the visiting industry understood that it could never pay really good

3 CASTLE TERRACE, CENTRAL
PROMENADE, DOUGLAS, I.O.M.

1870s interiors at 3 Castle Terrace. Keeping these elaborate Victorian rooms clean created enormous amounts of work for staff.

wages to everyone. There were only a few months of busy activity in which the industry had to make enough money to last all year, and this made well-paid or permanent employment for those below the level of senior staff unlikely.

Those most affected by low wages were the inexperienced, young or temporary staff, who worked a season or two, then moved on. This turnover of people hid the problem and avoided strikes and the sort of industrial unrest which became common in late nineteenth- and early twentieth-century manufacturing towns. Even during the General Strike there was no organised militancy recorded among the Island's boarding house workers. The amenities of seaside life partly made up for low pay. For seasonal staff, the fun on offer made summer boarding house work more than just a source of cash. For many proprietors with small houses, the cash profit over the course of a year was often

modest. However, the amenities of a large house, lots of free time in the winter, and a respectable social position all helped compensate for this. The best way to make lots of money was to run a very large boarding house or hotel, or to become a landlord and rent out buildings, which almost guaranteed a profit in normal circumstances.

The first great interruption of 'normal circumstances' and a strain on the system was the First World War. Once the immediate agony of conflict was over and visitors began to return, the post-war years saw a period of high inflation. Prices went up and this caused many problems for landladies and proprietors who were trying to rebuild their businesses. By the mid-1920s, wages bills had increased by an average of 100 per cent of their 1913 level, whilst the new system of National Insurance contributions cost 400 per cent more than before the war.[67] Tradesmen whom every boarding house proprietor needed such as joiners, upholsterers and decorators had also become much more expensive to employ. As the 1920s dragged on into the 1930s the British economy remained sluggish. The slump at least offered landladies a welcome break from the upward pressure on staff wages.

At their worst, the wages of a waitress in the mid-1930s might have reached only £1 a week. Such low pay led to allegations of young girls being 'easy prey for avaricious, tyrannical boarding house keepers'.[68] The allegation was denied by the industry, which was quick to claim that a few isolated incidents were being exploited for sensation. Average wages, as published officially by a group of employers in 1936, seemed somewhat better.

Average boarding house wages in 1936.[69]

Job	Wages
Male cook	90s per week, living in
Female cook	67s 9d per week, living in
Female head housekeeper	90s 3d per week
Male stillroom worker	83s per week
Female cleaner	37s per week, living in
Female cleaner	55s 6d per week, living out
Young maid of all work	34s 3d per week

The reason that boarding house wages were so often condemned as mean was that profits were often unreliable. Staff costs were the easiest thing to cut down. As the table above shows, it was also cheaper to employ women instead of men. Only the larger or more up-market hotels could afford to employ expensive male labour. The huge Douglas Alexandra chose to employ men simply because this was conspicuously expensive and projected the right image. The owner's daughter explains:

It was my father's idea. [He did it] because that was how a top-class hotel would have been run. In the smaller places waitresses would double up as chambermaids, which we didn't need to do because we were bigger, and he thought waiters looked nicer. They cost more, but nobody cost very much then. I always remember because I did the wages book and the average wage for someone would be £4 a week . . . in the late 1940s.[70]

Pay and conditions improved after the Second World War. The war provoked a change in the attitudes of government towards labour. Prices, wages and many other aspects of the market were heavily regulated and controlled in wartime, and this continued well into the late 1940s. The Isle of Man did not regulate as heavily as the British Government, but it adopted many of the same controls on wages, prices, and food. Public opinion was on the side of boarding house staff. As *The Times* admitted in 1949, 'exploitation is not too strong a word for the treatment to which some workers in the catering trades were, until recently, subjected'.[71]

With wages modest, tips were one way by which staff could improve their lot. Tipping was more widespread before the introduction of service charges and VAT. Visitors who stayed for a week or so often tipped their waitress as a gesture of thanks, and gratuities were usually pooled to be divided equally between all the staff

Waiters at work at the Balqueen Hydro, Port St Mary, 1950s. The traditional seaside holiday in these years was much as it had always been, with a full service of meals and busy communal dining rooms.

on changeover day.[72] From time to time, suggestions were made about eliminating tipping altogether and replacing it with a 10 per cent service charge. This was the case at the Douglas Boarding House Association annual general meeting of 1958. Those in favour said that it would lead to greater clarity in charging, but objectors reminded the meeting that an ordinary family coming to the Island often had a bill of £20 or £30, and a 10 per cent service charge could add an extra £2 – £3, which they would find heavy.[73]

Staff crime

From their earliest days seaside resorts saw their fair share of crime and petty theft. Victorian holidaymakers were regularly warned about seaside pickpockets who enjoyed a trip to the coast as much as they did. Boarding houses were not exempt. Some incidents happened when penniless staff felt a desperate need to return home, as for one fifteen-year-old girl who

came to work on Mona Drive in 1930. She had never been away from home before, and her homesickness must have been exacerbated by working from 6 a.m. until 9 p.m. each day. She stole the price of her fare home from a fellow chambermaid and ran back to her mother in Ashton-under-Lyne, only to be arrested and returned to the Island where the truth came out in court.[74] She was treated leniently, and only got probation, but other offenders in the 1930s were less lucky. A Liverpool girl who stole a watch and ran away from her job after only a week was met by the police at Liverpool pierhead, and was sent back to a month in the Island's prison.[75] The Manx authorities worried that girls sent away from home for the first time could be tempted into a life of crime. This concern meant that special attention was given to a young Dublin couple who stole from several boarding houses during the summer of 1939. The high demand for staff meant they were able to walk out of one job straight into another, making a chain of thefts easy. When they were caught, the man was found to be a hardened criminal who had compounded his sins by giving a false name. His accomplice was more innocent and collapsed in court, a tear-stained young girl, after being sternly warned of the risk of being drawn into a life of vice and degradation.[76] Boarding house keepers kept an eye out for this type of incident and talked amongst themselves and with the police. Muriel Cottier remembers that one summer in the 1940s:

> A policeman that we knew came round, and he said 'Have you got X working for you?' We said, 'Yes', so he said, 'Well take my tip, get rid of

her.' We asked why, and he said 'Oh — just take my tip and get rid of her.' Well she was pretty hopeless anyway, so we said 'Well, we're sorry, but we've found you're not suitable. You'll have to go in the morning', and she just replied, 'Oh, all right then.' And about two days afterwards she and her boyfriend were arrested for stealing out of shops. You know, things like that just happened. Another time, a mother and daughter came, and my husband went down to meet them off the boat. They had a huge suitcase and when he picked it up, thinking it would be heavy, it went right up in the air. You know, it was an empty suitcase. They told one of the other girls that they'd come with the intention of stealing linen and stuff, we found out later.[77]

When food was in short supply just after the war, even this was stolen. In the late 1940s, Mrs Cottier noted that one maid was using huge amounts of rationed tea. She investigated, only to discover that the girl was not drinking her share:

I used to think 'That tea is going down'. Do you know, she used to say, 'Can I have more tea, can I have more tea?' and I used to be dishing out the tea thinking 'That's going awfully fast'. She was sending it home! She used to get a newspaper, open the newspaper, put the tea in the middle, fold the newspaper over and over and make it like a parcel with our tea in the middle, and she used to say 'I'm just sending my mother the newspapers' but our tea was in the middle of that newspaper.[78]

Filching didn't stop at tea. Crimes involving stolen cigarettes and drink were a regular feature most Augusts in the Island's courts. It was not just staff who stole; visitors could be even worse. Thefts by youths as young as 15 were not unknown.[79] The free and easy atmosphere of the resort, with its carefree crowds and forgetful holidaymakers carrying plenty of cash, was too much for some to resist. However, crime remained only a small problem for many years, and it was not until the 1960s that Yale locks were fitted to bedroom doors in most boarding houses.

Winter unemployment

By early September, the tourist industry began to wind down, and staff were laid off. Visitors who only knew the Isle of Man in the summer would have been surprised by its very different winter life. Because the visiting industry only operated in summer, local workers had to seek alternative jobs out of season, or even move to England in search of winter work. In Walter

Greenwood's 1933 novel *Love on the Dole*, a hard-up Salford couple visit the seaside and start to wonder about who lives and works in the resort they're visiting. But when they ask about jobs, they discover that the seaside can also be a place of hardship where the winter sees most folk unemployed.[80] Bitterly, the young man exclaims: 'Unemployed, here, though! Did its stinking carcass foul the air everywhere? Was there no place where it did not lie in wait for your coming?'[81]

No one wanted to lay off employees earlier than necessary, so proprietors tried to make the best use of their staff at the end of the season. As visitor numbers began to go down, staff time was turned to maintenance and housekeeping. Beds were stripped, mattress-covers removed, and furniture cleaned.[82] Upholstery, rugs, curtains and bedding would all need attention, and there was plenty of mending to do. But the end had to come. Even the one or two essential staff kept on during the winter were a heavy drain on a business which earned nothing for months. The dilemma was perfectly summed up by Dora Broome in her witty 1939 *Sketch of Douglas Boarding House Life*. The landlady, Mrs Quaggin, is portrayed walking about her empty house in winter, looking at the empty promenade, and worrying:

What did it matter that the sunshine coloured the hills, and the sea shone blue and jade and purple, when folkses across the water was shutting themselves up in the great big towns, breathing the smoke and grime, and not caring in the least for Sea View's sixteen empty bedrooms? And Mona

there in the kitchen, eating the head off her, and nothin' at all to do but run up and down the stairs with a dustpan and a duster. Not that Mrs Quaggin grudged Mona her food, for the girl worked well enough in the summer, when Mrs Quaggin had to get them saucy pieces in from across to help, and needed two pairs of hands and feet and a head that never got tired to keep going at all herself.[83]

As winter ended, boarding houses would gradually take back staff to prepare for the coming season. If a landlady's husband held a regular job, then a trusted local member of staff would be the first to return. If both partners worked in the business, recruitment started later. Cleaning began slowly – perhaps a couple of days a week – until the final few weeks before opening. Then more staff would arrive to get the house completely in order. The ideal was to have as few staff as possible for the needs of any given time, as a landlady of the 1950s explained:

At the start of the season, if we only had six or seven, or a dozen [guests] in, Fred and I could manage them ourselves. But once you get over that you've got to have some help. So it depends on how many visitors you have when you do start. We usually

started the staff in the beginning of June and they would go 'til whenever we thought we could manage with less, because that was the idea, if you could manage with less. What we did was: if we had one floor that became empty as time went on, well, we would clean all that floor and cover it up again while we still had staff to do it.[84]

Past and present

The working life for staff in today's small hotels and guest houses is quite different from that of their predecessors who worked in the same buildings. Often, the kitchen sees less activity, because many only serve breakfast. By contrast, bedrooms have become more used and more luxurious. Today's en suite, fully-carpeted, comfortably-furnished bedroom demands more care and attention than its bare, lino-laid predecessor. Today's guests also come and go much more quickly, on all days of the week. Maureen Quirk at the Cunard has noted the effect on her staff, and reflects that 'the chambermaids are shattered, because it's a major clean every three or four days now with the way things have gone'.[85]

In the early twenty-first century, full employment and the attractive wages offered by the finance sector also present problems for Manx hoteliers. They cannot compete with office levels of wages and working conditions. It is not only young workers, once so plentiful, who are in short supply. The traditional part-timer is also increasingly rare, as more married women pursue full-time careers. As Shirley Birch of the Imperial put it, 'All we would really like for [cleaning] our bedrooms are housewives, that want a little job, but you can't get them. It's very, very difficult'.[86] Nor does bringing staff over from Ireland or Scotland solve the problem, for 'every year they say they'll stay until the end of the season, but they never do'. With the recent rate of growth in the Irish economy, even this traditional source of seasonal labour cannot be relied upon. A modern businesswoman remarks:

In the past two years we have found it difficult to get staff, because employment is much better in Ireland and much better in the Isle of Man . . . so there's not as many girls come looking for work now as they did.[87]

Those establishments still catering for holiday-makers (as opposed to business people) demand a wider variety of skills from their staff. In the Port Erin Hotels group, every permanent member of staff has at least two sets of skills; the chef is also a painter and decorator. The nature of the one-time seaside boarding house has changed for good. The jet-planes that started to take British tourists to the Mediterranean in increasing numbers in the 1960s and which changed the Isle of Man forever also changed the public taste. Many who now come to the Isle of Man enjoy foreign-style food, and expect more service from hotel staff. At the Douglas Hydro, the proprietor Ron Needham found:

We were introducing changes bit by bit, as the years went on. We'd introduced Italian tastes because we had an Italian chef and I remember one day some lady in the dining-room complained about the lasagne. Well, Salvo [the chef] heard about this, threw everything in the air, everything clattered down, and he was out into the dining-room screaming that his mama used to make it like that and he didn't go to Marks and Spencer! It went down very well you know, it was rather a cabaret act in fact.[88]

These human dramas, and the mixture of personalities between proprietors, staff and guests have always made hotel and boarding house work a little bit different. It is a life that leaves enduring memories.

Last week;
BANK

This week;
SWANK

Next week;
BLANK!

3

*Running a **business** and keeping a **family**[1]*

When the Island was full of visitors, its boarding houses seemed on first impression like little gold mines. Why, the proprietors often had to refuse bookings! But this impression of universal prosperity could be deceptive. This chapter looks behind the scenes to ask whether boarding houses really made a lot of money, and discovers what made the difference between business success and failure. The factors which affected profits can be divided into two groups. The first contained factors over which landladies had control, such as prices, staff, menus, buildings and decor. With hard work, skill, and perhaps a bit of luck, these ingredients could be balanced to create a place to which guests returned time and again, building up a thriving business. Of course, not all boarding houses were the same, so profits varied a lot. For example, there was more

money to be made in large houses than in small ones. Location mattered too, and establishments in inaccessible or unfashionable parts of town could not charge the prices of those on the promenades. There was a hierarchy in such things.

The second group was made up of factors that were not so easily managed. These related to conditions in the districts from which the Island's visitors came. Manx prosperity was linked as though by an invisible thread to the economy of the north-west of England. If this area suffered economic slump, unemployment or other distress, then the people who lived in it took fewer holidays. Running a boarding house in times like these was a challenge indeed. Even in the good year of 1906, the Douglas seafront Belvedere went bankrupt with debts of £139. It was a well-positioned and popular hotel,

Hilary Guard's office at The Hydro in 1961.

Alastair Birnie, aged 2, growing up at the Metropole Hotel as a landlady's son in 1974.

but this alone had never guaranteed success.[2] As the proprietor of one establishment said in 1912: 'the large boarding houses on the front are not the El Dorados that they appear'.[3] Fortunately, there was usually enough peace and prosperity in the north-west to keep the visitors coming, and the century from 1870 to 1970 was an era in which many did make a good living on the Isle of Man, though only a few became truly rich.

Entering the business

The 1890s saw a lot of new boarding houses built on the Isle of Man and there was no shortage of families

Joy Birnie of the Metropole Hotel in 1961.

Group of happy holiday makers at the Belvedere, c.1920
Photos like this, on the front steps, became a tradition.

For married couples, boarding house keeping was a means of securing two incomes in an era when opportunities for women were few and far between. It could also be a way of using the labour of a whole family if a husband was too ill, or had died or left, or if other financial troubles had brought the household income low. Keeping a boarding house was a 'respectable' occupation in the eyes of Victorian and Edwardian society, which was an asset for the newly poor, such as young widows, who could use the job to keep a hold on some measure of gentility. To others, it was a method of social climbing. Although it was important to be seen as 'respectable', seaside towns were places where people of all backgrounds could re-invent themselves, and where opportunities for quick employment with few questions asked could be found in the season. There were also more opportunities for women and a lucky few even rose to management level in large hotels.[4] Married women could also secure a better home than they might otherwise have hoped for by taking on a boarding house. For all these reasons, Victorian resorts had a large number of households headed by women.[5]

For those not born or married into the trade, a boarding house and 'ingoing' had to be acquired on the open market. The ingoing comprised furniture, housekeeping items, and goodwill in the form of contacts with tradesmen and a list of regular visitors. This was an important asset at the time of sale, though it was far from unknown for landladies to take their visitors' list with them secretly when they moved. The price of the ingoing was based on the earning potential of the business, which was of course open to debate. The building itself was normally rented, so there was no need to buy the building as well as the business and only a little capital was required to open a boarding

keen to run them. The Wakes Weeks were one attraction, for they brought a predictable flow of people every year, but this was concentrated into a short and frantic period. The Manx season was shorter than in many English resorts. Summer earnings had to last through the lean months, and when this was taken into account the middle and lower reaches of the industry only made a modest profit. Did this mean that many hopefuls were disappointed, or were there other reasons why so many people tried their hand at seaside enterprise?

house, for even an ingoing could be bought in parts, with former owners holding onto a share in the business. People living in England sometimes advertised in the Manx press to find a boarding house to run. In the 1890s a regular trickle of advertisers from Manchester, Bradford, Preston, Oldham and similar towns sought them in the 'wanted' columns. There is evidence to suggest that newcomers with money tended to look for larger houses. Whilst the majority of small boarding house proprietors in upper Douglas in the early twentieth century had native Manx surnames, those in the more expensive parts of town came from a wider variety of backgrounds.

If entry into the lower reaches of the trade was fairly easy, so was an exit. Some came to the seaside for a few years and moved back when they could not make a living or if they did not like the lifestyle. The Cope family, for example, moved from the Staffordshire Potteries to the Island around 1894. They rented Rose Villa on the Queen's Promenade, one of a large number of buildings created and financed by the speculative builder Alexander Gill. They returned to England for reasons unknown, but after a while came back to the Island for another attempt at the holiday trade. The flexibility of renting made such opportunities possible and opened up self-employment to a wide range of people. Renting was the key; purchase was an option only for a moneyed few. Those who bought boarding houses outright often did this as an investment to gain a regular monthly income. There were always a few properties for sale in the Manx newspapers from the earliest days of the industry. By the late nineteenth century there might be four or five boarding houses on offer each week in winter.[6] The situation changed over time as purchase eventually overtook renting and proprietors became owners of the buildings they

worked in. By the late 1940s up to forty boarding houses a week were advertised in February editions of the *Isle of Man Weekly Times*. A typical advert was that of Kyle House, at 2 Mona Terrace, which offered:

> Twelve bedrooms with hot and cold, bathroom and WC on each floor. Large dining-room and lounge. All the accommodation is well furnished, and bookings for the forthcoming season are excellent. The ingoing can be bought at a reasonable figure by a suitable person.[7]

Who was a 'suitable person'? He or she could be almost anybody, as a proprietor who wrote an advice column for one of the trade journals in the early 1930s observed:

> Regarding the would-be proprietors, it could be safely estimated that sixty per cent of them desire to rush straight into hotel or boarding house proprietorship from some totally different trade or calling which has hitherto been their life's work. Widows who have been left with a small capital and the need to maintain their own position of economic security seek to escape the sorrows of recent bereavement, at

the same time finding a new status of independence, in the Promised Land of hotel or boarding-house proprietorship. Middle-aged married couples seem to think that the husband will escape the irksomeness of being the servant to another, and the long hours of separation will be ended.[8]

The columns of *The British Boarding House Proprietor* and *Hotel* often took part in the general discussions on the question of how, when and whether to enter the business. For example, in 1935 *Hotel* printed a letter from a draper in the Midlands. He had kept a shop for 25 years and was thinking of moving to the seaside. He wrote:

As I consider that it is time my wife and I retired and began to take things easier, we are therefore contemplating a move to one of the resorts . . . and would like to open a small private hotel.

This did not find a warm welcome from the editor, who remarked that if the draper carried out his plan:

It will not be very long before he realises that he has done anything but

retired from business and that his idea of taking things easier will probably be much further off than before.[9]

Behind all this rhetoric, the real issue was all about the aspirations and reality of boarding house keeping. Some who worked in the trade found the assumptions of outsiders that theirs was an easy life very annoying. But it is true to say that there were factors not directly concerned with money which powerfully attracted potential boarding house keepers to seaside towns. These might be called 'quality of life' issues, which were hinted at in the draper's letter. They included the desire for more independence, to be one's own boss, or to make a break with the past and start afresh. The relative ease with which one could become a boarding-house keeper made the dream seem possible to many who had little experience of the reality of seaside business.[10]

Once the dream was fulfilled with the purchase of a business, practical concerns soon crowded in around a proprietor. One of the most important was the building up of a loyal clientele. A new landlady had the option to advertise, but the cost of a thorough campaign put this out of reach for many. In any case, many visitors preferred to return to their regular haunts year after year. So an accepted way of starting out was to build up trade around a nucleus of friends, relatives and former neighbours, whilst simultaneously trying to attract as much casual trade as possible and to retain it for the following season.[11] This worked well from the 1890s to the 1960s until the formula began to weaken as customers began to try new kinds of holidays or went abroad. With declining profitability in the industry, there were calls by 1967 for direct government aid to

'Building a loyal clientele' The Lansdowne Private Hotel, ' Very quiet and homely'. Recommended by clergymen, doctors, lawyers, bookmakers, and broken-down punters'. (An Edwardian joke.)

young people wanting to buy boarding houses.[12] This did not come. New entrants could however hope for cheap loans to help with the cost of improving old premises. There were also a few grants, though complicated rules and regulations made them tricky to obtain.

Keeping costs down

With many houses operating at the margins of profitability, keeping costs down was important. Furniture and fittings also had to last a long time. Hallways, sitting-rooms and dining-rooms had to put on a good show and give maximum 'respectability' for minimum cost.

But changing fashions made this harder when, by the 1940s, the Victorian style fell out of favour. Sleek modern simplicity became the trend and proprietors tried to follow it, doing their best to afford new interiors for their public rooms. Only a few could afford to stretch the budget to major improvements upstairs, and many Manx boarding houses still kept much of their Victorian bedroom furniture well into the 1950s. With margins tight, there was little chance of brand new buildings, so existing boarding houses were patched up, being repaired, modified and extended, instead of being demolished or comprehensively improved.

Alongside the issue of capital investment in buildings and their contents came day-to-day costs such as staff wages and provisions. Hired staff were a major outlay, so if family members could be used instead, this was a real saving. Under the old 'apartments' system, visitors had paid for their own food. But when full board as well as lodging became the norm, control of food bills became an increasingly important skill to master. Heavy summer demand for food from hordes of visitors increased local prices for meat, eggs and other essentials, so large amounts of food were imported to the Island from an early date. Cheap Irish bacon was a particular favourite. The President of the Boarding House Association declared in 1912:

The boarding house keeper can purchase goods, everything required, from the other side, often at less cost to himself than the price in the insular market. It is quite safe to say that from April to October, half the products, including vegetables,

poultry, flour, eggs, butter, lard, bacon, etc. come from England or Ireland.¹³

Economies in food handling through the use of labour saving devices such as mixers, peelers and refrigeration did not come for everyone until the 1960s. By this time, many of the small operators who needed them most already faced declining revenues and found the cost of buying new equipment a fresh worry. Other costs were forced upon the industry through government regulations such as fire protection. In the 1970s, much stricter standards of fire safety were introduced and the cost of modifying old buildings prompted quite a few struggling or elderly proprietors to sell up.

Keeping income up

Holding costs down was only one of the skills needed to run a successful boarding house. Keeping income up was even more important. Short seasons gave rise to the temptation to cram in as many paying visitors as possible. Overcrowding in August was a regular complaint during the 1870s and 1880s. The Wakes Weeks tradition, when whole towns took holidays at once, generated great surges of people and made overcrowding more likely, although groups of visitors who knew each other well were perhaps less likely to complain. To workers from many industrial districts, a degree of overcrowding was nothing new – they had it at home. There was a fine line in such matters which proprietors could walk. They had to be careful not to lose their good name, which was an important asset

for attracting and keeping business. A reputation for cleanliness and good cooking was essential to keep income up and the loss of either of these virtues was a major problem. A good name could be lost by carelessness, or lack of attention to detail, but it could also be put at risk by forces which were hard to control such as pests in food or bedrooms. One such pest was the bed-bug, now largely forgotten, but still a problem as late as the 1930s. If the dreaded pest infested a boarding house, the proprietor could:

> . . . lose the reputation of his establishment. The goodwill he has created by hard work and service evaporates into thin air overnight, his business becomes worthless; worse still, he is saddled with a lease and furniture which have suddenly become valueless. He can neither do any business, nor sell and get out. He is not only holding a dead loss, but must continue holding it, and paying rents and rates for the privilege.¹⁴

A rare survival of some 1950s office files from the Belvedere, on Douglas promenade, gives a fascinating glimpse into the efforts necessary to make an old boarding house more successful. The late 1950s saw a series of adequate but slightly lacklustre seasons. Visitor numbers showed a fall from around 600,000 a year to 500,000 – not enough to be a crisis, but sufficient to awaken grave concerns. Boarding house keepers were called upon to modernise their often elderly and

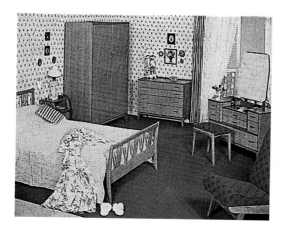

By the late 1950s, the original Victorian furniture of many hotels had fallen deeply out of fashion. Catalogues such as this tempted proprietors who could afford it to modernise. For some years, hated Victorian mahogany wardrobes were regularly burnt by Hilary Guard on bonfire night!

rather tired-looking buildings and facilities. When two new business partners took over the Belvedere, they were keen to move with the times and installed modern equipment such as neon lighting, improved dishwashers, aluminium fittings and cigarette-vending machines. They enlarged the public rooms, knocking out walls to make larger, brighter spaces. In bedrooms, Victorian wardrobes were thrown out and modern fitted units installed in their place, but at £17 5s 0d per pair, only a few could be afforded each season (a double room at the front of the hotel only cost 23s per night).[15] The partners also experimented by opening from February to September. This meant more cost problems. The highest earning member of staff, the chef, was paid £6 a week from February to June, and £8 a week from June to September, in an attempt to retain him for the summer. The hotel fell foul of the

Performing Rights Society for playing recorded music at meals, foreshadowing another conflict between the Society and the Guest House Association in the 1980s. Attempts to improve the facade of the building by installing neon signs turned sour when costs rose above the estimate. Other schemes also backfired when a free holiday competition went wrong. Price-cutting was tried, but this brought a curt letter from Len Bond, the popular secretary of the Tourist Board, stating that competitors had complained about unfair practices, and recommending that the hotel charge 30s per day like everyone else on the promenade.[16]

After just one season, the partners had discovered how hard it was to turn a Victorian boarding house into a small modern hotel. The bedrooms at the Belvedere held more people than the dining-room could seat.[17] The proprietors did not own the building, yet the landlord was not interested in spending money for modernising. The ground floor boards were rotten, and had to be replaced. Even the water-tank in the loft leaked! Of course, the Belvedere was only one of many such establishments suffering similar problems in the Isle of Man and further afield. Keen to cash in on the need for improvements, manufacturers offered a bevy of new products. In the kitchen, the latest electric hot cupboard could be bought for £65, whilst butter-pat machines and Kenwood mixers claimed to save expensive staff time. For the dining-room, paper and plastic cutlery could complement bright modern 'Link' furniture bought in Douglas from Cubbin & Bregazzi. If new tables were too expensive, eight old ones could be covered with green Formica from local timber merchants Quiggin and Company for only £3 13s 0d. 'Beauty-board' covered tired old walls, whilst vinyl asbestos floor tiles replaced polished boards with 'thirteen glowing colours and a real labour saving'.[18]

★

THE
BELVEDERE HOTEL

One of the most Recommended Hotels in the Island

Ideally situated opposite sunken Gardens, close to Landing Piers.

LICENSED

Hot and Cold Running Water in all Bedrooms.

Interior Spring Beds Fitted Throughout.

ELECTRIC LIFT serving all floors.

GAMES ROOM

SPACIOUS LOUNGE

Central for Shopping and Theatres

Chef Cuisine

WRITE FOR ILLUSTRATED BROCHURE

Loch Promenade :: Douglas

Telephone: Douglas 2274.   Guests: Douglas 412

RESIDENT MANAGER

Advertisement for the Belvedere Hotel, 1950s.

Many proprietors were keen to trade for a longer season and the Belvedere was no exception. However, autumn and spring opening at the hotel brought its problems, not least the fact that guests shivered miserably in unheated rooms, with long-disused coal fireplaces. A number of slot-meter operated heaters were hastily ordered for October 1954. Guests could then be as warm as they pleased, so long as they fed the meter! When winter came, some of the larger promenade hotels took on local functions to make a little money. There was not much business to be done and the Belvedere tried to poach the John Henry Lee department store show from the Sefton, but was unsuccessful.

Another change, which arrived in the 1960s, was the increase in small licensed bars for residents. There was a long history of protest and agitation over the sale of drink with meals in boarding houses in the early twentieth century, but by the 1960s the organised temperance campaign had all but died out. There was only a weak opposition, therefore, when many of the larger guest houses started to offer small bars in their lounges. The supply of alcohol was a handy way for proprietors to make a little extra income and offer an amenity which it was hoped would add a touch of modern sophistication. The chic little bars of this period, often crammed into odd corners and fitted out in the teak veneer and padded leather that was high fashion in their time, can still be seen in a few establishments.

The introduction of bars was a sign of how the nature of business changed in response to changing times and public taste. Other changes involved bedrooms. Maximum profit once depended on cramming bedrooms to the limit, but by the 1970s higher quality began to be sought by even the most loyal customers. Improvements chiefly involved knocking small rooms together, and the installation of en suite facilities. The old rules about how rooms were booked had to change too. Acceptance of shorter bookings was forced on the industry by the changing market and greater flexibility in other departments such as mealtimes and menus became essential.

The new Spanish Lounge at the Crescent Hotel, 1960s. This was an attempt to keep up with changing fashions, set by those who could afford to travel to Spain. This style was found in many bars and restaurants in the British Isles during these years.

Moving up

Improving the profitability of an existing business was one way to make more money, particularly in the period of decline from the 1960s. But in the heyday of Manx tourism before this point, it was easier just to move to a larger house, preferably on the promenade, where rooms commanded higher prices. After a few years' work in upper Douglas, the successful small boarding house keeper might look to move from, say, Circular Road or Christian Road to the Loch Promenade or Church Road Marina.[19] In Peel, Marine Parade was the smartest area, whilst in Port Erin the prestigious boarding houses above the bay were popular. For those active in the early boom years when the Island's promenades were being constructed, there was even the opportunity to have a house built to one's own specifications. The McAdam family, who successfully traded on the Loch Promenade in the 1880s, moved to the brand new Silvercraigs on Queen's Promenade at the turn of the century. They boasted to customers in their brochure that the hotel was specially built for the proprietors in

a 'select' part of town. Safeguarding the peace, amenities and social tone of a desirable area was important, because these qualities made it a good place to trade. But sensitivity to social tone was not just for the few. The correct price had to be offered in the correct part of town, and a balance had to be maintained between the proper exercise of the social graces versus homeliness, licentiousness and holiday fun, to fit the preferences and pockets of different types of visitor.

Not everyone aspired to the promenades. Some were happy to enjoy the life of a small business. Others found that extra help made the difference and enabled them to step up. Letty Edgar kept a house with fourteen bedrooms in Buck's Road, and was at first nervous about her husband's plan that they take a house on the front. She only agreed to make the leap when he chose to give up his job to work alongside her.[20] Help from within the family was often given in this way. Another source was the once powerful Douglas landlord Alexander Gill, who for thirty years around the turn of the century proved himself a friend to many hard-working landladies who wanted to advance themselves but lacked capital. If he had confidence in a tenant, Gill often helped her to rent one of his houses by offering a loan to buy the ingoing.[21] In 1910, the ingoing of a good sized boarding house in Douglas cost about £300.[22] This was a one-off sum and did not include rent. Rents varied widely; in the popular areas of the Island's towns they could start at £50 per annum, rising to as much as £160 for a big promenade boarding house.

Managing a business

Long before the Manx Government started a system of grading to raise standards in the holiday industry, advice

on improvement passed between proprietors. It was generally agreed that successful proprietors had to have a real interest in their work and to care about the good name of the house and the welfare of guests. As with any small businesses selling services, much depended on the personality and interest of the proprietor. Not only could a strong landlady shape a business by her personality – the business could shape her. The problems of running a house which did not make much money, or which was full for only a short summer season, could make their mark. A strong spirit was certainly advisable and many of the best landladies were memorable people. This meant that the character of the British seaside landlady was often found in plays, jokes or sketches. The cultural historian Fred Inglis wrote of her that:

> At her best she was an ideal mother – cheerful, welcoming, generous, resourceful, a good cook of well-loved dishes, keeper of a hygienic household; at her worst she was mother's just as necessary negation, queen of the music-hall joke and seaside postcard, demon mother-in-law, tyrannical, mean, avaricious, permanently enraged.[23]

The attention of outside observers was not lost on those who kept boarding houses. Cheeky picture-postcard jokes about their habits, characters and treatment of visitors really got up the nose of most

boarding house keepers. Many also came to dislike the term 'landlady', preferring a more genteel title. One wrote sniffily in the 1930s:

> If one refers to a dictionary, we will find the word 'landlady' defined, amongst other things, as the female keeper of an hotel, inn, or lodgings, but, in spite of all this, I do feel that I am not alone in my intense dislike of the term when used in this respect. From recent observations, it seems that whenever the term is used in the press, it is applied to a lady who may be conducting a boarding house or private hotel. I have never been able to understand why newspaper reporters continue to use such a phrase as 'the landlady of a boarding house' when the substitution of the term 'the proprietress of a boarding house' would be more attractive.[24]

Such objections notwithstanding, the old word continued to be used by almost everyone else until the 1960s, when the re-structuring of the industry and the upgrading of premises finally purged the terms 'landlady' and 'boarding house' from everyday use.

The loss of the word was symbolic of a changing world and a lifestyle which went with it. So who was the typical landlady at the height of her fame, both lampooned and loved? Analysis of the 1871 census returns for resorts across the British Isles reveals that the average Victorian landlady was middle-aged. If she led the household, she was frequently a widow. There were young children in only one-third of establishments; most landladies lived with adult relatives who helped them run the house. By the census year of 1911, things were much the same, though areas that specialised in working-class visitors were more likely to employ entire families. Widows had become less numerous, and more married couples ran houses together.[25] This trend remained evident, though only the larger houses on the Isle of Man tended to be run by both partners because the short season led most men to seek a year-round job. When the folklorist Agnes Herbert wrote about the Isle of Man in 1909, she combined an interest in myths and stories with an eye for contemporary culture. She may have had a romantic view of the Island's fairies, mists and legends, but she stopped with a bump against the realities of modern life when she got to the tourist industry. 'Romance and lodging-house keeping', wrote Herbert, 'do not go together. There is no connection between a seaside landlady and romance. She is quite the most realistic thing in nature.'[26]

The popular image of the landlady as a hard-bitten creature who bound visitors with rules whilst fleecing them blind was an enduring one, and sometimes the aggrieved industry hit back with its own complaints about 'whining grumblers . . . labouring under a species of melancholy mania – a chronic delusion – that the mission of every person in public business in Mona was to rob and plunder the visitors'.[27] No wonder a leading boarding house trumpeted in opposition that 'We have succeeded by good food, good beds, and adequate liberty'.[28] The popular Silvercraigs

During the 1920s, the craze for dancing led to the construction of this dance floor, at the Waverley hotel, with its chic potted palms and parquet.

boasted of 'Four C's: comfort, cuisine, camaraderie and cleanliness'.[29] Liberty and cheerfulness were explicitly linked to business success, and not without reason. In Victorian times this meant, for example, providing a piano in the parlour where guests could sing and play. Some larger establishments went further, and the Waverley was noted for the excursions and games arranged for guests, and even for printing keepsake programmes of the entertainment. Music and dancing remained central entertainments into the twentieth century to provide the fun that holiday-makers enjoyed.

Losses

Losses could affect both single businesses and the resort as a whole. Some were related to larger social or economic circumstances, because people only took holidays when times were good. Trade recessions in a resort's catchment area reduced the number of available visitors. For example, if the West Riding cotton trade had a bad year, Douglas had a bad year. Or when the General Strike of 1926 occurred, the Island lost hundreds of thousands of visitors. Its romantic geography, though attractive to tourists, could also be a

The Upper Douglas Cable Tramway, constructed in 1896 to serve boarding house and other businesses in the fast growing town.

severe problem because the tourist industry was totally dependent on a cheap and reliable sea link. Any disruption was disastrous. Both the First and Second World Wars virtually closed this link, with ruinous results. To the gall of the Manx visiting industry, rival resorts on the north-west coast of England, which needed no dangerous sea crossing, managed to continue trading through both wars. In later years, the rising cost of shipping fuel and the seamen's strikes of the 1970s lost much business. Periods of inflation after both wars and in the 1960s and 1970s also made life harder for business. For example, the sharp rise in the cost

of labour in the period of full employment after the Second World War made business more difficult. The worst period was when competition from foreign holidays really began to bite in the 1970s. This time, many landladies who could afford it decided to retire, and they were not replaced.

Going right back to the heyday of the industry, even in the boom times of the mid-1890s, it was not always easy for small boarding house keepers to make ends meet. What is often called a golden age was not always golden for those who had to live through it. A public meeting in 1895 revealed the shocking truth that

many proprietors in the new terraced houses around Tynwald Street were unable to meet their annual rents of £40. The extra bedrooms with which the houses had been built were not paying their way. Even rent reductions to £25 per year were not always enough. It was the complaints of the boarding house keepers and other businesses in the upper parts of the town which were the main reason for building the Upper Douglas Cable Tramway in 1896.[30] Unfortunately, the new service led to another construction boom, so for a few years 'an excess of building' in the area meant that some of the new houses were not as successful as their builders hoped. However, speculators gambled on the hope of further growth in the visiting traffic and this produced enough demand for new boarding houses to rescue them.[31] The president of the Boarding House Association, James Ducker, remembered that business in the 1890s was not always easy. During a space of only fifteen years, he noted, the available accommodation in Douglas had nearly doubled. As a result of the boom, property on the Loch Promenade had lost nearly thirty per cent of its value, and in the upper town falls of up to fifty per cent had been seen. In Buck's Road, around one third of property was available to let, even in 1910. This hints at a large number of failed businesses and even on the promenade around twelve of the large houses changed hands that year. 'People have been ruined on the front', lamented Ducker.[32] Yet right up until the 1970s, there were always enough new people ready and willing to take the place of those who had retired or gone bust. A former Tourist Board inspector reflects:

> You had to remember that the lower end of the hotel industry in Douglas

was always supplied with an endless new supply of would-be owners who dreamed all their working life in the north of England or in the Midlands of owning a little boarding house in the Isle of Man. This had one good effect: it meant that there was an endless supply of new people to take over houses when the present owners were too old to run them. It meant they could always sell the place for their retirement and this new money was coming into Douglas all the time, almost like new blood refreshing the industry.[33]

Another loss-making problem was caused when visitors left without paying. It didn't take many such incidents to seriously dent the profits of a small boarding house. Proprietors had to take a firm line, and some were prepared to go to law. The political influence of the boarding house lobby came in useful over the matter, because it was able to persuade Tynwald to pass a law allowing hoteliers to seize property from guests and sell it for payment of bills. By the 1920s a regular trickle of hoteliers could be found in court, serving summonses. Unfortunately the jurisdiction of the Manx courts did not extend to England, so a summons was not binding outside the Island. But the mere sight of legal papers being served on the doorstep often had the desired effect. As Mrs Corris of Murray's Road curtly stated, 'the summons usually makes them pay up'.[34] More controversial were actions for breach of promise,

taken when reservations were broken. But most people did not turn to law under normal conditions. A few used debt-collecting companies operating in England if the loss was substantial or if they felt confident that a little pressure would do the trick.

Health problems

Poor health was an occupational hazard of the long hours, hard physical work and hot kitchens in which many landladies had to work. For those not blessed with a good sound constitution, it was easy to lose health under the strain. Before the NHS was created in 1948, all medical attention had to be paid for, which compounded the problem. Many people were unable to afford doctor's fees, so huge numbers of patent remedies were advertised in popular newspapers to fill the gap or to attract those for whom ordinary medicine had failed to cure. There was little regulation of this market, and nothing to stop wild claims of 'miraculous cures'. An advert of 1910 featured Mrs Gibbin, the landlady of 8 Christian Road, who put her faith in Doan's Pills. She had been a martyr to her bowels for many years. But Doan's cured her constipation, and the firm published her story under the headline 'Well known residents of Douglas do not hesitate to speak out frankly'.[35] We can only hope that Mrs Gibbin's visitors made no connection between her little problem and the food she cooked.

It was not just quack doctors who tried to take advantage of the fear of bad health. Everyone from insurance companies to evangelists was in the game. A tract of 1888 aimed at seaside residents told the story of a sick boarding house keeper, lying abed and attended only by her faithful maid. Persecuted by the spectre of 'the old sinner', 'Care', the proprietress worried:

I suppose that things downstairs will all
    go awry
That the waste will be great, that the
    money will fly.
I suppose, too, that the boarders will
    very soon find
Little comforts are missing, if mistress's
    mind
Is not at the head, to control and direct,
And that 'notice' from them you soon
    may expect.
'And', said the old sinner with many a
    smirk,
'Your husband just then, too, may be out
    of work,
A weary and downcast in trouble's long
    fight —
Well! Yes, I confess things don't look
    very bright.
'Then, how will you manage to pay up
    the rent,
The rates and the taxes, when you
    haven't a cent
Coming in all the week, and the doctor's
    bill too,
Running up to high figures? Things look
    black, it is true.'[36]

The poem being written by evangelists, it went on to reveal how prayer was the salvation of the sickly boarding house keeper. Through her faith, the healing Christ supplanted Care, and with her mind much eased, her health returned. Some real-life proprietors were less fortunate. In August 1933 Margaret Carpenter of the Knowsley cut her throat with a carving knife in her own

boarding house kitchen. It was a hot night. The season was at its height, and her husband was sleeping on the couch in his office, too exhausted even to undress. At one o'clock in the morning Kathleen McArdle and Peggy Hart, the cook and kitchen maid, both from Liverpool, were awoken in their basement bedroom by Mrs Carpenter's swearing and shouting. The pair lay still, scared by what they already knew about Mrs Carpenter's history of mental illness. They heard the landlady run into the kitchen and rummage in the dresser. Shortly afterwards, Mrs Carpenter went into the toilet and 'a terrible gurgling sound' was heard by the staff. Too horrified to investigate, the women sat awake until daylight before venturing into the toilet where they found Mrs Carpenter lying in a pool of her own blood.[37] The press recorded the coroner's verdict: suicide whilst of unsound mind. In the adjacent column, advertisements proclaimed the Island as a carefree fairyland.

Children

Boarding house keepers had to balance the demands of work against family life. Living and working in the same building brought both benefits and problems to those with children. A lot depended on the time of year. In winter, family life could be enjoyed in a huge, if rather chilly, house, with lots of room for youngsters to explore and play in. However, in summer every room had to be let and all hands old enough turned to work. Churches in Edwardian Douglas even closed their Sunday Schools in high season, because most children were working.[38] Those too young to work were often sent to live with grandparents, or to stay with family over the water if no local relatives were handy. The newly-married Violet Bridson, inexperienced in keeping a boarding house,

was lucky and had the advantage of a local mother- and father-in-law. Mrs Bridson recalls:

> We were married in the May and we went into the boarding house. Well, I had absolutely no experience at all of it, so my in-laws offered to stay with us for a couple of years. We said yes, would they stay on for a little while. Then baby Joan came along of course and [my husband's] mother didn't think it was fair to leave me with such a big job and a small baby to look after. So they decided to stay for an extra year. Then they bought a house up in High View Road and took Joan home with them at night and brought her back to me in the day-time in the season. Children and boarding houses don't really mix you know.[39]

The Aylens and the Hydro

The stories of people such as Mrs Bridson, who worked in tourism from 1920 to 1980, are still within living memory. Much less is known about the lives of individual boarding house keepers from earlier years. Many left no trace other than a small advert in the *Official Guide* and a census return stating their age and name, and perhaps a family photograph. There is certainly no archive full of old boarding house paper-

A pair of young holidaymakers enjoy the simple pleasures of Peel beach. A competition-winning photo taken by a visitor during the 1950s, during a regular series of Tourist Board competitions.

work from which to reconstruct the details of everyday life, or to tell us exactly how the finances of most small boarding houses worked. Only a few larger enterprises have left enough paper records to tell their story. One such is the Douglas Hydro. It is unusual for a Manx boarding house in that its complete history can be told, from construction to the present day. It was first run by the Aylen family. Thomas Samuel Aylen and his wife Emma Lilian moved to the Island in the late 1880s.

Thomas first set up in business as a tea, wine and spirit merchant at number 59 Victoria Street.[40] His wife ran a boarding house, Seabank, round the corner at 31 Loch Promenade. The success of the two businesses enabled the couple to move up in the world, and soon they moved along the promenade to number 4 in the brand-new Metropole Mansions.[41] Aylen's contacts in the provision business favoured the boarding house enterprise, and he was able to support a large family.

After only a few years at the Metropole block they moved again, to rent the freshly-built Hydro on Queen's Promenade from Alexander Gill in 1910.[42] The Aylens had arrived at the top of the boarding house tree. The Hydro was one of the last hotels to be built on the promenade, and also one of the largest. Aylen made a good living by it for several decades, until in 1922 he formed the Hydro into a private limited company.[43] After the collapse caused by the First World War, the now elderly Thomas must have worked hard to rebuild his hard-hit business. It seems likely that he created the company to secure a future for his daughters Emma, Elsie, Marion and Dora. All had reached their early thirties without marrying and their best hope for a dignified existence was to remain at the hotel in business together.

On paper, the value of the business was of course very good.[44] Aylen sold it to a company of his own making, and paid himself in shares rather than cash. We do not know how much money his daughters subsequently made from running it, since private companies did not have to register their accounts. It was certainly enough for them to move out of the hotel in 1930 to the Red House, a genteel villa on Victoria Road, away from the promenade crowds. After this move, some of the daughters did then marry. Emma became a Corkill and moved to Onchan; Elsie also found a husband and moved to Colwall in Worcestershire. Their father died in 1934, their mother four years later. In 1934 one of the younger daughters, Marion, took over from Dora on the family board of directors and the running of the hotel. In business she had the advice of her brother, also called Thomas, who was the manager of Lloyds Bank in Peel, and who served as the company secretary through the difficult years after their father's death.[45] The unmarried Marion lived at the Red House

for some years. When the Second World War broke out, the requisitioning of the Hydro left her without a business to run. She was an elderly woman and died in 1946, just after the war's end, but not in time to see the return of prosperity to her family's hotel.

Despite its long association with the Aylens, the Hydro building was still owned by the executors of Alexander Gill's estate who kept his assets in a trust. With the dilapidation caused by yet another war, the trust faced a huge burden of repairs and maintenance, so selling some of its property was a way to raise funds. In 1947 Thomas and Emma Aylen finally bought the building they had rented for so long, taking out mortgages on the real estate and business of the Hydro with the Gill Trustees for £14,000, and the Isle of Man Bank for £6,000.[46] No doubt Thomas's banking credentials were of great help in arranging the matter smoothly. But Thomas and Emma were themselves no longer young. They decided to sell the business to a new operator named John L. Breadner and his sister, whilst keeping most of the shares. The Breadners were, like the Aylens before them, on the up. They moved from a boarding house in Palace Terrace and were keen to operate a larger establishment.[47] After a while, they bought out the Aylens' building and ingoing in full and ran the company until 1959, when it was sold to Hilary Guard and his wife.

Guard had £3,000 in hand after selling the ingoing of his previous establishment, the Grasmere, but this was not enough to secure the ingoing of the much larger Hydro. A further £3,000 was needed and had to come from a bank loan. The usually cautious managers of the Isle of Man Bank agreed to advance him the cash he needed on the evidence of his profitable working of the Grasmere. Guard prepared to make Breadner a cash offer for the ingoing of the

The Hydro, Douglas, built 1910, 'one of the last and largest hotels to be built on the parade'.

The Queen's Promenade at Douglas, 1920s.

Hydro, but this caused consternation. Breadner had envisaged a more old-fashioned mortgage arrangement, such as he had made with the Aylens, where Guard would borrow the money from him and pay it off gradually. Such private mortgages were a common way for retiring hoteliers to secure an income for their old age, and they also enabled people of limited means to enter the trade. Eventually Guard and Breadner arrived at a settlement. A mortgage was arranged, secured on the new Hydro Limited Company of 1959 which was created to hold the assets of the hotel. It obtained 'all the goodwill of the company in the hotel or boarding house business carried on at the Hydro

Mr and Mrs Guard, who ran the Hydro from 1959.

Queen's Promenade in the Borough of Douglas; and all plant, fittings, fixtures, furniture, stock-in-trade and effects'.[48] This transaction, however, was only for the business and did not include the land or structure, which still belonged to Breadner. When the ambitious Guard wanted to improve the property, he was confronted with the problem that new works might become Breadner's property if he moved on. After hard negotiation a price of £24,000 was agreed.[49] To execute his plans, the proprietor had racked up a total of £30,000 of debt – a huge sum in the 1960s. His bank manager even asked him how he could sleep at night.[50] But trade was good, the hotel was on a valuable corner site and all the improvements bore fruit. Some of the cost was borne by Isle of Man Government loans especially for hoteliers. These schemes, though heavily criticised by the trade for their bureaucratic restrictions, nevertheless made £9,000 available to Hilary between 1964 and 1969.[51] In the early 1960s business was still good, and the Hydro Limited steadily reduced its debts, a fact recorded each year on its record with the Companies Registrar.[52] By his twenty-eighth year as a hotelier, Hilary had paid off all his debts. After a prosperous and busy career he retired, selling the hotel to the Needham family, who continue to operate it today.

Bigger businesses

When the Hydro was first constructed, it represented the highest class of boarding house by its size, architectural splendour and good position. To go better, one had to operate a large hotel, of which the Island boasted several. The larger hotels served as landmarks of the Island's promenades, around which the boarding houses clustered. They offered a level of accommodation far above that of a boarding house, and were even more diverse. Some, such as the Falcon Cliff, the Douglas Bay or the Sefton, were true providers of high-class board and lodging. Others, including the Villiers and the Grand, specialised in making money from their bars and restaurants, though they also let many rooms. Yet others – among them the Regent, the Port Soderick, the Crescent, and the Creg Malin in Peel – were hotels in name alone, making nearly all their profits from selling drink.

The hotels and boarding houses complemented each other and catered for different needs so were rarely in competition. As a Douglas Commissioner explained in 1891, 'the large boarding houses can take on three [guests] for every one in the hotels'.[53] Boarding houses were for the many; large luxury hotels for the fortunate few.

Profits and prices

The small number of luxury hotels on the Isle of Man showed that an affordable holiday was very important to most visitors. Setting a tariff was, therefore, amongst the most vital and difficult decisions for an hotel or boarding house proprietor to make. In its earliest days as a watering-place, the Island's low taxes and isolated situation gave it a reputation for cheapness, which helped to offset its rudimentary facilities.[54] As the resort developed, it had to remain affordable and long debates on the subject were often aired in the Manx press. Opinions and accusations about the price of a holiday on the Island were of deep interest to most local business-people. Sometimes letters from disgruntled visitors were printed, alleging that the Island was costly, only to be answered by hoteliers or happy visitors who

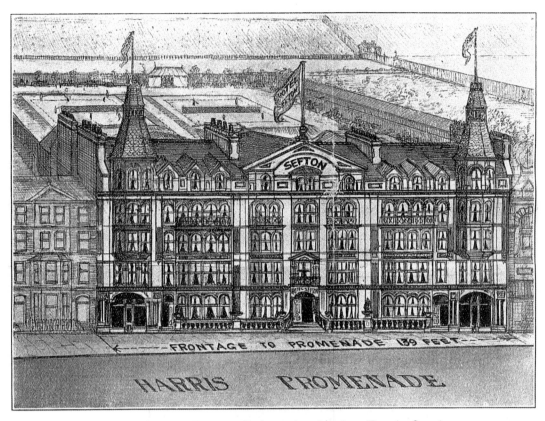

Elevation of Hotel to Promenade, showing Tennis Courts
at rear.

The Sefton, Douglas c.1880–90: 'a true provider of high class board and lodging'. Note the carriage arches which can still be seen in the façade, though long infilled to make extra rooms.

argued to the contrary. The *Isle of Man Times* certainly thought that the Island offered good value for money, and even suggested in the heat of debate that some people arrived with fixed ideas that local landladies were out to fleece visitors. One furore in the early 1900s was caused by a group of holidaymakers who tried to eat their own bread in a Port Erin hotel dining room. Nothing was guaranteed to annoy the landladies more,

though the press tried to pass the practice off as an 'eccentric habit', joking that some people would soon start bringing their own beds, pots and kettles with them. The reality was that many working-class visitors in the 1870s were only just able to afford a holiday. Consuming their own food was a perfectly understandable dodge. Indeed, it was formalised through the survival of the apartments system well into the

A c.1920s postcard from the Villiers, demolished in the 1980s to great local outcry causing a terrible gap in the architectural harmony of the promenade.

twentieth century. The money saved by buying one's own food was highly valued by many families.

Such incidents reminded the Manx that their growing tourist industry was not particularly genteel. Some still hoped that the Island would become 'a resort for a superior and moneyed class of visitors . . . of good breeding, position, and wealth'[55], but the reality was that its lot was firmly cast with the mass market. Such a market was highly sensitive to accommodation costs, so it was no surprise to find that twenty years later the same accusation of high prices was still being made. A typical response found that:

. . . prices are below the English level: the lodging–house business seems to be carried on at a positive loss under present conditions: not as a recognised trade, but mainly as an auxiliary to the employments which are looked on as the chief family support.[56]

This was a possibility for small boarding houses, which could be run by women whose husbands had full-time work, but it was not true of larger establishments,

which had to employ both married partners and pay staff. Such places had a real balancing act trying to make money whilst setting their prices keenly enough to offset the cost of a sea voyage to the Island. In 1896, most houses on the Loch Promenade were charging between 5s 6d and 6s 6d per day, depending on whether they styled themselves as boarding houses or private hotels. In hilly upper Douglas, one paid around a shilling less than in the lower town at 4s 6d per day. Only a few could afford the luxurious Sefton with its 150 rooms at 7s 6d, which would have cost £1 4s 0d more than the average promenade hotel for a couple staying six nights.

Some money-spinning strategies tried by hotels were firmly frowned upon. When Douglas police found out in 1900 that the financially troubled Grand Hotel was not only selling alcohol after hours, but also exhibiting 'certain pictures' in a cinematoscope machine, swift censure resulted.[57] Most boarding houses did not have the option to try such tricks even if they had wanted to, which many landladies would not. They simply provided basic accommodation and personal service, which meant that periods of rising prices – inflation – proved particularly difficult. The Island's first boom had been helped by years of stable or even falling prices, but this long period of deflation ended by the turn of the century. In 1906 *The Caterer* advised its readers:

> Profits have been adversely affected by the high price of provisions and supplies and by the ever-increasing public demand for the maximum of convenience . . . [we need]

> enterprise in advertising, close buying, stopping leakages, adopting improvements, and keen personal supervision.[58]

There is evidence to suggest that this time of inflation must have hit profits, because prices for accommodation hardly rose. Rooms on the Loch Promenade could still be had in 1913 at the 1890s price of between 5s 6d and 6s 6d per day. The Belvedere, the St Elmo, the Oban and the San Remo all offered full board at this tariff, as did the houses on the Marina. For those who did not require lunch, Mrs Cretney and her neighbours on Church Road Marina would accommodate you for 3s 6d. Rooms off Broadway could be had from 4s 6d full board (with the slightly illiterate but charming promise of a 'liberable table') or descending to 3s 6d for tea, bed and breakfast, and a mere 2s for nothing but a bed. This was also the rock-bottom price on the other side of town, where Mrs Quayle on Peel Road would give you a bed for 2s per night – with no hidden extras.[59] It is difficult to see what extras there could have been, unless she charged for baths.

Prices remained remarkably unchanged until the First World War, which brought the worst period of inflation the industry had seen, combined with a collapse in visitor traffic. When the steamers started sailing again in 1919, landladies struggled to raise prices to a level sufficient to make good business without alienating customers. By the early 1920s, the *Isle of Man Times* claimed that low tariffs had 'ruined the trade' by making it impossible to modernise due to a lack of surplus for investment. It stated (to an audience which included many proprietors):

Such charges would never have been possible unless the people who kept the house were content to labour without adequate help in the house and without any profit. The women folk worked and slaved themselves to death, and at the end of the season . . . it was common to find women occupying beds in the hospital suffering complaints from excessive work. This state of things arose from the ridiculous state of prices. Every boarding house keeper seemed bent on ruining his neighbour and capturing his business, forgetting that such a thing was impossible, because as soon as one tenant was ruined, another one came along to take his place.[60]

The relative ease of entering the business made sure of this, and the boarding house keepers of Royal Avenue, in the village of Onchan, were well aware of the situation when they met in March 1919 to consider the tariff question. They resolved that new people coming into the district should be approached and advised on how to set their tariffs to avoid price cutting. The Douglas Boarding & Lodging House Keepers' Association was also thinking along the same lines because everything had increased in price since the war. Candles, still used in many bedrooms, had gone up from threepence-halfpenny to 1s 4d, coal from 26s to 52s and gas from 2s 8d to 5s.[61] The Association declared that for the 1921 season minimum charges would be 10s 6d per day for the promenades, and 9s 6d for other areas. Apartments could be had for 4s per day on the prom, with a charge of 1s 6d per week for cooking – similar to the price at Blackpool. Those prepared to stay in cheaper country areas could keep the cost under 4s per day.[62] These prices were also set at a time when the public began to demand higher standards, such as electric light in bedrooms and running water. One proprietor sighed:

It is all very well to talk glibly about reconstruction and modernising, but few of the critics who speak or write in this fashion understand either property or the business . . . Whatever views regarding the possible profits and income of boarding houses and small hotels may be held by the uninitiated, the truth is that only by the utmost care and rigid economy do they ever show a profit at all. The perpetual call on the financial resources for the purpose of maintaining an old property in a habitable condition makes these pretended profits not only fabulous but utterly ridiculous. Modernising may seem very nice on paper, but in reality it is controlled by the amount of money the residents will pay.[63]

Little over a decade after the First World War came the Great Depression, posing more challenges to all kinds of businesses. Boarding house keeping was no exception. UK unemployment rose to over two million in the summer of 1930, a new and horrifying figure. However, the depression was not uniform across Britain. Some areas, such as the north-west and north-east, suffered far more than others. The Island was invisibly linked to the regional economy of the places from where its visitors came, so this was bad news indeed for Manx tourism. It was made all the worse by the fact that the holiday industry *as a whole* across the British Isles managed to weather the slump fairly well, for along with other leisure pursuits such as the cinema and dancing, it remained very popular with those who managed to keep their jobs. The introduction under UK law of holidays with pay in 1938 also benefited resort towns. But, as in other industries, the overall picture of prosperity in services concealed some hard times. Whilst resorts on the south coast of England in particular continued to prosper, the Isle of Man did not. Unemployment in the north-west was simply too severe for either the 1938 Act or the growth of commercial leisure to come to its aid. Visitor numbers fell from 555,000 in 1929 to a low of 451,000 in 1931. They did not return to the pre-depression level for several years.[64] The value of seafront property fell with them. When the Regent Hotel on Loch Promenade changed hands in 1921 it was worth £9,500, but when an auction attempt was made in March 1932, no buyers could be found for less than half that amount.[65]

With the economy so depressed, accommodation prices were held down. Pleasant rooms in the Belvedere on Loch Promenade, or the Cliff View on Palace Terrace, could still be had for 10s 6d per night – the same price as ten years previously. Even the Villiers offered its cheapest rooms from only 12s 6d.[66] The real problem for the Island remained the sea journey. In 1933 a Londoner could buy an all-inclusive week in Blackpool from Thomas Cook for £5 16s 6d. The same holiday on the Isle of Man cost exactly £1 more.[67] Nevertheless, there were visitors who could still congratulate the Isle of Man for being 'at least twenty five per cent cheaper than a mainland holiday'.[68] Once again the debate about whether a holiday on the Isle of Man was more expensive than its English equivalent came to the fore. So it is instructive to see how the costs of running a fifteen bedroom boarding house (open for a four-month summer season) worked out in 1935. A margin of 5.5 per cent net profit was available after the following outlay[69]:

Food	32 per cent
Wages	15 per cent
Light, heat, water	7.5 per cent
Advertising, printing, stationery, post	7.5 per cent
Renewals, replacements, depreciation, sundries	12.5 per cent
Rents, rates, taxes, insurance	20 per cent

After food, wages represented the second highest expenditure. After the Second World War, the British Government established Wages Boards to oversee levels of pay in the catering industries with a view to protecting workers. But whilst pubs, holiday camps, restaurants and even staff canteens were controlled, the Wages Board planned for boarding houses never came into operation.[70] On the Isle of Man, where such government intervention was rare, there was even less regulation. In any case, such a board would have foundered on the rocks of local politics, for the holiday industry had a strong arm. The issue of how much

PHONE:
Douglas 271

Melrose
~~" ST. ALBANS "~~
~~94 BUCK'S ROAD~~
18 Clarkston Rd

DOUGLAS *19/6* 19*59*
Isle of Man

Mr Albert Hope

To Mrs. P. HANNAH

	£	s.	d.
To Board Residence .... Days			
.... persons @			
per day each			
Tea, Bed and Breakfast ....*7*...... Days			
......*1*...... persons @ ....*12/–*.... *per day each*	*4*	*4*	*0*
3 Dinners monday Tuesday		*10*	*6*
Bed and Breakfast *Friday* ...... Days			
.... persons @ .... *per day each*	*4*	*14*	*6*
Less 10/- deposit			
Received with thanks Total £	*4*	*4*	*6*
P. Hannah.			

Cheap at the price! Mr Bert Hope's honeymoon bill from the Melrose, 1959.

holiday businesses paid their staff was surrounded by silence and there was little collective bargaining. The UK Government's own earnings surveys showed that hotel and catering had the highest concentration of workers earning poverty level wages of all its twenty-six industrial groups.[71] But the 90,000 people estimated to work in boarding houses across the country in the post-war years had little protection from the considerable number of employers paying 'pitifully low' wages.[72]

Campaigns for hotel workers to unionise only created pockets of activity. High labour turnover, small staffs and the number of seasonal or casual workers remained obstacles to workers' organisations. Employers found it difficult to recruit and retain staff, often complaining of their low calibre or lack of interest. But low pay and little job security meant that staff often saw catering as a short-term job, especially at resorts which only opened in summer. Commentators with left-wing views urged the industry to 'tackle the problems at their root cause and pay decent wages', whilst those on the right-wing suggested freedom from regulation was the only way to operate, unless customers wished to pay more for their holidays.[73] Only the most valuable and sought-after staff, such as experienced chefs, were usually well paid.

By 1957, the year in which Harold Macmillan famously proclaimed that 'most of our people have never had it so good', the battle against inflation was still very real. The Suez crisis had not helped, and the *Isle of Man Examiner* gloomily proclaimed 'Up, Up, Up Go Holiday Costs' in January.[74] This time, the tariff increase of more than 2s per night implemented by many hotels and boarding houses only reflected inflation in the economy as a whole. Fortunately, this inflation was accompanied by a more general prosperity and rising standards of living. This seemed to promise more demand for holidays. However, if traditional boarding houses offered little more amenity than in 1900, except perhaps hot running water, then visitors with improved homes would not be satisfied. They began to expect higher standards of accommodation on holiday. In addition, the threat from foreign travel, though distant, was growing more real.

4

Hard times

The tourist industry seems far removed from politics or trouble. Its enduring memories are happy ones. Sepia photographs of sunny days on the beach or promenade somehow suggest that life was better years ago. But many of these photos were taken for publicity purposes and they deliberately showed the more pleasant side of life. When the camera was not looking, many people who worked in tourism knew hard times. The Island went through several painful slumps as well as exciting booms. It struggled through two world wars and the Great Depression. It constantly had to compete with bigger rivals such as Blackpool for customers. Even its clear waters and bright air were polluted by sewage and coal smoke as a result of the coming of thousands of visitors. Yet there is no question that the visiting industry brought modern lifestyles and new prosperity to a once-backward place which had for so long been terribly poor. Did economic growth compensate for the

fact that many of the jobs it created were seasonal, or paid only just enough to live on? Did the good times outweigh the bad? This chapter dares to take a look at the fascinating and forgotten history of some of the worst times in the history of the Manx visiting industry.

From 1765 until the 1870s the Manx Government was hampered by a terrible lack of money. Much of its revenue was sent to the UK Treasury. Financial reforms made under Governor Loch improved the situation a good deal and laid the foundation for big infrastructure projects, especially harbour works. These fuelled a faster pace of private development. The Isle of Man got caught up in the booming tourist industry which was seen all over the British Isles. New houses, piers and promenades sprang up in an atmosphere of entrepreneurial excitement. Some of the businessmen who built and ran them entered local politics and became members of Tynwald

Drying sheets on Douglas beach in 1885.

or local Commissioners. As a result, the tourist interest got a good hold on the levers of power. This was fine as long as the boom continued. But as the local economy settled down, the politicians seemed less good at strategic planning or long-term thinking. Whilst visitors kept coming it was not too much of a problem. However, even in the busy years the politics of tourism had a tendency to lurch into sudden crises.

Drink

One of the first big political crises was about alcohol, once a very controversial subject. In the late nineteenth century, many Manx people held temperance principles; however, most visitors did not. This was one of the reasons why the visiting industry began to generate social friction and resentment as well as income.[1] By

the 1890s the question of drink, visitors and boarding houses was the hottest potato in Manx politics.

The amazing boom in tourism had outstripped the capabilities of existing licensed hotels and public houses and led to the construction of large unlicensed boarding houses which could house up to a hundred people. Many of these visitors wanted beer with their dinners. However, the law stated that if the visitors requested beer with meals, it could not be sold without a licence. A servant had to go to licensed premises such as a grocers with an off-licence or a pub, buy the drink, and take it back to the customer.[2] This was awfully difficult to do at busy times, so many boarding houses ignored the law. As more and more proprietors began to break the law, a scandal started to brew up.[3] The scale of the problem defied attempts at regulation. It was estimated that in August up to 14,000 people per night were served in Douglas boarding houses, lodging houses and hotels, and only a few places serving had licences. How long could the law be openly flouted?

There were other issues which began to be talked about. One was drunkenness. Extra policemen began to be needed in summer to control the increased number of drunks in the Isle of Man and this was thought to be rather a scandal. A more complex part of the issue involved tax. Taxes on alcohol became a big source of income for the Manx Treasury, which quietly took a lot of money from the legal and illegal trade. Those in the know realised that if drink sales were to drop, then government spending on amenities would also have to fall. It was no surprise that the drink question became a big issue around which a lot of other arguments revolved. It was symbolic of the late nineteenth-century problems of how the law was enforced, how the Island was taxed and governed, how boarding houses should be regulated, how visitors were expected to behave and be controlled, and how a new industry had changed everyday life.

Well-established temperance campaigns began to take a higher profile. The movement had made gains in the UK from the 1830s, and an Isle of Man Temperance Association was formed in 1845.[4] The British movement had managed to influence the law and restrict the sale of alcohol somewhat by the 1870s and its Manx adherents hoped to do the same. It was a time of great social changes, and new tensions. Many campaigns – of which temperance was only one – tried to point out the various 'evils' affecting society. The most spectacular were the labour and socialist movements, but there were many others, including secularism, Marxism, republicanism, vegetarianism, feminism and co-operation.[5] Many of the campaigners found a great deal to do in seaside towns because they seemed to be places where a lot of opportunities for immorality were found.[6]

The Methodist church, which was a strong force locally, preached hard on the subject of morality and drink. This benefited the biggest Manx temperance society which was known as the Rechabites. It recruited around 4,600 members by the 1890s – a remarkable one-twelfth of the entire local population.[7] Their campaigning led to the creation of a Tynwald Licensing Commission in 1891. It looked into the whole question of the boarding houses, and concluded:

It having been shown to the Legislature that a law enacted by them is daily and almost universally violated by the boarding-house keepers, it has become an imperative

duty to take steps to prevent this scandal.[8]

The Commission suggested that there were two courses of action open to the Government. Either enforce the existing law more rigorously, or accept the way the wind was blowing and give 'reasonable facilities' for the sale of alcohol in boarding houses. A Boarding House Bill was put forward which favoured the second option. Whilst Tynwald considered its options, campaigning rose to fever pitch. Some opposition to the Bill came from outside the temperance movement. The Douglas Ratepayers' Association, which was essentially a group of ratepayers who opposed anything which might cost them money and who favoured cheap and non-interventionist local government, thought it 'unnecessary and uncalled for'. The Association thought that change would mean their members had to bear the cost of policing any system of regulation. They decried the Bill as 'a direct blow to the liberty of the subject; and an invasion upon the privacy of their homes'.[9] This was only one of the lobby groups pressing Members of the House of Keys. J.A. Mylrea, a director of the Steam Packet and businessman, explained that if he looked after boarding house interests he would offend the temperance party, but if he urged that existing laws should be enforced, the boarding house keepers would be incensed.[10]

Finally, in 1894, a Boarding House Act was passed. It enabled larger houses to serve drink between noon and 11pm from May to September. It was pushed quickly through the Legislature by Governor West Ridgeway, because he needed to maintain his tax revenues which came from selling drink to tourists. These were all the more important because income tax

did not exist at the time.[11] The Government also feared that if they legislated to cut off the drink, the number of visitors would decrease.[12] No wonder that Ridgeway used the very considerable powers of his office to promote the Act.[13] It was passed in only six days, and established the uniquely Manx 'permit system' for the sale of drink in boarding houses.

It should be said that not all ministers of religion were fervently anti-drink. The Roman Catholic church was a lot more liberal than the Methodists on the subject. The priest of St Mary's, Finch Hill, admitted that although temperance was a good thing, a clampdown on drinking would cause suffering to those of his parishioners who depended on a legitimate trade for their living.[14] Some members of the Anglican church thought that the new legislation would be better for public order because the law could once again be enforced. This was also the view of the British government.[15]

Even after the Act, not all boarding houses were keen to sell drink. Some made their business specifically from serving teetotal holidaymakers. There was a long history of teetotalism and seaside holidays. Temperance campaigners were initially very keen on arranging mass seaside trips as part of their social activities, because travel and nature were supposed to take people away from the temptations of public houses.[16] Thomas Cook himself claimed that 'the attractions of cheap excursions have in many thousands of cases been employed to counteract the demoralizing influences of the bottle'.[17] For many years the Isle of Man offered a number of boarding houses run on temperance lines and Cunningham's Holiday Camp began on temperance principles.[18] But, to their extreme annoyance, the temperance campaigners never seemed to really win over the mass of

the people. Deemster Drinkwater reminded what he called 'extreme temperance' idealists that:

> You would really banish a very considerable proportion of visitors from the Island if you prevented a man from having a glass of wine if he was dining at an hotel, or whether he was at any other place, if you prevented him from having his reasonable enjoyment that he expects . . . We must take care that we do not imperil an interest amounting to . . . possibly hundreds of thousands of pounds in this Island.[19]

Soon around ninety boarding house permits were in force in Douglas.[20] The system seemed to be a great success. Yet the experimental legislation on which it was founded was deliberately designed to expire after three years. When it did so in 1897 a new Bill was launched and a fresh battle ensued. Those who thought the experiment had gone well proposed that smaller boarding houses, with a rateable value of £24 or more, might join the permit system. When it came to the vote, the House of Keys (dominated by Methodists) voted fourteen to seven to throw out the Bill. The Legislative Council disagreed, and constitutional deadlock resulted. There was no alternative but to call a general election on the issue. It had brought down the Government!

The general election returned even more temperance supporters to the House of Keys.[21] Two attempts to pass a new Bill in 1901 and 1902 both failed, despite claims by supporters that:

> The order obtaining in the boarding-houses over the last three or four years has exhibited a marked improvement. There is better order kept, the houses are shut earlier, and there is less noise . . . there is every indication that the condition of things in Douglas is decidedly improving.[22]

The permit system never returned. The old system was modified to issue short-term summer licences instead in 1896, and these became increasingly widespread.[23] The anti-drink cause considered itself the victor. Although Rechabite membership steadily declined, the cause went on for years. Even in 1929 there was strong chapel opposition to moves to allow the guests of boarding house residents to take drink with meals.[24] In the 1930s members were still campaigning, calling the fourteen licensed premises on Douglas seafront an 'excessive' number.[25] Police raids also continued as Joseph Barker, proprietor of the unlicensed Rothesay, discovered. He was caught selling whisky to his guests and fined. His excuse – that they all had colds – was at least imaginative. At the popular Alexandra Hotel, Carlo Raineri also received an unwelcome visit from two plain clothes policemen who bought drinks then charged him with breaking the law for serving them. It brought cries of 'entrapment' from his advocate.[26] Even the quieter areas such as Hutchinson Square were raided, with similar results.[27]

Large hotels such as the Alexandra
and Douglas Bay specialised in events,
such as this party for Mrs Richards in
the 1950s. But what did the ladies
drink, and the drivers?

It seemed that many places thought that selling drink on the quiet was still worthwhile.

A tradition of drinking on the steamers also continued to thrive. When Sunday excursion sailings began, many churches feared that these would not only tempt people away from the services but that they would also encourage all-day boozing in floating bars, unregulated by the licensing laws. Visitors on the excursions laughed off such concerns as 'a lot of rot'.[28] The potency of the drink question can be seen by the fact that as late as 1948 the Isle of Man accommodation guide divided boarding houses not by quality or any grading system, but into licensed and unlicensed premises. In 1951 only three boarding houses out of 51 applicants were granted spirits licences – a sure indication of how long the temperance issue continued into the twentieth century.[29] [30] Only in 1954 did a legal challenge from a

small boarding house proprietor result in more small establishments gaining the ability to sell spirits as well as beer and wine.[31]

The 1950s were also a time when young people began to take group holidays without their parents in greater numbers. This was blamed for an increase in cautions for public drunkenness, which caused the authorities to worry about threats to the image of the Island as a family resort. Some blamed drink for the slow fall in visitor numbers.[32]

The morals of Douglas

Image was all-important for a seaside resort. In Victorian and Edwardian times, and even into the 1950s, the Isle of Man tried to maintain an image which mixed

pleasure with respectability. This was done because without this virtue, the social tone of a watering-place might decline, and valuable paying business would be lost. In the early days of popular tourism the Island's rugged and undeveloped nature offered the quiet, thoughtful and slightly austere type of holiday which the mid-Victorian middle classes thought proper. But this soon changed. Austerity was not the tone by the 1890s. Instead, Douglas danced to the latest tunes and the August crowd was firmly working-class. The Government was slightly scared that these visitors might give the place a reputation and bring it down. The Official Board of Advertising kept trying to reach the 'respectable moral [and] moneyed' classes instead.[33] One of its first efforts was to send a lithographed circular to 30,000 'professional men', a tactic which cost almost half the amount it spent on more effective and modern poster advertising.[34] Eventually it accepted the situation and used popular newspapers to print over one hundred million adverts a year.

It did not take much to re-kindle all sorts of fears about the morals of holidaymakers. The year 1894 was already ablaze with the drink scandal when an explosive new incident occurred. The Reverend Thomas Rippon, a Wesleyan minister, preached two highly controversial sermons which got widespread press coverage and were later printed and sold under the title 'The Morals of Douglas'. They were about the behaviour of visitors in the town's dance-halls during the season. Rippon claimed that he had seen over a hundred prostitutes in the Palace Ballroom night after night. The story was too juicy to miss and the UK press seized on it with glee.[35] It posed a real threat to the visiting industry, so denials were swift and vigorous. Angry local people who had financial investments in the dance-halls and boarding houses got an injunction in the Chancery Court to

stop the publication of the sermons. But this didn't stop Rippon from proclaiming that Douglas had been 'shunned'.[36] The scandalous affair was one of the main reasons why the Government backed its new Board of Advertising. Good publicity was sorely needed to maintain prosperity. The sermons had done a lot of damage, as a newspaper editorial admitted:

> The Blackpool pictorial posters are plastered all over the Island. Douglas remains unsung — except by the Ripponites. Is it still too late . . . to bring prosperity to the Island this year?[37]

The affair clearly showed how issues of politics, morality and money-making became bundled together in a resort. The scandal didn't die quickly. Even after six years, the Manx press reported with horror that the Island's rivals on the Lancashire coast were still running a whispering campaign. They were even claiming:

> . . . in Blackpool, Southport and Morecambe that Douglas is flagrantly immoral; that the whole of its inhabitants . . . openly connive at encouraging frivolity, and appeal to the low and sordid tastes of our visitors; that our places of amusement are dens of infamy, and our hotels and singing rooms are haunts of wickedness. The most forcible

An unusually quiet Douglas beach in 1895.

Edwardian paddlers in Peel, 1895, with the new Marine Parade.

argument . . . heard is 'Don't let us get as bad as Douglas'.[38]

Critics of the Ripponites argued that the accusations had taken on a life of their own and done a lot of harm to the Island.[39] This seems unlikely – buoyant visitor figures suggested that they hadn't affected arrivals at all. This being so, why was the debate so fierce and important to so many people? It was central because of what it revealed about fears surrounding development. The drinking, dancing and boisterousness criticised by the moral reformers were clear evidence that Douglas, at least, had become a popular resort. Some people did not like this fact at all. Whilst it is highly unlikely that a hundred prostitutes ever came anywhere near the Palace Ballroom, it is clear that Douglas in particular offered holiday activities of the sort which the lower middle and working classes preferred. Businesses such as the Palace risked a lot of money and invested heavily to cater for the tastes of the mass market, not for a few aristocrats. Investors in these companies were not prepared to see their trade put at risk. This is why they kept up such a vigorous opposition during the 'morals of Douglas' affair. Douglas was certainly not the only place to suffer convulsions over social class and about what kind of town it ought to be and how visitors should behave.[40] Debates like this raged in many places all over the British Isles at the time.

A generation later, as the tourist industry matured, most resorts had settled into catering for their own particular clientele. On the Isle of Man, Douglas was known as the place for the young and lively. Ramsey remained genteel. Peel, Port Erin and Port St Mary catered for families. But thirty years after the morality

scandal, the desire to keep Douglas 'decent' could easily be seen. The *Isle of Man Weekly Times* argued:

> It is worthwhile to lose a visit from a warship or an excursion-party from a big factory, if discouraging these people is the only way of keeping the place not 'select', but just ordinarily decent. Douglas at one period found itself possessed of a reputation . . . we trust that now it has shed that reputation and become known as a suitable resort for happy, healthy holidaymakers.[41]

'Happy and healthy' had taken the place of the old 'respectable and moral', but the message remained the same. Boarding house proprietors kept an eye on the behaviour of visitors within their houses. This led to all sorts of grumbles about landladies snooping about, looking for evidence of sexual misconduct or secret drinking. However, there were reasons for doing this. It wasn't necessarily a personal crusade. When landladies snooped, they were usually making sure that their livelihood was not put at risk by scandals which could give their house a bad name. Unfortunately this tactic sometimes backfired and some new kinds of holiday developed because visitors became frustrated with the rules and regulations of the typical boarding house.

Rivals!

For the holidaymaker of 1900 who was not rich, there were very few alternatives to staying in a boarding house. Some farmers took in summer visitors. A few organisations began to offer hiking and fresh air holidays, but many people thought that these were just for cranks. However change was just around the corner. On the Isle of Man it took the form of Cunningham's Holiday Camp. It was started for young men in 1894 at Howstrake and was only a couple of miles from Douglas. It soon moved to Little Switzerland, a more central site on the brows above the promenade. Within five years it was a well-established part of the Island's visiting industry and soon the boarding houses started to see it as a rival. Cunningham's built its success on three great attractions: it was cheap, there was lots of food, and it was relaxed. It could offer cheap holidays because the camp's tents were a lot less expensive to keep in repair than the permanent buildings which boarding house keepers had to maintain. The large size of the camp also made holidays cheaper. The huge quantities of food and supplies that it bought allowed the business to negotiate good prices. Its kitchens were modern, too. It produced hundreds of meals a day in large, industrial-size kitchens unlike those of the boarding houses. In addition, the low cost of buying empty land away from town allowed Joseph Cunningham to develop his site just as he wished and to adapt it as he pleased. This flexibility was denied to those who ran terraced boarding houses, who were stuck with whatever the landlord had built.

The camp didn't just offer visitors a cheap holiday. Apart from its temperance principles and the requirement to be in by locking up time it had few rules. It offered lots of fun and games, all available on-site. This was a far cry from the average boarding house.

Only the larger establishments had dance-rooms and in-house entertainment even in the 1920s. Smaller houses might offer a piano if visitors were lucky. No wonder the camp seemed so free and easy. Its advertising even made a point of telling campers that they could enjoy themselves away from the 'watchful eye of a boarding-house landlady'.[42] Camping, claimed Cunningham, was not just cheaper than a boarding house holiday, it was more fun.[43] The camp had the resources to manage its image and it advertised efficiently. It regularly published the *Camp Herald*, and posted it to customers old and new. This sort of publicity was advanced for the time. There was no way that most boarding houses could match it. Only the largest or most enterprising establishments had begun to print small booklets which were sent to enquirers. The best hope for many was the *Isle of Man Official Guide*. Later the Boarding House Keepers' Association created the *Douglas Weekly Diary* to act as its own information sheet.

The boarding house keepers tried to use their political influence. There were, after all, thousands of them and many local politicians had a hand in the trade. In 1909 the local press invented the term 'campophobia' to describe the attitude of hoteliers who were also members of Douglas Corporation. They insisted that the camp was unhealthy. Boarding house keepers who had invested heavily in the idea (if not always the reality) of 'perfect sanitation' and their friends at the Corporation argued that the camp could become a source of infection and disease. When the camp remained healthy, critics turned their attention to its morals – but Cunningham's strict temperance principles and camp rules withstood criticism.

The frustrated boarding house keepers turned to arguments about tax. The camp enjoyed very low rates

because local rating assessments were made in the winter when it was closed with the tents packed away. Only permanent buildings were assessed and the tent site was used as grazing land. Boarding house keepers, on the other hand, paid rates on large permanent houses all year round. They were furious that the camp seemed to be getting off so lightly – it even paid a very low water bill because assessments were made on permanent and not temporary structures. To the frustration of the lobbyists, they did not win the day and the camp continued much as before.

The camp was certainly a target for the fears and resentment of boarding house keepers. Yet it seems to have affected their trade less than they suggested.

Metropole Mansions, 1910, showing the sheer perfection and harmony of the promenade façades at their best.

The Rutland Hotel, 1910. Note the sumptuous curtains and blinds. The boats were 'painted in' with 'printers' white'.

Many of its customers wouldn't have been able to afford a boarding house holiday.[43] Many landladies were also rather ambivalent about the large all-male groups in which Cunningham specialised. They were apprehensive about rowdiness, drinking and damage to the furniture. Most were quite happy to cater for families, who were more reliable, came year after year and who were easier to manage. The biggest reason for the anti-camp protests was caused by the imbalance in profits between it and the boarding houses. To the exasperation of many hard-working hoteliers, the camp was simply able to make money more easily than they were. The high fixed costs of the hoteliers, who had to maintain their premises all year round, were easily undercut by the camp. Its size also made for efficiency by creating economies of scale.

The Isle of Man's hoteliers were, in the 1910s, among the first to confront new forms of development which spread throughout the British Isles. In the 1930s and 1940s there was a massive development of holiday-camps, camping holidays, and later caravanning. In many English seaside areas sprawling caravan sites sprang up on the edges of towns to the horror of most local residents.[44] The lobbying of the Manx hoteliers at least saved the Island from this. No static caravan parks were allowed.

The First World War

Despite several local political scandals and rows, the early twentieth century was still a period of peace and prosperity for the Isle of Man as a whole. Annual passenger arrivals broke the half-million barrier in 1910 and the Board of Advertising declared that the resort had permanently turned the corner into

undreamt-of growth. It even dared to predict that the Island would take one million a year during the next decade.[45] But all this ended abruptly in 1914. Attorney-General R.B. Moore told a government financial committee:

> When war broke out, the Isle of Man was full of visitors, and we were promised the best season we ever had. It had been a record season up to that date. We were full of goods ready to sell to the visitors, and ready to do our best to bleed them of every sou they had. News of the outbreak of war came, and within a week the Island was empty. That season was ruined, and for the next four years there was no season at all.[46]

Boarding houses stood empty and their proprietors soon faced ruin. The Lieutenant Governor, Lord Raglan, advised them to sell up and seek work elsewhere.[47] This was foolish and useless advice to many people for whom the holiday industry was their sole livelihood and the vessel in which their life savings were contained. Many proprietors had nowhere else to go. Nor could visitors come even if they wanted to: the ships on which the tourist industry depended were quickly requisitioned for war work. The Isle of Man Steam Packet Company's fleet was reduced from fifteen to four small vessels within a few months.[48] This rendered mass tourism impossible. In any case the threat of U-boat action in the Irish Sea turned the journey to the Island into a scary one which few risked for pleasure.

Financial losses mounted by the week. Boarding house furniture was sold and shipped to England, where the second-hand furniture market was booming. The sales were a sign of desperation, for furniture was an expensive investment for proprietors who could not do business without it. It was the biggest asset of proprietors who did not own the houses they traded in. Once this was sold, it became impossible to pay the rent. One Douglas boarding house owner later explained how the decline set it. She took £168 rent per year from her tenant up to 1913. She received the usual money in 1914, then only half of it in 1915. By 1916 she was glad to get £25 and for the tenant to stay at all. In 1917 the tenant simply paid the rates and kept the house aired. The landlord lost £555 in rents, but had no relief from mortgage interest. At the end of the war it cost £100 to repair the house, and the most she could rent it for at first was £120.[49] The largest owner of boarding houses in Douglas, Alexander Gill (who owned 160 properties in Douglas at the outbreak of war), was also forced to reduce his rents to one-third of their normal level. Large houses went down from £200 per year to £65; smaller ones from £75 to £25, or less if tenants were unable to pay even this small sum.[50]

Whilst Gill and his tenants cut back, other businesses made money out of the war. This only made the boarding housekeepers' plight more noticeable. Those who prospered most made their money from internment. The internment of 'enemy aliens' began in August 1914, and over the course of the war 29,000 German and Austrian men were held on the Isle of Man.[51] At the start of the war, Cunningham's Holiday Camp was pressed into service and around 3,000

Beach view with bathing machines, c.1880.

profits thrust into their hands, both by the demands of the aliens' camps and by the soaring prices of their produce in the world markets.[53]

were held there. The site at Douglas quickly revealed its inadequacy for the task, so a much larger camp was built at Knockaloe, near Peel, which held more than 20,000 at its height.[52] The political campaigner and MHK Samuel Norris saw how many suppliers made a good profit on selling goods to the Government. He wrote:

This was all the more horrible to those who worked directly in the holiday industry. By 1915 the position of the boarding house keepers was desperate. A group of women banded together and started a campaign. They wrote to the Manx Government and to many influential British figures, including Members of Parliament. A letter of April 1915, sent by Mary Dyson and Eleanor Thomas from the Clifton on Central Promenade, explained:

To help local trade, all the goods used at the camps were, as far as possible, purchased in the Isle of Man. What this meant to local tradesmen will never be fully known, but that policy saved tradesmen generally from absolute stagnation and bankruptcy, and, in many instances, meant wealth beyond their wildest dreams. The farming section of the community, too, had enormous

We, the women boarding-house keepers of Douglas, feel that something should be done to alleviate the distress of our Island. Last August we were in the midst of our season when war was declared and the season collapsed . . . our life-savings are invested in our houses, and we feel that we are being unjustly treated.[54]

They looked enviously at the resorts of Blackpool, Southport and Morecambe, where their opposite numbers could billet troops, convalescents or evacuees.[55] When the war started, Blackpool's landladies had feared ruin, but full employment in the textile industry actually created a boom which meant that war-weary visitors

had plenty of money to spend. Large numbers of troops were also billeted in the town, and although the Government only paid 3s per day for each soldier, the money was available all year round.[56] But on the Isle of Man there was nothing. By May an official Boarding & Lodging House Keepers Women's League was formed to campaign for the suffering landladies. It was no longer just a question of rents and rates: things had got worse.

> The tradespeople are refusing us any further credit for food supplies, we see no possible means of providing ourselves with even the bare necessities of life. [We are] panic –stricken as to the prospect immediately before us, and all this through no fault of our own.[57]

Local reformers held the Manx Government responsible, but senior local figures in the wartime administration blamed delays at the British Treasury in releasing money for assistance. A plan was created to help boarding house keepers by paying one third of their rent, on condition that landlords demanded no more.[58] Some assistance also came from the extension of the National Relief Fund to the Isle of Man, and 700 women made appeals for the allowance of 8s a week.[59] However, the position of the landladies was not helped by their refusal to consider billeting Germans in their houses. Some said that they would rather starve than suffer that.[60] Samuel Norris remembered:

> I walked along the Douglas promenade from end to end — two miles — on August Bank Holiday Monday 1915. En route I passed eight people . . . In peacetime, thirty thousand visitors would have that day come to find health and pleasure and bring industry and prosperity to the Island . . . [now] the closed houses and hotels, the shuttered shops, the silent dance halls and theatres spoke eloquently of the war.[61]

As Norris noticed, it was not merely boarding houses that suffered. Entertainment companies large and small also ran up losses. The Palace Company, the Island's largest, made a profit of £14,000 in 1913. But over four years of war it ran up losses of more than £53,000, despite using many of its premises for war work. When depreciation and dilapidation of buildings were taken into account, the company estimated that its loss was more like £100,000.[62] At least the company had the resources to survive. Smaller businesses had less in the bank to fall back on. Pressures for action to assist those in need grew stronger. A government Loan Scheme to Distressed Boarding House Keepers was proposed and laid before Tynwald in June 1915. But the terms of the scheme were denounced by its intended beneficiaries as harsh. Discontent led to the formation of a War Rights Union, mainly composed of boarding house keepers and owners.[63] They campaigned for reduced rates, for the billeting of troops or convalescents in their houses, and

for practical assistance to pay the rates by grants, not loans.[64]

This was asking for something which the Manx Government had never done before. It had never directly intervened in private businesses. It had not levied any income tax but it had never given any grants either. Therefore the idea of loans was seen, at least by Lord Raglan, as very generous and rather radical. But the reformers wanted something different. The loans scheme was hated and only £3,000 of a projected £50,000 was borrowed at first.[65] With more than 200 empty premises in Douglas alone there was an air of crisis. The reformers campaigned for the Government to help the local authorities so that they could act more leniently towards defaulting ratepayers without becoming insolvent themselves.

The thorny issue of income tax added an extra complication. The British Government – which had great influence over Manx affairs at this time – was quietly keen to introduce it. However, Governor Raglan's management of the Island's wartime finances was expressly designed to avoid the move. Tensions grew as some thought that property holders were bearing too much of the tax burden whilst the wealthy got off lightly. A leading boarding house keeper complained of:

The unsympathetic and almost antagonistic attitude of our own officials towards us . . . the centre around which so much trouble moves is, of course, taxation. Our officials seem to be prepared to tax tea, tobacco — anything, in fact, but

themselves . . . we are not asking the wealthy people to bear our burden . . . we are only asking them to play the game and take their own share.[66]

As they grew disillusioned with Tynwald, over which Raglan seemed to have a stranglehold, the campaigners turned to Whitehall and Westminster. They wrote to English MPs about the 'humiliating' loan scheme.[67] With the boarding houses as its cause célèbre, the League evolved from being a single-issue campaign to a wider political programme with the slogan 'redress, retrenchment and reform'. The Manx government was accused of apathy and neglect. To the reformers, its reliance on indirect taxation placed a disproportionate burden on the poor. An open letter reminded the governor that commodity taxes borne by the visiting industry had preserved the rich from income tax 'for the past fifty years'.[68] This, combined with a lack of interest in social welfare (there were no old age pensions or health insurance), was fully exposed by the pressures of war. There were criticisms of the 'singularly illiberal' constitution of the Isle of Man which the reformers claimed had failed in its duty to the people.[69]

The most needy remained women who kept boarding houses. The failure of the tourist industry left them far fewer options than male workers who could join the forces or do other essential war work. Unlike in Britain, unemployed women from the service sector were not always able to move into war work on the Isle of Man because it had almost no factories. Eventually some textile workshops were made in the Derby Castle Ballroom and a Manx Industries Association produced

knitwear. This was only a drop in the ocean – there was just not enough work to lift the resort out of financial depression.[70] Nor did farmers use female labour on any scale because there were plenty of internees if extra hands were needed.

With nowhere else to turn, landladies remained keen supporters of the War Rights Union. They continued to call for the tax revenue from the camps to be used to pay rates and relieve war distress. On Tynwald Day in 1916 the Union urged all Manx people to 'assert your rights and defend your liberties at . . . a great national protest meeting'.[71] Socialists and trades unionists became involved in the campaign which the landladies had started.[72] The ancient right of presenting a petition of grievance was used to make a demand for Lord Raglan's resignation. The events of that day created increased government opposition to the campaign. Leading members were prosecuted for unpaid rates as a way of trying to silence them. Douglas Corporation changed its policy and urged the boarding house keepers to accept government loans to pay outstanding rates.

The campaign gained new strength when the UK newspaper the *Manchester Guardian* became interested. It wrote articles about the 'outdated' Manx constitution and drew the attention of a wider public to the Isle of Man. One of the most dramatic events it reported was an official attempt to seize boarding house furniture to pay outstanding rates in October 1916. As the coroner's van went from house to house, it was followed by crowds of angry people. Some rang dinner bells and banged saucepans to call attention to what was taking place.[73] When the furniture came up for sale, the reformers urged citizens to attend the government auction to protest. Hardly any lots were sold. However, several boarding house keepers were charged with

contempt of court, and Samuel Norris, the leading light of the campaign, was sent to prison. The British Home Secretary – who was the superior of the governor – was petitioned for the reformer's release, but he just referred the question back to Lord Raglan. The best the British Government could offer was to reassure campaigners that it had sent a Constitutional Reform Committee to the Island in 1911 and that progress on its recommendations would resume after the war. For the time being, it said it was working with the Manx Government to help the boarding house keepers.

Norris was released after a few weeks, and resumed leadership of the War Rights Union, which continued to agitate on questions such as the price of food, poor relief, and other issues which affected all citizens as well as unemployed workers in the holiday industry. Manx income tax was eventually imposed as a temporary measure in 1918 to pay for government subsidies on bread.[74] By this time, a small visiting season had begun which gave some hope to the landladies. The campaigns which they had started had also borne fruit, and marked a real step forward in making the Manx Government more genuinely democratic and more accountable for the well-being of its people.

As the war drew to a close in winter 1918, the visiting industry turned to the job of reconstruction. The prompt closure of the internment camps and government factories on the Island soon after the armistice brought a last bout of hardship to 800 women workers, who were suddenly unemployed.[75] There was a lot of making good to be done. On Loch Promenade, almost half the houses stood empty. Even the landlord Alexander Gill who had done much to look after his tenants had eighty empty properties.[76] In Ramsey, Port

Modwena Hotel, Loch Promenade, 1920s.

En route to Douglas by the Steam Packet in the 1920s.

Central Promenade, Douglas, I. o. M.

"THE WARRINGTON."

The Warrington, Central Promenade, Douglas, c.1920, built in the 'Swiss' style, influenced perhaps by Gill's travels on the continent.

Erin and Port St Mary, the situation was the same. The Island's boarding house keepers owed the Government £11,000, through debts secured on their furniture with interest at 5 per cent.[77] The industry placed all its hopes in the pent-up demand for holidays which had built up during the war years. Fortunately this began to make itself felt very quickly. By August 1918 the tiny war-reduced steamer fleet could hardly cope.[78] Full employment during the war made many industrial areas prosperous. When 96,000 visitors arrived in 1919, followed by a flood of 500,000 for the 1920 season, they spent money freely and created a short boom that rescued the fortunes of the Isle of Man.[79]

The trauma of the war was not quickly forgotten. Memorials to the dead were built, of which the largest was in the centre of Douglas on Harris Promenade. Some worried that it would make visitors feel depressed, but most people felt that the war dead deserved every honour.[80] Some good publicity was needed to cheer people up and to counteract the bad reputation that wartime Manx politics had attracted in the British press. The Board of Advertising took up its work again with new enthusiasm, and the *Isle of Man Times* sent a reporter to the AA and RAC to talk up the first post-war TT Races.[81] A liberal programme of political reform was put in place by the Government

The war memorial seen through the Villa Marina Colonnade.

Aerial view of the Savoy Hotel, 1920s. New and old meet: the modern use of aviation shows the traditional bathing machines, which would be used for only another ten years or so.

Carisbrook, Central Promenade, Douglas, 1920s.

which included the introduction of old-age pensions for the first time. The seasons began to pick up. Visitor arrivals rose steadily, until by 1923 they were up to a healthy 448,000, enough to see most boarding houses full during early August, with a fair proportion well-booked until the end of the month. It took four or five years for the visiting industry to recover fully from the after-effects of war. Visitor numbers never again rose to the high levels of the 1910s and they began to fluctuate more year by year.[82]

One event which caused a big fall in numbers was the British General Strike. There was a lot of industrial unrest in the 1920s and it usually centred on wages. The war had caused a huge inflation problem, and workers made demands for higher wages to cope with the rising price of food and goods. The tourist trade was not exempt from the problem. This table shows how the cost of running a boarding house had risen in 1925 when compared to 1913.[83]

Item	% increase
Hotel's wage bill	Over 100
Employees' insurance	400
Meat	70
Flour	55
Fish	50 to 100
Poultry	50
Glassware	40
China	100
Joiners' and upholsterers' wages	150
Decorators' wages	100
Table and bed linen, approximately	50
Carpets	50
Stationery	85
Furniture	65

In times like these, it was difficult for proprietors to judge their prices. Inflation had to be taken into

account, but the Island could ill afford to gain a reputation for high prices because some visitors were already put off by the cost of the sea journey. It was difficult because for many years before the war inflation had been very low. An editorial in the *Isle of Man Times* – which was always a strong supporter of the holiday industry – put it this way:

> There can be little doubt that the low tariff charged by the boarding-house proprietor in the past was the main cause of [our] general insecurity . . . the charges were ridiculously low, 3s. 6d for supper, bed and breakfast . . . the women folk worked and slaved themselves to death, and at the end of the season were often as not in debt to their tradesmen or landlord, or both. At the end it was common to find women occupying beds in the hospital suffering from complaints due to excessive overwork. How can this state of things be remedied? The easiest and most natural way is by an agreement to raise the tariff.[84]

By the standards of today there was little help or guidance from the Government for struggling land-ladies. When a committee of the UK Privy Council came to the Island to try to get more money from the Manx Treasury to pay off war debts it was told that there was none to spare. Normality had returned but prosperity

was very fragile. Despite the annual flow of visitors, the Island still faced many problems. Investment levels in new hotels and leisure facilities were low. Debts incurred during the war were still being paid off. Many buildings had become dilapidated and cost a lot to repair. This was also true for many British resorts. Even Blackpool, which had a very good war, built very few new hotels in the 1920s. Most boarding house keepers managed to find the money for electricity and hot water to be installed to modernise existing buildings but that was all. The Government did a similar job when it improved the Loch Promenade by making it wider and adding sunken gardens in 1934. This was a winter works scheme designed to combat seasonal unemployment as well as to provide an amenity for visitors. At the opening ceremony it was pointed out that it had employed over 19,746 man-weeks over six years.[85] Sadly, Douglas was not particularly noteworthy as a corporate investor. Its promenade scheme cost £30,000 – a substantial sum but rather unremarkable when compared to the work done by some English resorts. The most lively municipalities oversaw a flowering of investment in public works such as gardens, open-air bathing pools and lidos during the 1930s. Bexhill's stunning De La Warr Pavilion was acclaimed as an architectural master-piece at the cost of £80,000. Morecambe's swimming stadium, next to its modernist-movement Midland Hotel, cost £120,000.[86] Sadly, this exhilarating modern architecture was little seen on the Isle of Man. The most notable buildings of the inter-war period were the Crescent Cinema, the Crescent Hotel, and the Villa Marina Arcade. The Villa was Douglas Corporation's showpiece and its 1931 improvements, particularly the colonnade, did much to enhance the sea front.

The wider political and economic situation in Britain still looked worrying. The Wall Street Crash of

1929 ushered in the Great Depression which spread from America to Europe. Textile and heavy industrial towns such as those which formed Britain's traditional hinterland were especially hard hit. By 1929 one cotton worker in two was out of a job, and a quarter of all coal miners were unemployed.[87] Their plight gave the period its nicknames of 'the devil's decade' and 'the hungry thirties'.[88] British unemployment reached three million by 1932, and did not fall below a million until the Second World War.[89] However, economic problems were unevenly spread across the British Isles and the Isle of Man was tied to many of the old industrial areas which did not do well. By contrast, many new jobs were created in light industries such as motor and electrical products. Most of the new factories were in the south of England, which was a boon to south coast resorts linked by modernised fast electric railways. The most exciting development for these resorts, and for the people whose living standards improved, was the spread of paid holidays. In 1931, only one-and-a-half million people enjoyed paid holidays; by 1939 over eleven million were entitled to them. This opened up the seaside to working people who had never been able to afford a week or more away. Across Britain, twenty million people visited the seaside each year, of which fifteen million stayed at least a week. A new leisure culture boomed, and the resorts played a big part; others elements were cinema-going, football, dancing and hiking.

The weak economy and short seasons meant that Victorian and Edwardian seaside buildings were patched up instead of being fully refurbished or replaced. The Chief Industrial Adviser to the British Government, H.D. Henderson, thought that tourism would become a growth industry and advised that some of the attention being given to the depressed areas should also be spent on improving hotels. However, he admitted that there was little that could be done in the short term.[90] Therefore when we think of the 1930s as a golden age for the British seaside holiday we should be cautious. It was a busy time but there were some important problems facing the industry. Nevertheless, compared to the 1940s, the decade was reasonably good. Whatever the problems of navigating a boarding house through the depression, they were as nothing compared to those which were caused by another world war.

The Second World War

As the clouds of war gathered in the late 1930s, the newspapers and wireless bulletins grew ever worse but the British public were determined to enjoy their holidays despite the troubles. The British Health Resorts Association ran a campaign urging people to take their holidays, as an antidote to nervous strain. The pulse of resort life was taken by the *Daily Telegraph,* which noticed a definite reluctance to let the international tension affect the holiday season. Yet it warned grimly that the future looked bleak for the many thousands whose livelihood was at the seaside.[91] This was all the more unfortunate given that the 1939 season promised to be the best for years. The economic depression had begun to lift and bookings in the Isle of Man were good. The resort experienced a very successful August bank holiday and 45,000 people were landed in twenty-four hours from an amazing twenty-five inbound sailings to Douglas. It was to be the last such August for years. When war was declared, there were only a few panic departures. Most people kept calm but everyone knew that the season was wrecked.[92] A boarding house keeper from Empress Drive remembers that day:

Douglas promenade in World War II.

The house was quiet at the time. I remember that we had a speaker in the lounge (we didn't have one downstairs of course) and I remember that [Chamberlain's] speech was going to come on. So we went up. I was just stood inside the lounge door when he said the war was declared. It didn't really hit me at first, you see, and then one or two of them said 'Well that's that, I suppose.' And they soon left and I shut the doors and saw all the, kind of emptiness, you know. We [the boarding house keepers] were very despondent, nobody knew what was going to happen. For so many of them, that was all they did. I was fortunate; my husband was working, he had a job, but there was a lot of

them didn't. Nobody knew what was going to happen.[93]

History had taught the boarding house keepers some lessons and the memory of the First World War was strong. They were determined that the Government should act quickly to prevent another bout of destitution. 'We know', went up a great cry, 'what happened last time.'[94] The local newspapers also campaigned for the hundreds of men and women who were too old for the forces or war work who had lost their livelihoods.[95] At first, the boarding house keepers asked the Government to send them wounded soldiers. They also tried to get evacuated children and even suggested a tariff. Not everyone was sympathetic and some criticised the price of 8s 6d per child per week as further evidence of proprietors' grasping natures.[96] When the campaign seemed to be going nowhere, the Douglas Boarding House & Apartment Association placed advertisements in the London press announcing:

> ISLE OF MAN: a really permanent place of security. Safe accommodation to suit all pockets. Very reasonable terms. Home farm produce. Regular mail boat services to and from Liverpool.[97]

By October, the bankruptcy of Edith Ryer, proprietor of the Adelphi Hotel, showed in no uncertain terms how the war had again brought economic crisis to the Island.[98] The new boarding houses in Hutchinson Square stood idle and unsold. Landladies who had borrowed for improvements such as plumbing began to default on their debts.[99] The situation would have been worse had a Rent Restriction Act not been passed in October 1939 to keep a grip on inflation and homelessness.[100]

Salvation of a kind came in an unlikely form. The British Government, fearful of spies and fifth columnists, began a hurried programme of internment without trial. It rounded up thousands of civilians who were classified as 'enemy aliens'. They included many thousands of Jews who had fled from Nazi persecution, as well as Germans (and later Italians) who had lived in Britain for many years. Other internees were German visitors or sailors who happened to be in Britain when war was declared. While the Government recognised that many were probably harmless and even supported Britain, it nevertheless took a deeply cautious approach. This led to mass internment. The hasty and sometimes unwise decisions taken in the early days were not an honourable reflection on British democracy and this aspect of the war led the historian A.S. Stent to call internment a 'bespattered page' in our history.[101] Connery Chappell, a writer on internment, said:

> At first few people argued about the policy to intern the aliens . . . the majority of newspaper readers accepted that the risk of a fifth column in Britain could spring from the freedom of thousands of enemy aliens who might include Nazi agents and saboteurs. The popular press was not on the side of the aliens. They were an easy target. It made good copy.[102]

The Government needed a large and easily secured place to house the people it had so rapidly interned. The Isle of Man was chosen. By May 1940 internees began to arrive in large numbers. There were 1,000 at the end of the month, and the number swelled to 8,500 (excluding women and children) by the middle of July.[103] Because of the speed at which the situation had arisen, and the numbers generated by the internment policy, which had affected 23,000 people in July 1940 alone, there was no time to build camps. Empty boarding houses were requisitioned instead and at great speed. The first properties to be taken over as a camp were on the Ramsey Mooragh. During the first requisitions, boarding house keepers and householders were given only six days to vacate their homes. They were officially told to leave even valuable items such as cutlery and almost all their furniture. This was bitterly resented, and it caused a scramble for second-hand furniture which could be left to the tender mercies of the authorities. Later requisitions saw more realistic treatment, and only an essential minimum of furniture and utensils was demanded.[104] After the Mooragh Camp, which opened on 27th May 1940, the next area to be enclosed with wire was the part of Loch Promenade surrounding the Granville Hotel in Douglas. The wire spread along the promenade, and by the end of 1940 the Sefton Hotel area, the Metropole, the Palace and much of Central Promenade were all enclosed. Hutchinson Camp, opened in July, encompassed the whole of Hutchinson Square. Onchan's Royal Avenue, one of Alex Gill's last developments of small family boarding houses, became Onchan Camp. Peel's only large tourist accommodation block on Marine Parade was swallowed up by Peveril Camp.[105] Compensation terms for householders were fair but not generous. Usually when a house was commandeered the contents left behind were valued by an assessor appointed by the Manx Government. A percentage of the value was then paid as a yearly rent divided into quarterly instalments. The rent was set at fifteen per cent for the first £100 and went down to seven-and-a-half per cent on any value over £1,000. A landlady who felt aggrieved could appeal against the valuation.[106]

The problem of disappearing furniture and meagre compensation was not just a Manx problem. It occurred in many English resorts along the same lines, as seaside towns all over the British Isles gained army camps and evacuated government departments and hostels for workers.[107] But however much the Island's population complained about the conduct of the Government and military on the Island, they knew that they were faring better than in the First World War.[108] At the height of internment, there were 20,000 internees and service people on the Island, most of whom were billeted in hotels and boarding houses which would otherwise have stood empty, their owners ruined.[109]

The largest area to be enclosed encompassed Port Erin and Port St Mary. Most of the villages were turned into a single camp named Rushen. Unlike the Douglas and Peel sites, it was reserved for women and children. Security was looser, but the peninsular area was still cut off by a barbed wire fence. It also differed from other camps in that boarding house proprietors and other locals were not evicted. They remained in their houses and catered for their obligatory 'guests' for whom the Government paid £1 1s 0d per week. Some landladies made the best of it and tried to treat their unusual visitors humanely.[110] Others hated the situation and were bitterly resentful. A report observed that:

The management and catering
remain in the hands of the
householders and the comfort of
the arrangements and the quantity
and quality of food depend very
much, therefore, on the size of
the house and the personality
of the individual proprietor.[111]

One who did her best to accommodate the internees was Mrs Olive McFee. She bought a house in Port Erin in 1943. She balanced the risks of entering the boarding house business during an uncertain war with the advantage of being able to buy the house for a low price. She had a six-week-old child, and her family told her she was mad. At the time, the house was filled with married Italian couples of middle age who did most of the work of running the house themselves. Mrs McFee established a good relationship with most of them. Nevertheless, there were tensions, and none of the Italians were there out of choice. Women used to the dignity of running their own houses resented the presence of the young landlady and took a stand on principle:

Well we were supposed to be able to
go into the bedrooms and see that they
were kept fairly clean. Each family
did their own room, but to get in was
terrible, you couldn't. They always
had an excuse, and though we'd no
locks on the bedroom doors, I never

went in unless they said 'Yes, you
can come in.' But that was very,
very rare.[112]

Mrs McFee also had to face internees who complained of inadequate food and the hours they had to work. Her troubles worsened as the stoic Italians were replaced by Germans who were younger and very bitter. Times were hard for both sides. Mrs McFee could see perfectly well that they were taking out their frustrations on the system by being horrible to her. But, she sighed, 'it had nothing to do with us [landladies] . . . they were interned and that was the end of it'. It was a long way from the usual happy crowds of holidaymakers. German-Jewish internee Dr Leo Khan remembered that his first impressions of the Island and his camp were grim. It was one of the few rainy days of the long hot summer of 1940, and as he approached he saw 'a lot of not particularly beautiful small boarding houses behind barbed wire; which is not a pleasant sight'.[113]

Though all the internees were held humanely, this did not reduce their mental distress. The policy operated in its early days with a remarkable lack of discrimination, and war emergency conditions resulted in the internment of a wide mixture of people. German-Jewish refugees, loyal but war-hating Germans, and outright Nazi sympathisers were initially all tarred with the same brush and even interned together. A parliamentary debate held in 1940 did open serious questions about the waste of human potential that this crude mass internment created and the damage it did to Britain's reputation.[114] It resulted in the first releases for people who were deemed low-risk. However, decisions about release were often slow in coming, and those who remained interned had to work hard to fight

boredom and despair.[115] To make life more bearable, the internees organised their own educational and artistic activities. Arts and crafts of remarkable quality were often the result, and the Amadeus string quartet first met in the camps of the Isle of Man.[116]

Visits from wives and families began in the autumn of 1940 and these provided an unusual sort of visiting trade for landladies whose houses were not requisitioned.[117] Many were Italian-Scots, who had worked in the catering trade in Scotland for most of their lives. Mona Atkinson's mother accommodated several at Pitcairn House on Church Road, off Douglas Promenade, and found them often fearful and grateful for a visit.[118] Very few were as bold as the woman who stayed with Mr and Mrs Cringle:

> One night, in either '43 or '44, a lady came and asked to be put up. She said that her husband was an Italian, who was one of the Italian internees in the camp at the Metropole. So my mother took her in, and was very glad to have her. She [the visitor] went to visit her husband and was going to stay for a couple of days and visit him. On the second night we were there, my mother and I, sitting in our front room in the sort of semi-basement which was the living quarters . . . listening to the Home Service on the wireless. Then our front door opened outside the room and somebody walked in, up the corridor outside the living room and then up the stairs up towards the bedrooms! Well, my mother obviously guessed who it was, and she was right, it was the Italian prisoner. He'd escaped and obviously his wife had told him where the boarding house was and where her bedroom was. So he'd gone up to see her to make up for a good deal of lost time while he had been in incarceration. Well the only thing my mother could do was to ring up the police and she did so. The police and the army came and they took this poor fellow away, but I would like to think that before they did they sat down and thought 'Well, we'll give him five or ten minutes before we go'.[119]

By this time, a few visitors from the blitzed cities of the north-west once again began to make their way to the Island for a holiday, and extra weekend sailings were laid on. This was a relief to boarding house proprietors because the number of internees was falling. There were 7,000 men interned on the Island in July 1940 but this fell to 5,300 by April 1941. Numbers declined further to 4,700 by early May.[120] They rose slightly as early releases were offset by 800 Fascist detainees brought to Peel from May 1941. There were also 2,900 Italians held in Douglas at this time, split into Fascist and anti-Fascist groups.

As the numbers of internees declined, Sefton and Central camps closed in 1941, and Rushen reduced in size. Central became an RAF station and the British armed forces used many other hotels and boarding houses for training or billets. The Granville and Regent hotels were turned from internment camps into a Royal Navy shore training establishment named HMS *Valkyrie*. Douglas gained air-gunnery and radar schools, and a naval training base, whilst country areas saw other installations, from small radar stations to large RAF airfields. There were other hush-hush jobs to be done. Pamela Bradley, a journalist only nineteen years old, enrolled as an ATS Private and was sent to the Island for secret training in wireless interception. Working on Douglas promenade under the Official Secrets Act, she learnt to intercept with total accuracy German Morse transmissions encrypted with the Enigma code. After training, the intercepts taken by these girls were sent to Bletchley Park for deciphering by Alan Turing and his remarkable code-breaking organisation.[121] The daily routine for Private Bradley was busy and exacting. She was billeted in the Almeda, but would breakfast in the Hydro, which served as a mess, after which she would proceed to hotels such as the Rutland for training. The training was a total immersion in wireless, especially Morse code, and it started to affect the operators. However, life was exciting and lively off-duty:

We'd go out and when we'd see an advertisement on a bus or anything we would automatically be sending it [in our heads]. You couldn't help it: your brain was going dit dit dah, dit dah dah, dah dit dit all the time. And that was the only way that they could really pound it in, and it took six months. It wasn't a short course; we had to do all the electro-magnetism and wireless procedures, [as well as learn] what certain signals meant. ERQRN for example was 'This is control calling all stations'. It was fascinating and it was interesting, and of course being on the Isle of Man, particularly as I arrived in the summer, it was wonderful. At the end of the day we could just slip across the road and go and have a dip in the sea. We thought we were in paradise. The Island was blacked out, of course, but there were plenty of dances and there was a wonderful NAAFI somewhere in Douglas, I can't remember where it was. Cinemas, dancing, and because we were all boys and girls of eighteen, nineteen, twenty, that's all, and all of the same level of education, it was just wonderful. It was a wonderful camp.[122]

After the tin huts and army beds of many military encampments, the ATS girls found the hotels and boarding houses a paradise. Simple things such as wardrobes, real mattresses, and washbasins in bedrooms were much appreciated. They were a link to

pre-war life, although other aspects of the boarding houses saw changes which would have startled peace-time visitors. Windows were blacked out, and doors that once concealed nothing more than holidaymakers stood locked and guarded with wireless intercept sets hidden behind them. For Miss Bradley (later Mrs Clark), who had known the Island from holidays before the war, it was a strange contrast. But youth and camaraderie kept the girls going.

Violet Bridson's boarding house was used to billet troops. She remembers:

One day a man came round — I can see him yet coming up the drive with a sheaf of papers in his hand — and he said, 'You are going to be billeted with some soldiers that are coming in on the boats and you have to get these rooms ready'. It was the soldiers coming from Dunkirk, they'd had to get out, and they were being put in all sorts of places. All these soldiers. They were so weary-looking with packs on their backs. I'll never forget one going up the stairs wearing his pack with a mug slung on it. As he was going up [stairs] with it at my level I saw a bullet hole, right through one side of the mug and out the back. I suppose he kept it for a souvenir but, to me, oh, that was awful. The problem came after

they'd been in some time [with] the big army boots in and out and the lino coming off in chips. Well every room finished up down to the bare canvas underneath.

Then I couldn't understand where brown stains were coming from on the ceilings and round the basins: eventually I found out it was the army blanco, they used to do [uniforms] with the blanco, you know, and of course the soldiers would be standing at the basins scrubbing to clean it and the spray from that was all going up and every room had to be done over. The wall in the yard went from white to khaki. Eventually they went and we took others in. But I said to my husband 'I don't know', I said, 'I think we'll pack this in'. So we decided, anyway we gave the boarding house up, we didn't own it . . ., it was a write-off you see, we gave it up for that reason because we just hadn't the cash to carry on.[123]

This story shows that even when money of a sort came through work for the army or government it might not be enough to stay in business. As the war drew to a close, both military and internment camps

began to wind down. Palace Camp closed as an internment centre as early as November 1942. The year 1943 opened with 2,990 men interned on the Island, and by January 1944 only 2,068 remained.[124] August 1944 saw a large-scale repatriation of women internees, and a holiday season was even seen. That summer actually saw queues for the boats and severe delays as would-be holidaymakers overwhelmed the much-reduced Steam Packet Company, which even had to place posters at railway stations to warn hopeful people how difficult it was to reach the Island.[125] By D-Day only Port Erin, Mooragh, Metropole, Peveril and Onchan Camps were still operating. Hutchinson was prepared for a return to civilian use, and did so in November.

Rehabilitating the boarding houses and their contents was a long and costly job. In 1942 the British Government bought outright most of the furniture it had requisitioned (though at 1940 prices) and at the end of the war it was sold to the Manx Government for half the sum. The authorities then repaired what they could to help the Island get back in business. They used the Palace Ballroom as a clearing-house where owners could reclaim their property and use a small grant to replace missing items.[126] The ballroom was stacked with more than two thousand chairs, hundreds of tables, and a huge pile of wardrobes which were cleaned and repaired over many months.[127] Despite precautions, the issue of furniture was nevertheless very controversial. Some displaced householders protested that their property had been stolen by camp guards or burnt by the internees for fuel. Nor was the grant as useful as it appeared. There was a terrible shortage of furniture. New items were almost impossible to find and this drove up the price of second-hand ones, if these could be bought at all. There was a real temptation for boarding house keepers to be a little

hazy about which item belonged to whom. The result was something of a free-for-all. A story survives that one proprietor cunningly wrote the name of his boarding house underneath and inside all his furniture the night before it was requisitioned and that after the war he reclaimed his property from the most unlikely places.[128]

The cost of repairing boarding houses which had suffered from wartime use was considerable. A surveyor's report on the 43-bedroom Windsor House on Port Erin promenade revealed that after the war it needed at least £803 to be spent on redecoration, the repair of furniture and the replacement of stolen or damaged kitchenware to bring it back to pre-war condition. A simple inflation index suggests that this sum would be about £15,000 at today's prices, without taking into account the rising cost of skilled tradesmen.[129] At £2 (now £38) per bedroom and £5 (now £97) per hallway, the redecoration was clearly far from lavish, but with so many rooms the cost soon mounted up.[130] Multiplied by hundreds of premises the challenge was enormous. At one hotel, puzzled lift engineers had a lot of trouble trying to get the machinery going after being shut off for the duration. They found that wily internees had taken many of its parts and wires for their own purposes. It was not obvious because fake ones had been put in place to conceal the subterfuge. Even the call buttons had been stolen and replaced with papier mâché ones. Some hoteliers, such as the proprietors of the Grasmere, had left locked rooms containing valuables, but internees had got into them and much was lost.[131] Many came to the conclusion though that the army was far worse than the internees.[132] The extent of war damage was felt in other ways as well which could not be measured with money. Betty Kelly recalls:

I never had a room of my own until after the war, because the internees came. I was nine, and I was sent to boarding-school at the Buchan . . . because my mother thought it was the best thing for us, because things were so uncertain with a house full of Nazis. I don't think they were Nazis really, but they had said when they came in that they wanted to go back to Germany if they had a chance of repatriation. So of course they were immediately branded as Nazis. So people didn't know whether they were going to be murdered in their beds or what! That is how my mother came to send us both to boarding-school right away.[133]

After the Second World War

Unlike many of its competitors on the north-west coast of England, the Isle of Man suffered badly during the Second World War through lost trade. By contrast, some Blackpool boarding houses trebled in value during the war years.[134] Fortunately the immediate post-war years were good ones. They were the last golden age of buoyant demand in traditional seaside resorts.[135] There were few durable goods to buy in the shops but wages were relatively high and there was full employment. Taking a holiday was one of the few ways for people to spend money on pleasure. The British tried to forget

the bitter memory of war and the grim reality of living with austerity when they went on holiday, though it was not until July 1947 that many of the Manx boarding houses stopped asking visitors to bring their ration books with them.[136]

For the first time economic and social planners began to give serious thought to the issue of holidays and how the sector worked. The holiday boom made them ask some interesting questions. A report mused:

Twenty-five or thirty million people will, after the war, want to spend a week or more of leisure away from their home streets. They will be workers by hand or brain who are entitled, by law or agreement, to a week or two weeks' annual holiday with pay. Where are they to go to and who will put them up? . . . There is little doubt that the total accommodation available after the European war will fall very short of demand . . . we hope that those who make their living from this business will be able to expand their provision for tourists and holidaymakers, as soon as war restrictions permit and war damage is repaired.[137]

Visitors to the Island couldn't help but notice the restrictions and the strains of war. Caterers struggled to cope with the demand for food: many items were in

1950s girls enjoying the view from the Villa Colonnade in pearls, perms and halter-necks. The last golden decade of full seasons for the Isle of Man.

short supply. Fortunately the Isle of Man had a good source of meat and vegetables from its hard-working farmers. Boarding house keepers somehow seemed to find what they needed. Whilst the Island was blessedly free from bomb damage, many of the facilities of tourism were very run-down. Glens and pleasure grounds had become half-wild again with no gardeners to tend them. Cafés and tearooms went unpainted and un-repaired. The trams kept going only by ingenious improvised repairs.[138] Some facilities which were closed in 1939 never re-opened. Only in the 1950s did full prosperity and normal business return.

Jobs, strikes and government

Manx tourism was never entirely free of the spectre of unemployment in the UK. It relied for most of its visitors on a core of towns in the north-west of England, so when these areas had a bad year the industry could do little to improve its prospects. It had to ride out trade depressions, strikes and slumps as best it could. The Manx Government investigated from time to time the possibility of creating a more diverse industrial base but, apart from encouraging some light manufacturing, there was little it could do. By the time this happened in the 1950s other resorts with the same unemployment problems were competing for attention from factory owners, and the offshore location of the Island sadly did not help.[139]

One of the worst years was 1966 when a long seamen's strike paralysed the visiting industry. The strike followed a dispute between English shipowners and their seamen, and had nothing to do with the Isle of Man Steam Packet Company. But in accordance with the practices of the union, when a national strike was

Staff at the Crescent Hotel, 1960s.

approved all members had to withdraw their labour, wherever they worked. For a small holiday island, this was a disaster. Early in May 1966, the visiting industry realised that mediation was unlikely to stop the bitter dispute. It seemed that unlike in a previous unofficial strike, the Steam Packet crews would not continue working just to save the season.[140] Tension grew as the Government announced that it had plans to keep food and fuel supplies going. With the start of the strike two days off, hoteliers became more and more fearful.[141] Everyone hoped that it would be short and would end before the TT started. The Government's Strike Emergency Committee warned that if the strike went ahead the Island would suffer over £1 million in lost business.[142] At first, the Douglas Residential Hotel and Boarding House Association reported relatively few cancellations.[143] The local newspapers reflected what was on almost everyone's mind when they said:

> The Isle of Man is being crucified in a cause in which it has little part . . . for an Island which is a self-governing country it is paradoxical that it should be drawn into a situation to which it has contributed nothing . . . can anything be done to get the visitors here?[144]

HOLYROOD

Interiors at the Holyrood, early 1980s.

Mr and Mrs Curtis in the Palace Ballroom, 1960s.

Hoteliers reported that visitors were watching and waiting, but reports of cancellations began to flow in faster and faster. Westlake's hotel reported a loss of 30 bookings at a cost of £30, whilst a party of 100 cancelled at the Villiers and another 60 were lost to the Alexandra.[145] Plans to improve and modernise buildings, never quite as far-reaching as they should have been, were put on hold.[146] Local builders grew apprehensive that a very lean winter lay ahead for them. A delegation of boarding house keepers wrote to the Governor rather like their forebears had done in 1916. They met the Strike Emergency Committee at the Villa Marina and told how they were becoming more vulnerable as their debts to printers, grocers, and mortgage-holders went unpaid. Most had kept their staff on full wages. Rates, taxes and National Insurance all had to be paid. Hoteliers began to criticise the strikers for hurting the trade which employed many of their own friends and families. The strike and the sad plight of the Isle of Man attracted international attention. An American observer described 'an emerald sea devoid of ships . . . the wide promenade of Douglas sprawled empty, café tables waiting in vain for customers, [whilst] 2,000 hoteliers and landladies face ruin'.[147]

Essential food was allowed in by the National Union of Seamen but this was all. As the strike dragged on, the Island tried to arrange more flights to bring in visitors and save the season. It was a strange Whit week, the first since the war to see no steamers sailing in and out of Douglas. By contrast the airport was a hive of activity and over 12,000 air seats were made available to holidaymakers; but this was not enough to stop the cancellation of the TT. The loss of the races was mourned as a crushing blow. It was said that it was

bringing the industry crashing about the ears of the boarding house keepers and hundreds of others who could do little more than look on in bewilderment and horror.[148] Hoteliers feared regular visitors would lose their habit of coming every year and find other resorts to which they could grow loyal instead. Sensibly, the Government made loans available to troubled businesses as early as 9th June, a sure sign of how attitudes had changed since the first time it had reluctantly helped them almost fifty years before.[149]

The strike ended after a punishing six weeks. August was saved but more was needed. To try to make enough money to support the Island through the winter an ambitious season extension campaign was set in motion, supported by a £50,000 government grant. Advertising charges for the official Isle of Man guide were deferred to help hoteliers concentrate on new business.[150] Licensing controls were relaxed and entertainments ran on longer than usual. A slogan of 'June-in-September' was announced and everyone did their best to keep the place lively.[151] 'Sunshine insurance' was invented for September visitors, and the Tourist Board paid Douglas cinemas to open for free on rainy days. Free golf was provided on all the links. Two hundred hoteliers joined a competition to offer free rooms to winners. Of course the air services had done a good trade during the strike. Some 57,300 people travelled by air when it was on, a figure that was 20,000 more than the previous year.[152] However, the gradually falling price of air travel, which had proved so handy during the shipping strike, would, in the long term, work against the Isle of Man as the Mediterranean became an ever-cheaper holiday destination.

5

The visitors

As the Isle of Man grew more dependent upon tourism, increasing numbers of visitors shaped the way local people lived and the towns they lived in. By the 1890s, it seemed like the season had always been vital to prosperity; but within living memory agriculture had supported most of the population.[1] Of course, farming continued to be a thriving part of the Manx economy, not least because thousands of hungry visitors needed to be fed, but the fast growth of mass tourism meant that the younger industry soon eclipsed the older one. Tourism contributed by far the largest proportion of the Island's tax base and supported a larger section of the population.

Of course, the question of how tourism made its impact on the Island's economy and society was far from the minds of most visitors. The British upper-middle classes, with their rising incomes, were able to make trips to the coast in large numbers by the mid-

nineteenth century. Their holidaymaking preferences were influential and they helped to create a culture of holidaymaking which favoured quiet and 'improving' activities such as sea-bathing, promenading and nature study. However, it also included plenty of time for gossip, showing off and social activity. It was an alluring combination and stories about seaside holidays quickly made their way into newspapers and magazines. A mid-century edition of *The British Journal* portrayed a middle-class family in hot, dusty London, longing for a change. The women of the family complained of all sorts of vague illnesses and aches, which would be relieved by a seaside holiday if only Father would allow it. He soon gave in, for after all:

What would we English do, without
a sea-coast? Once a year, like

Edwardian holiday-makers at the Snaefell Hotel.

swallows, or woodcocks, the emigrating fancy seizes us. The instinct is universal; it pins the Papa on his counting-house stool, it pervades the Mama in her sultry parlour, it seizes ruthlessly on the young ladies of the household who begin forthwith to trim up old summer dresses for 'sea side things'.[2]

The desire for such pleasures grew steadily and was not just restricted to the middle classes. By the 1860s, summer excursion trains for workers were available, and statutory Bank Holidays began in 1871. Holidays were certainly not yet for all: only the better paid and more skilled workers could take them at first. Fortunately the Isle of Man was close to one of the most booming and heavily industrialised parts of Britain, the north-west. This region was at the forefront of holiday developments for two main reasons. First, it had many large factories densely clustered together. Those who worked in them were organised in the most modern way with fixed work and leisure hours. Second, workers in the wool and cotton trades maintained an old tradition of 'Wakes' – taking time off for holiday – to secure an annual week off. This often meant a carefree community spree with plenty of eating, drinking and fun. Holidaymakers could conveniently be transported by the same rail network built to move their manufactures. Groups of workers or neighbours sometimes saved together in 'going-off clubs' to make the unpaid holiday easier to organise.[3] This was the system in Lancashire and the West Riding. Other industries with skilled artisans or strong unions also won holidays fairly early on. These included shipbuilding and iron- and steel-making.[4] No wonder holidaymakers treasured their time at the seaside. For example, in the town of Colne in turn-of-the-century Lancashire:

> When the Wakes week came round each year there was a general exodus down the long road to the station, where the town well—nigh emptied its population into the trains that carried it to Blackpool and Morecambe, the more prosperous journeying as far afield as Douglas.[5]

This shows how the Island benefited from the custom of the better-off workers and the middle classes in such industrial areas. Like many late Victorian resorts, it tried to cater for a broad range of demand. At the top were a very few of the wealthy. Then came an army of middle-ranking administrators, subordinate professionals, tradesmen and clerks; the sort of people which industrialisation had produced in large numbers. Then came the skilled working class and those like the mill workers who could afford holidays.[6] These groups often wanted different things from a holiday but the size of 'Manxland', as guide books liked to call it, meant that it was possible to cater for many different kinds of

person without too much conflict. This was why, from early on, the Island's towns were marketed as offering slightly different social tones. Douglas was for the young and lively, Ramsey for the genteel, Port Erin and Port St Mary for families and Peel for those who liked old-fashioned charm. The Victorian Isle of Man rarely attracted upper-class visitors; such people preferred the south coast of England, the spas, quiet rural locations or, increasingly, the Continent. It depended on better-off workers and the middle classes because the cost of the sea journey (or indeed a holiday at all) was too high for those on low incomes. There were so many mill workers that locals nicknamed holidaymakers from Lancashire 'cottonballs', but despite the hint of dislike in the name, levels of tension between residents and visitors were much lower than in some English towns, which had interests divided between tourism and other industries. This was not the case in Victorian Douglas because the rebuilt town was very largely a creation of tourism. It was, one writer put it, 'an El Dorado for the respectable working class'.[7]

Because so many Manx made a living in the industry, local interest in the numbers coming to the Island was always strong. From 1830 to 1850, some 20,000 to 30,000 visitors were thought to land each year, before numbers rose steeply to between 50,000 and 60,000 by the mid-1860s. The opening of the Victoria Pier transformed harbour facilities in Douglas, so that by the year after its opening, 1873, 90,000 passengers were landed. The introduction in 1887 of a small tax on the fare of every person landed, to fund harbour improvements, allowed the compilation of more accurate arrival statistics, which run to the present day. These were published annually by the Board of Advertising (later the Tourist Board) from 1894, and show that the period up to the First World War was one of great growth; by 1913 over half a million people a year came to the Island. This remarkable season was never bettered. The inter-war years saw many good summers but also some bad ones, caused for example by the General Strike of 1926 and the Great Depression. Nevertheless, around 500,000 visitors a year were recorded for most of this period before the closure of the industry once again in 1939. After the Second World War, the half-million figure was generally sustained until the end of the 1950s. After this, a decline not only in numbers but also in the average length of stay and spending power was clearly to be seen.[8]

This decline was not foreseen earlier in the century, when the future looked nothing but bright and the number of visitors seemed capable of almost endless expansion. Much of the growth was driven by a gradual improvement in working conditions, which made holidays available to more ordinary people. Legal controls on the exploitation of workers were gradually extended. Employers also realised that offering leisure time was an alternative to putting up wages, which some unions found useful in negotiations from around 1910 onwards. By the late 1930s around one-third of the population were able to holiday for a week or more. It was not until 1937 however that the breakthrough of the Holidays with Pay Act made paid holidays available to most people. This was one of the reasons why, despite the Great Depression, the holiday industry did not suffer too badly.[9] The effect of the depression was uneven and, despite savage unemployment in many industries, those who still had a job often found their conditions gradually improving. These were the years of booking rooms months in advance, which was good news for proprietors and tended to make demand seem very stable. It was a golden age for resorts such as Douglas and Blackpool, which offered affordable plea-

sures to the many. However, even in the mass market, there were distinctions of social tone. Bolton workers told an early market research organisation called Mass-Observation that Douglas was considered slightly up-market, saying it was like 'the difference between the vault and the lounge in the pub . . . there is a "class distinction"'. The people in each case were apparently of the same origin and lived in identical houses, but some made a little more money than others or saved more carefully. Holidays were not exempt from questions of social class.

When war broke out holidaymaking was cut back, but planning for peace continued. Scientific studies of holiday patterns and holiday resorts were carried out to help understand and plan for post-war demand. In one such report, a northern industrialist remarked that Lancashire factory and mill people had, for generations, been accustomed to take an annual holiday, often at Blackpool or Douglas.[10] This was encouraging news for the Isle of Man. But the question asked by the planners was: how long would the habit continue? It seemed that in the foreseeable future there would be no change, or that demand might rise further. However, by 1945 some far-sighted researchers began to wonder if the habit would change if living standards rose. What would happen if everyone could afford a car? Would ordinary people abandon their fortnight in the same resort every year to travel further afield?[11] If living standards rose as hoped, would the traditional resorts still be able to provide the comfort and pleasures that would bring customers flocking in?

Health and pleasure

This gives a good opportunity to reflect on why people chose to come to the seaside for their holidays. Resorts traditionally offered a diversity of attractions; some were obvious such as dancing, theatres and other entertainment. Another, which now might be called a 'unique selling point', was health. From the earliest days of resort visiting in the eighteenth century, doctors stressed that a visit was not merely a source of pleasure; it was also good for you. A Manx guide book of 1824 proclaimed that:

> Douglas [offers] comfortable accommodation for genteel families disposed to take up their summer residence for the benefit of sea-bathing. The salubrity of the air and the cleanness and strength of the waters are very powerful inducements for invalids to visit this place.[12]

Sea-bathing from bathing-machines, which were small huts on wheels drawn into the water, was a central part of the nineteenth-century 'cure'. The sea was supposed to enhance vigour, stimulate circulation and heal all manner of diseases. As the years progressed, the rigour of the regime (which only the middle and upper classes could afford) was relaxed, and bathing became more of a pleasure. It was not just the sea itself which was said to be healthy. The advantages of ozone-laden sea air were also announced in many a guide and poster. The town of Skegness found such success with its poster of a jolly sailor announcing 'Skegness is so bracing!' that he was used for decades. Many other resorts tried a similar approach and for more than two hundred years the seaside has been promoted as a

1950s entertainments listings for Douglas.

Entertainer at the Crescent Hotel, 1960s, with CND guitar strap.

Jimmy Nelson at the Crescent Hotel in the 1960s.

'Puppet on a String' at the Crescent Hotel, 1968.

The TV room at the Hydro, 1965 – the beginning of the end for traditional communal entertainments such as guests singing around the piano together.

healthy place. Over time, fashions have changed. At first, the emphasis for visitors was on healing waters. Then came fresh, bracing air. By the 1930s, sunshine and the sun-tan came into popularity. Prior to this, sunbathing was unfashionable because to earlier generations a tan was a sign of poverty and manual labour. Nowadays, healthiness is still promoted, with resorts marketing themselves as refuges from the modern hazards of stress and pollution. This has been a long-standing attraction of the Isle of Man and visitors from blackened and coal-fuelled industrial cities always appreciated its clean environment. This was true even in the 1950s, as Bill Watson remembers:

The air was so much fresher, as you stepped off the boat everything seemed to be clean, the air very fresh, the sun always seemed to be shining in those days, different than Liverpool. When you were going back from the Isle of Man as you got to the Bar Lightship you'd see the haze over Liverpool, a thick smog sort of thing and you thought, well, I've been living in that for so many years

August 1952, Bathing Beauty contest, Villa Marina Gardens.

Swimming at the Traie Meanagh Swimming Pool, Port Erin, 1958.

and you come to the Isle of Man
and everything is so fresh and clean
– it was very nice.[13]

The long legacy of the 'improving' middle-class Victorian holiday allowed health-seeking to remain a grand excuse for pleasure. For many years the two were combined in one slogan and the Island marketed itself as a 'health and pleasure resort'. Pleasures certainly abounded at the seaside. With a trip to the Island a once-a-year treat, it had to be enjoyed to the full. The normal rules and restraints of society were often relaxed a little, as an American observer noticed in 1890:

In the warm summer months the Isle
of Man is a colony of hotels and
boarding-houses in which the sturdy
Britisher luxuriates in unheard-of
costumes and with an abandon in
startling contrast to his usual staid
and methodical habits.[14]

Resorts were places with a difference, away from the everyday routine. The resort was – in a metaphorical sense – half way between town and country, between sea and land. The Isle of Man, by the virtue of its geography, was even more unusual and special than most. To cross the sea was to make a trip of both body and mind into another place, to a magical holiday island which could offer every thrill from the latest electric amusements to wild storms and rugged nature. Douglas specialised in entertainments on pier, promenade and

beach, with plenty of theatres, concerts, fair grounds and later cinemas to make an exciting social whirl. Other Island resorts stressed that they had few of these noisy diversions, and emphasised their high social tone and quiet, peaceful atmosphere. Whatever a visitor chose, holiday pleasures were sweeter because they were so different from the everyday routine. Some were happy with the simplest, as a Manchester woman cheerfully said of the Douglas horse trams:

I always put me mother on the tram
. . . let her go up and down from half
past ten 'til lunchtime. Ooh, she luvs it
up and down the prom. Sees all kinds
of people, and it doesn't tire her.[15]

Messing about in boats, 1950s style.

The sea crossing

Coming to the Island was always a small adventure because of the sea journey. Many guide books attempted to make the crossing seem romantic, which is a marketing device still used today. This was sometimes true and in good weather the sea crossing to the Island could be wonderful. However, the writer's grandfather (and no doubt many another grandparent) was so sick on a journey to Douglas in the 1920s that his holiday was ruined by the awful dread of a queasy return. Whether for good or ill, the sea crossing certainly set the Island apart and made the resort unlike almost any other. A guide book summed up the voyage at its happiest:

Whatever the 'middle passage' may have been in the past, at the present time . . . the passage has been so shortened by improvement in the boats employed, that the voyager has hardly had time to realise the fact that he has actually left the land behind him before he is in sight of his landing-place. The boats themselves have been so increased in size and weight as well as speed that the motion of the sea is hardly felt, except in rough weather, which is rarely experienced during the season. The time occupied by the voyage is so filled up with music and sight-seeing, with pleasant conversation, and with music and amusements, that visitors even . . . look upon it as the pleasantest part of their trip to Mona's Isle.[16]

The Steam Packet Company became adept at moving large numbers of people quickly and in reasonable comfort, despite long summer queues. Before the Second World War, the August crowds attracted the attention of journalists and analysts alike. During the peak season at the start of the month, vast numbers of people had to be transported and newspapers often reported with amazement the great numbers travelling. A high point was reached on August Bank Holiday 1937 with a remarkable 68,000 people moving to and from the Isle of Man.[17] Many of these were day trippers. They were good news for the Steam Packet, but did no business with the boarding house keepers, and spent little money outside Douglas. The cheap day trip fares meant a frugal journey in third class. Bill Watson remembers several trips in the late 1920s, when some of the old paddle-steamers were still in use, and the classes were kept firmly apart:

When we were coming over on the boat we used to go steerage class which was the stern end of the boat; first class was in the bow. Now we were kept in the steerage part by barriers, only about an hour before they got into Douglas they opened the barriers and we could go into the first class saloon then — so different! It was 12s 6d for a three-month ticket then, and when I first came over, in 1926 I think it was, I came over on a paddle-steamer, the Mona's Queen. There were just open decks and the seats round and across the deck and the paddles went across. It was really cold and miserable, you know, we were treated like cattle coming across in those days. And the other boats, the Victoria, and the Viking and those sort, when it was rough they used to have canvas to pull down at the side. And even though the canvasses were pulled down there were always gaps and if it was rough the water would come through like a hose pipe and you would get soaked. Everybody on deck would be soaked, but that was the fun of it you know![18]

THERE ARE PLENTY OF
GOOD OPPORTUNITIES
AT DOUGLAS.
BUT I'M SO SHY.

The bashful romantic, 1920s style.

Romance and morals

There was romance in the crossing, perhaps even in surviving rough weather. Both beauty and danger were also summed up in the seaside pursuits of flirtation and love-making. Edwardian popular songs celebrated the sexual element of holidaymaking, and were lustily sung all over the Island. These lyrics, specially written for the Palace Entertainment Company, must have been a boost to bookings in boarding houses all over the resort as young hopefuls wondered whether this would be their lucky year:

Maidens beware,
There's love in the air
That you breathe in this beautiful Isle.
Each rustling breeze
That sighs through the trees
Sings music, your heart to beguile.
Oh, have a care,
O maidens – beware!
For the fairies have joined in a plan:
Your hearts to ensnare,
If you ever should dare
To come to the Isle of Man.[19]

A great venue for romance was the promenade. Here the eyes of the idle, romantic or just plain lustful

Romance, 1950s style, over Port Erin.

had plenty to fall upon. It was a place which existed for seeing and being seen. Ladies could show fashion in the latest dresses; courting couples could enjoy a walk arm-in-arm. The beach and the promenade provided an endless free show for each other. Despite strict rules and regulations governing bathing, there was many a mini-scandal in season as gentlemen tried to get the best possible view of female bathers. The more respectable waxed lyrical about beautiful 'sea-nymphs' with long hair and elegant curves frolicking in the water. The end was the same.[20]

Romance had always been on offer at the seaside, as many a postcard joked and a 'romantic' view suggested. For couples who wanted a more peaceful venue than the bustling promenades, the Island's glens were perfect for flirtation, and their owners took pains to promote them as idyllic trysting places. Some even had accommodation close by, as at Glen Helen where the Swiss Cottage offered boarding house facilities as early as 1869.[21] Up to the Second World War, cheap labour meant the glens could be maintained and run at a profit. With a turnstile at the entrance, and a tea-room

A crowded Douglas beach in the 1930s.

to hand, waste lands and gorse-covered ravines became 'El Dorado glens' to their owners.[22] 'Manxland' was certainly a popular venue for romance, and the Board of Advertising delicately encouraged the image in its booklets and lantern lectures.

Dancing was another great attraction for courting couples, or those who hoped to become part of one. Dancing at the Palace Ballroom is a happy memory for many and for years live entertainment in Douglas was dominated by the Palace & Derby Castle Company, which bestrode the business with its colossal venues. By the 1920s it could entertain almost 23,000 people at any one time: the Gaiety Theatre could seat 2,300, the Derby Castle 5,500, the Palace Opera House 1,800, the Coliseum 3,000 and the Pavilion 6,200. The Grand Theatre accommodated another 2,400, and the Buxton's complex 1,600. The Company boasted that this was more than the permanent population of Douglas and nearly half the population of the entire Island.[23] The Company was a business like any other but its activities certainly gave happiness to many. Singing and dancing feature in many reminiscences, with their last flowering just after the Second World War. The return of peace brought happy memories, remembered a visitor:

I couldn't get here quick enough! Everything was so light hearted compared to what we had gone through during the war and everybody seemed to be happy. People used to go along the prom, the youngsters singing, arm in arm. They'd be ten deep along the prom all singing and dancing. They were good times.[24]

Sadly not everyone got lucky. A Miss Braithwate of Sheffield wrote in 1895 to a friend about the young men in her digs, Osborne House. There were about thirty of them, 'but nothing very attractive!'[25] Holiday affairs amongst guests posed a perpetual problem for women trying to run a 'respectable' boarding house, because strict standards of behaviour meant that any scandal could ruin a business. Not until the 1930s did society become relaxed enough for a few jokes to find their way into the hotel and boarding house press, such as this wisecrack of 1935:

Guest: I am expecting a heavy mail in the morning.
Hotelier: Yes madam, shall I send him up when he arrives?[26]

Such flippancy caused grave concern to those who held traditional views. The Bishop of Sodor and Man regularly warned young females about the hidden dangers of the Island. In his open-air sermons at Kirk Braddan, he explained to them the dangers of 'getting into the wrong set', and the fate that would result from 'going wrong', meaning scandal and pregnancy at worst or an unhappy marriage at best.[27] Even intended postcards were censored for sexual content by a special committee, which left a vast archive of material considered too racy for publication in the early twentieth century. This was another sign of how keen the Manx authorities were to ensure that the Isle of Man was a morally respectable holiday resort.

When young single people first began to take holidays apart from their families in large numbers in the 1930s much potential for tension was created. In one incident of 1939, cited in a call to maintain high moral standards, a promenade landlady was informed by a young female guest that she would not return until 4 a.m. The hostess replied that her house was locked at midnight; should the girl not be back by then, her parents in Lancashire would be informed – at once![28] The morals of young visitors were a matter for public debate in most seaside towns. The Douglas Dilettante Debating Society acknowledged this in 1928 when it discussed the motion that 'the visiting industry is responsible for every evil' that stained the Island's moral reputation.[29] But the fire of the great Victorian temperance debate had died down, and there was too much at stake for the Island to risk a moral reform campaign which might stir up trouble.

One of the regulations required to maintain respectability was control of Sunday trading. This was common all over the British Isles. The legendary dullness of the British Sunday was attacked in resorts from an early date, for what was a pleasure town without pleasures? Many visitors had to sit in their boarding houses, on benches or the beach with little to do. 'Sacred concerts' with music of a supposedly spiritual nature were one Sabbath relief, whilst country walks, made possible by the Island's extensive light-railways, were also popular. Religion could be an entertainment as well as a duty, and open-air church services at Old Kirk Braddan mingled Christian endeavour with a hearty walk and a good sing. But the severity of Manx Sundays were a cause for complaint for many years. There were no buses in the town on Sunday mornings even in the 1930s, and visitors from upper Douglas had to walk down to the promenades in all weathers.[30]

This was especially irksome to the young. The Isle of Man and especially Douglas attracted a youthful clientele from the late nineteenth century onwards. The Lancashire textile industry offered good opportunities for employment to the young, especially women, and organised labour combined with the tradition of saving for Wakes holidays made it easy for large groups to holiday together. Social change in the years after the First World War also made the practice more acceptable and it was noticed that Douglas was 'becoming more and more the Mecca of youthful pleasure-seekers'.[31]

Cycling holiday visitors outside the Melrose, 1956.

Many other resorts witnessed an increase in single-sex groups of young wage-earners.[32] Some observers worried that 'father and mother are not taking the journey to Douglas'[33], but family holidays remained important to the Island's trade. Most landladies preferred family parties to large numbers of the young and single, given a choice, because they were quieter. Thankfully, fears about the behaviour of young people were often exaggerated. After a searching look at the question, the *Isle of Man Times* reported in 1930 that:

> Never before was the visiting population of the Isle of Man so largely composed of young people – very charming young people, too, very healthy and happy and well behaved, whom it is a pleasure to see.[34]

1950s holiday-makers outside Studley House, Queen's Promenade – on holiday, but still in jackets and ties.

Choosing a boarding house

Most visitors patronised the same house year after year because it was difficult to choose between a multitude of almost identical places, so once they found a place they liked they stayed with it. Families of modest means could ill afford to risk their precious holiday being spoiled by a bad choice of accommodation. The remark of a spinster schoolmistress in 1935 reveals how a sense of community – of the right sort – was also essential. She found: 'I had bad luck last year with seaside lodgings. The people were not my sort and I had to go on my own all the time'.[35]

There was little information to help customers make the right choice. Most small boarding houses could not afford to advertise using expensive photographs or glossy brochures. They made do with a few lines of text in the Tourist Board guide which, resulted in long listings of similar businesses in similar streets, differentiated only by price. The nature of manufacturing work for most of the twentieth-century also influenced holiday habits.[36] Until the great changes of the 1970s, which saw great contractions in Britain's manufacturing economy, most customers of the mass resorts led working lives of regularity, rhythm and routine. Many of them came on holiday at the same time, so early booking made sense. This is shown in one family's problems in choosing a boarding house as late as 1971, in the last decade of the old ways. Just before their holiday to the Isle of Man, tragedy struck. The ten-year-old son wrote in his diary:

30th July. Our [usual] landlady Mrs Moore has died! Our holiday is cancelled because we have nowhere to stay . . . we need a new boarding-house as well. Fast.

31st July. Dad said it might be too late to get into another boarding-house. He said everywhere might be full. He said we might not be able to go to the Isle of Man . . . I said I'm not going anywhere except the Isle of Man.

7th August. Still not booked anywhere and I warned Mum and Dad that time is running out.

9th August. Two brochures for the Isle of Man arrived! One of them is full of hotels and boarding-houses. I want to stay in a big hotel that has a big advert with a colour picture. Mum and Dad only looked at the small adverts at the back. There are no pictures.

14th August. We booked the Isle of Man today! Tommy Bracegirdle, a man at Dad's work, has been to a place called Bay View and says it's really good. His sister is going at the same time as us.

4th September. Dad told Mrs Bracegirdle that Tommy had done us proud by telling us about Bay View and she said that he does have his uses.

10th September. Tommy Bracegirdle's sister is leaving tomorrow. She said that this was her first time at Bay View and it had been simply charming. She said she is going to come again next year and bring mother. She said she would have stayed here last year but didn't know about it . . .[37]

Community pleasures

If the boarding house system was riddled with the class distinctions that permeated life in the British Isles such as rules, codes of respectable behaviour and a detailed hierarchy of status, it was also tempered by some of the friendlier traditions of community. One was the habit of sitting out on the front steps of promenade houses, for there were no promenade gardens until the 1930s.

This practice, which survives today, seems to have been in existence as long as the houses themselves. In a lantern lecture of 1913, the Board of Advertising commented that: 'The steps' are picturesque institutions, and the sight of porches filled with gaily-dressed boarders, especially before the various meal-gongs sound, is great.'[38]

It was a comradely activity well suited to a resort with a zeal for respectability but not too much gentility. The Douglas spirit, said a Cumbrian visitor in 1930, 'is a free and friendly spirit. No one need be lonely at Douglas'.[39] Such remarks, seized upon by those responsible for resort publicity, helped to counteract the problem that the boarding house could be a place of rules and regulations. Yet comic postcards, firmly established as part of the holiday routine from late Victorian times, made light of the archetypal landlady with her rules, suggesting that although visitors put up with them they did not like them much. Some were jokes about prices, others made fun of poor food or small portions. Many joked about relations between the sexes as boldly as the censor would allow. They were hugely popular and the Manx Postmaster-General reported that in 1929:

Holiday makers in the Island have been writing and dispatching postcards with greater industry than ever this season. During bank holiday week in August, three hundred thousand cards were posted . . . the comic variety easily outstrips the more sedate views.[40]

Jokes about the meanness of proprietors were keenly directed. Sitting out on 'the steps', for example, was grand in fine weather, but when rain came, not all landladies allowed visitors to use bedrooms during the day. A few houses offered open access lounges, but many did not, a policy which seems remarkable today. Even at the time, this habit generated resentment. There were sometimes underlying economic reasons for the perceived meanness of proprietors, as explained in Chapter 3. By the inter-war period, the larger

Jessie Quirk and great aunt Jane in 1938, enjoying a daring motorcycle pose!

boarding houses offered greater openness and freedom, to imitate the success of the holiday camps. A well-known Douglas example was the Hotel Alexandra, which was one of the largest. It was created from several smaller boarding houses and specialised in accommodating young people. Even the quieter resorts such as Peel received such groups and they were often free-spending, to the pleasure of local traders such as Harry Watterson, who was the proprietor of a souvenir and confectionery shop on Peel Promenade. He was both by necessity and inclination a student of human nature when visitors called into his shop, as he remembers:

> Sometimes you'd get an influx of three or four boys who would come in and say, 'I don't suppose you've got swimming trunks, have you?' So I'd say 'Yes, what size are you?' 'Oh, I'm 34' or whatever, you see, so I'd get the box down and I'd look at them and think 'You're no more 34 than me, mate! Try this 36.' You wouldn't say anything to them, you'd stand around and they'd say 'Oh yes, those are fine, yes, thanks very much, how much is that?' So I'd say it's so much and you'd get their money and 'What about a towel, have you got a towel?' 'No, do you sell towels?' So you'd say 'Yes, quite reasonable . . .'[41]

Motoring

If the advent of independent young holidaymakers was one new phenomenon of the 1930s, motoring was another. Motorisation opened up new possibilities for exploring the countryside, which entrepreneurs were quick to promote. A car of one's own was still a luxury and this was the heyday of the charabanc, when many coaches touted for trade. Boarding houses often made arrangements with coach firms, offering tours to the popular destinations, such as Peel, which had a charm all of its own. The liking for continuity already touched on above was also something which traders noticed. As Harry says:

Alf Duggan's beloved 1930s Armstrong Siddeley 3 hp motor landaulette used to take visitors on tours.

The Savoy Hotel's Sun Saloon motor coach, 'Lady Pat', 1930s.

Coaches packed with visitors line up for a photo during one of their popular 'Mystery Tours' in the 1950s.

The people that came to Peel used to say we were so friendly, everything was the same year after year. You know, they didn't want change, they wanted to come back to Peel and still to stay in the same places, the same houses maybe; they didn't want it to be changed in any way. They wanted to be able to go across the road onto the beach; they wanted to have the coach [trips]. We used to get people who were staying in Douglas who used to come in year after year and you'd say to them 'Oh, hello, you're over again I see' and they'd say 'Oh yes we wouldn't miss Peel for the world.' They used to love to come to Peel; the beach was a big attraction with people from industrial areas. They must have thought they were in heaven when they could walk along the beach and they could look out and see for miles right to the horizon, rather than looking out on brick walls or slate roofs or chimneys. They used to really love it. And they used to say to me . . . 'You get money for doing this, do you, Harry?' and I'd say, 'Aye, yes, yes, a few bob, not too much, but a copper or two' and then they'd say 'Well I don't know, I think you should pay for this, this view' and I, at times, used to more or less agree with them. It was lovely, there was everything. You'd see the sea in all its moods, you'd see the sun out and the people on the beach and kids enjoying themselves in the water and oh, all sorts of things used to happen.[42]

Douglas Esplanade, late nineteenth century.

VERY FULL HERE - BUT I DID GET A ROOM.

6

High and low season

August in the Isle of Man was surely a thought to wreathe many a prospective visitor in smiles and dreams of happy holidays. August was also, for a hundred years, a matter of the gravest importance to all boarding house keepers, whose smiles came only when the house was full! The tourist season, which peaked in August, was much discussed in seaside society. A 'good' season, a 'short' season, a 'poor' season and 'season extension' were terms that remained a part of everyday conversations until very recently. Everyone was interested in the season because it was so crucial to local prosperity. No wonder the busy days of August were celebrated in such detail, as in this account of 1933:

Last weekend the many fine ships of the Manx fleet landed something like forty or fifty thousand persons at

Victoria Pier in a space of twenty–four hours . . . a stupendous achievement. Buses, trams and hackney–cars were in readiness on the pier to convey visitors to their final destinations. Villa Marina and the Arcade were thrown open to those who had omitted to book 'digs', and the cafés were soon busy supplying meals to the weary but contented travellers.

The beach at Douglas on Monday afternoon presented one of the most amazing sights . . . as far as the eye could reach, there were people, people everywhere. People of

and conditions of summer dress, from bathing-suits of the least possible proportions, and startling, flashily coloured beach-pyjamas, to the more sedate frocks, and attended by grey flannelled and fiery shirted swains.

  With the rush and bustle of journeying to Manxland and securing accommodation, which to quite a number was an all-day job on Saturday . . . the thousands of visitors made the Isle of Man generally, and Douglas in particular, one of the liveliest places imaginable.[1]

High spirits – over the beach and Loch Prom, Douglas, c.1890s in a rather racy image. Women waving bottles of beer were not 'respectable' at all!

Summer days started early for boarding house keepers and their visitors. New arrivals could be on the doorstep at six in the morning. A 1939 account of Douglas claimed:

all descriptions, young, old, tall and small, some hatless, others with headgear of unconventional types in this gay multitude. Ever present, as usual, on the promenades and the shore, was gay femininity in all sorts

  If you would see thronged Douglas aright, on a peak Saturday morning, don't stroll down the promenade as early as half past six. At that advanced hour, the town, in a sense, is not busy; it has settled down after its first rush. Half a dozen boats will have landed thousands of travellers, and most of them will have found their lodgings. All the doors on the promenade will be

open, and the majority of those in the other principal company-house thoroughfares; but there will still be thousands of people quietly walking along with their bags, sitting outside doors which have not yet opened.[2]

These accounts were written in the heyday of the season when it seemed as if the annual cycle would go on for ever. But there was a time before the season existed: and now the seasons as they once were have gone for ever. Let us look more closely at how some of these changes occurred and find out what it was like to run a boarding house in high and low season on the Isle of Man.

The history of the season

The Isle of Man was making money from visitors by the late eighteenth century, but many of these people were semi-permanent residents rather than tourists. Mass seasonal tourism arrived in the late nineteenth century. New and improved steam-ships made the Irish Sea crossing reliable and speedy. The Island was fortunate to be close to the north-west of England, an area of dynamic new industries and factories which gave rise to new ways of working and new ways of relaxing, such as official holidays. In addition, changes in the financial relationship between the UK and the Isle of Man made under Governor Loch resulted in a more vigorous Manx Government. It became able to raise and spend far more money on public works. The new harbours, promenades and roads, which were so essential to the development of nineteenth-century

mass tourism, were set in train. Speculators quickly built boarding houses and entertainment entrepreneurs created new companies and attractions. The success of the new industry was, however, at the cost of older forms of business. The historian John Belchem explained:

Loch's reforms were to squeeze out the gentlemanly rentiers, pensioners and half-pay officers whose year-round presence (albeit on a fixed income) had kept the economy afloat. Their departure imposed a new seasonal pattern which brought, at best, its critics bemoaned, a brief ten week period of tourist prosperity. A.W. Moore noted a 'new problem in the way of pauperism, as distinct from poverty'.[3]

So, not everyone was delighted with the way that seasonal tourism affected the local economy. It created tensions and differences, and it was unsettling. Prosperous summers gave way to even leaner winters. A wedge was driven between those who successfully made money from the changes and those who did not. Some towns boomed and seemed to be doing very well: other areas felt that they did not share in the benefits. These problems were detected as early as the 1860s, at the time when local commentators were still astonished when packed steamers had to leave visitors behind at Liverpool quayside.[4] The season, gushed one reporter, had become the goose that laid an annual golden egg

COPYRIGHT P.S.M.13.   BALLAQUEENEY, PORT ST. MARY, I. OF M.   LILYWHITE LTD.,
I.M.   THE PHOTO PRINTERS.

The newly built Ballaqueeney, Port St Mary, c.1890s.

for the Isle of Man. Many a stocking, bank book or hiding place was said to hoard 'the evidence of a profitable summer'.[5] There was no getting round the fact that in a remarkably short space of time the Island had become dependent on the season. A local newspaper remarked in 1871:

> On Monday evening next our visiting season commences, and we badly need the money. If our tradesmen could not reckon upon the speedy relief that our visitors bring, ruin would stare us in the face.[6]

Gradually the Manx people came to take the season for granted. Thirty years on, the worries of the 1870s were forgotten in the height of a remarkable boom. The MHK Mr W.M. Kerruish assured the Tynwald Constitutional Commission in the course of a discussion about the local economy that the season was so reliable it might almost be reduced to a mathematical formula.[7] Kerruish's optimism was shared by many, and Douglas Advertising Committee could declare confidently in 1918 that:

> During the month of August, Douglas is thronged with a cosmopolitan

Morrison's Grasmere from the beach, c.1890s.

crowd of visitors, and the season is at its height. The Palace and Derby Castle ballrooms are crowded every evening, the other places of amusement are full, and gaiety is supreme. The mirth and jollity seem infectious, and there is a spirit of bon camaraderie in the air that helps to make Douglas so great an attraction to young people.[8]

The Wakes Weeks of Lancashire and Yorkshire saw the Island at its busiest. By the turn of the century

they had become so important that the dates of Wakes were published on the Island for the convenience of boarding house keepers. The earliest were Macclesfield and Warrington, from 17th June. The floodgates opened on June 24th with numerous medium-sized towns; by early July, Burnley and Chorley were moving en masse to the seaside. Glasgow Fair holidays introduced a Scottish element from July 21st, and from that date until the end of July towns such as Bacup, Keighley, Hanley, and Hebden Bridge held their holidays. Crowded into the month of August were no less than forty-four Wakes, from huge conurbations such as Wigan, Bradford and Oldham, to smaller towns including Preston, Oswaldtwistle and Brighouse. Dates of particular significance for the holiday industry

included Whit Monday, Easter Monday and the August Bank Holiday.[9] The pressures on resorts in August were severe enough for the Manchester Cotton Exchange to propose staggered holidays by 1900, to ease boarding house overcrowding. It met with limited success; the situation was still acute in the late 1940s. Even the efforts of the official British Tourist and Holidays Board to stagger demand by liaising with industrialists did little to solve the problem.[10] Advertising and publicity were used to try to spread out the August peak to less busy times, but the deep cultural habits of the Lancashire Wakes were too strongly ingrained. Joan Pomfret, a regular visitor from Lancashire who loved the Isle of Man and who wrote poetry in her local dialect, vividly recalled the annual ritual in *Wakes Week*:

Wakes Week

Summer meant packin' th'owd tin trunk
An' tekkin' t'cat nex doar;
T'gas turned oaf, th'aspidistras degged,
Buckets an' spades on t'floar.
Mi mother i'her Sunda' best
Shivin' up eggs an' beet
Fer t'sanwiches – an t'last mad rush
As t'cab crawled up eawr street!
Summer meand fidgetin' i' t'train
As t'teawn wor left behind,
An' gerrin' slapped fer muckyin' up
Me honds on t'strap o' t'blind.
We allus knew when t'say wor near,
T' sky seeomed so blue an' breet;
An' once on t'ship mi Dad ud say:
'We's be i' Peel toneet!'
We allus lodged at Missis Moore's,

'Sea View,' on th' edge o' t' Bay;
Went charra thrips to Douglas Head
An' Ramsey an' Glen Maye.
Summer meant smellin' kipper smooak,
Sand-pies an' songs an' fun –
Mi mother, set on t' castle rocks,
Her bonny face set to t'sun.[11]

Season extension

At the time of Joan Pomfret's childhood in the 1930s, huge demand for holidays had long been crushed into August, whilst many boarding house beds lay empty the rest of the year. The season seemed to be becoming shorter if anything. This worried the proprietors of small houses, many of whom made only a modest living. There was a real need to try to extend the season so that the industry was not sailing so close to the wind. Official Manx government season extension efforts had begun as early as 1894. The pioneering Isle of Man became only the second resort in the British Isles to fund advertising through local taxation. A Tynwald Commission on Advertising the Island recommended that:

> Prolonging the visiting season would undoubtedly be of great advantage, for it appears that, except for two or three weeks at the height of the season, lodging-house and hotel accommodation is greatly in excess of the demand.[12]

Publicity was designed to nudge visitors towards the early summer, advising that for:

> Those who profit by experience and who desire to see Douglas in comfort, at its best, and above everything to obtain COMFORT, August is the one month they DO NOT visit. The time to spend a holiday in Douglas is in the glorious month of June.[13]

In 1924 a public meeting in Douglas resolved to carry out a voluntary season extension campaign to complement government efforts, although many people worried that the task was nearly impossible.[14] The trauma of the First World War had brought the Edwardian boom to an abrupt end and sharpened Manx awareness that running a mass-market offshore resort was a risky business. Locals saw how, in difficult times, holidaymakers retreated to areas that were cheaper, closer to home or more secure. Post-war industrial troubles, including coal strikes and the General Strike, made the problem clear. Mr G.F. Clucas MHK scarcely exaggerated when he told a British commission of enquiry in 1925 that:

> Quite apart from the inability to extend our seasons, because the people who come here take their holidays at a definite [Wakes] time, our seasons are more precarious than they used to be, because of the great labour

unrest. Take the present industrial dispute. Suppose one prominent English newspaper were to say . . . 'a coal strike will take place in a fortnight'. That would be quite sufficient to ruin our season.[15]

Extension efforts continued, from the inauguration of electrical illuminations in the 1900s to

" THE HYDRO," DOUGLAS,
in the Merry Month of June.

A particulary fine group photo at the Hydro, Douglas 1920s.

women's health and beauty gatherings at the Nunnery in the 1930s and beyond.[16] Bursts of optimism tended to degenerate into weary efforts involving 'the same old subscribers and the same old critics' by the end of the inter-war period.[17] By then, the largest voluntary season extension committee was calling for more support from local taxpayers to underpin the movement. No one could find a way around the problem. The climate was one factor, but the limited leisure time given to most potential visitors by their employers was the real problem. Nevertheless, with resorts all over the country advertising against each other, season extension efforts were still thought necessary to stop the Isle of Man falling behind. By the late 1940s hoteliers were blaming the Government, the Government blamed the Steam Packet, which in turn blamed the hoteliers and anyone else it could. So when the chairman of the Publicity Board, J.D. Qualtrough, spoke to the Boarding House Association of the need for the shipping line to provide more early season services, no one was surprised.[18]

There was one event, however, which became a resounding success and is still the definitive season extension effort. This was TT race week. The races were inaugurated in 1904 and proved far more successful than anyone dared to hope. The ability of the Manx Government to take steps to boost tourism by road closures and the enthusiasm of the local authorities (once they realised that money was to be made) was vital. By the 1920s the races were an established part of the season and proved ever more successful in attracting June crowds at a time when there was plenty of space to accommodate them. The races generated interest from the large numbers of young men who came to own motorcycles in the inter-war period and who might not otherwise have come to the Island.

Having learnt from the TT that sport was a good way of attracting special interest groups, the Tourist Board went on to encourage other events such as cycle race weeks and sporting festivals, many of which were quite successful.

Problems with the season

Apart from the problem of the season being too short, occasional crises occurred as we have already seen. The first great blow to confidence came in 1914 with the outbreak of the First World War. The war led to four years of closure, and ruined many landladies. Even the loss of passenger steamers through the war made it hard for the industry to spring back in 1918. Although by 1923 most boarding houses were full for early August, with a fair proportion booked until the end of the month, it took the Island fully four or five years to recover all its customers. Throughout this critical time the shortness of the season was keenly felt. One post-war observer noted:

Come over in July, and you find the whole place flourishing; there are thousands of visitors everywhere, and it looks as though you had come to a little gold-mine. But how long does that last? Cut out July and August, when the Isle of Man is full, and June and September, when it is half full, why there is not a living soul [visiting] for the rest of the year . . . you can walk two miles along the

promenade and not meet a living soul.[19]

Only a few years of boom followed before the severe depression of the 1930s. Unemployment and a lack of money for holidays was all too evident in the Island's catchment area of the cotton towns. Resorts in the south of the UK had an easier time but it was harder in the north, and when times were hard, hoteliers came off badly. The revenue of the Manx state was also highly dependent on taxes generated from visitors. Income tax was low and had only been introduced a few years before. Most local taxes were levied on goods (such as alcohol and tea) which visitors bought in large quantities. So the bad season of 1930 caused fears of a shortfall in the Government's income as well as those of small businesses.[20]

During the depression, families who could not afford a normal holiday often managed to take a day trip or two. Although this profited transport companies and cafés, it was no good for boarding houses. Still, it kept the place busy. August Bank Holiday, which was the peak time for day trips, saw 29 sailings in 1929 and 24 in 1930, rising to 42 by 1933, when an astonishing 55,000 people sailed to the Island in 32 hours. The Isle of Man Steam Packet Company boasted that its thirteen ships had sailed a total of 2,700 miles.[21] But these visitors were not staying many nights. Even worse for the boarding house keepers was that they were being undercut by private householders offering bed and breakfast. In July 1939 it was said that:

> The truth is that Douglas has a greater [bed] capacity than ever before. The only new boarding-houses since the war are going up in Hutchinson Square now: but tenants or owners on the instalment system in [the suburbs of] Bray Hill, Ballabrooie and Ballakermeen, Olympia, Hillside Avenue and other areas where houses have been erected mainly for the reception of small wage-earners, are absorbing very large numbers of visitors, and are very glad to get them.[22]

Only a few short weeks after this account was written, the Island was again shut down by war (see Chapter 4). Fortunately the post-war demand for holidays was immense and the seasons remained busy enough to keep the economy fairly healthy for three or four decades. The government did its best to help keep the boarding houses filled by encouraging advance bookings through the Tourist Board. It also ran a bureau to fill last-minute vacancies in Douglas, and in smaller resorts such as Peel, the town clerk did the same job. These schemes helped landladies to make the most of the busy months.

Remembering the good times

There is no doubt that June, July and August were often times of excitement, satisfaction and fun. June Hope, who kept a house on Christian Road, found that no two weeks were ever quite the same.

You would have the Irish families one week, Glasgow Fair families the next. It was always a different atmosphere with a different set of people. It used to amuse us for Glasgow Fair, because at that time — I'm talking about when beehive hairstyles were in — the Glasgow women used to come on the first day of their holiday with their beehives sprayed solid with lacquer and they would still be up a fortnight later! But they were nice people, good fun people. We also found there was a difference between the northern English and southern English. Whereas northern English, they would come up the stairs and they would say 'Eeh that's grand love' and they'd put the cases in and shout 'We're off now . . . we're off to the Prom', the people from London would arrive and they would inspect their room first. But once they'd settled in and they were satisfied that everything was all right, then they were fine. But they weren't like the northerners.[23]

With so many visitors, there were always jobs for young people in the high season. Girls of school age used to wait at tables, whilst boys worked on trams, buses or hired out deck chairs. After leaving college in 1956, Dollin Kelly drove a coach in summer to supplement his wages as a teacher. It wasn't quite as easy as it looked. The driving part was quickly learnt, but drumming up business was rather harder. Some tours were booked in advance, but certainly not all:

Board and lodging – literally! This card was rejected by the Manx government censors as unsuitable, to protect the good name of the boarding houses, as the letter 'R' indicates.

You had to take pot luck, you had to entice the people into your coach. The Douglas Corporation had inspectors going round so that you were not allowed to tout — touting was an offence. Of course we did tout. I hated it. I didn't mind trying to talk to people and talk them into a thing, but not to actually tout when I knew it was against the law. Mumbling away to the people and at the same time keeping an eye open for an inspector didn't suit me; but it was very difficult to fill a coach . . . you had to get the backsides on the seats. That was up to the driver, so a driver was adjudged to be good if he could load a coach . . . One thing I learnt pretty quickly [as a young man] was that it was very easy to get girls onto coaches, but it was a heck of a hard job to get fellows on. They wanted just to booze, but the girls were trying to get off with the drivers so actually it was really quite easy!

It was also very difficult to forecast what time your coach would leave, so you would just say that you were going 'round the Island' and they would say 'What time are you going round the Island?' Well, 'Mumble, mumble, mumble, 10 o'clock' you know, but you mightn't get off until 10.30 because the truth was, you went when you got a full load, or as near a full load as possible. So the bosses would go round to landladies in the winter and sort of sign the landladies up, so that we could go in and talk to the people over their breakfasts. A lot of our bookings came that way.[24]

At the end of a day spent cleaning, driving, cooking or waiting on tables, most young workers like Kelly were keen to enjoy some social life. The dance-halls and entertainments in Douglas were freely patronised by boarding house staff. A young woman working on Douglas promenade would have counted herself unlucky if she could not go dancing twice a week in the 1930s. There was fun to be had for all ages in the season, even for those who didn't care for night life. In Peel, Mrs Sheilagh Barlow on Marine Parade found that the pleasure of being her own boss was a reward more tangible than mere dancing:

It was very rewarding, that was one thing about it . . . you were getting your money on the spot. You weren't like the grocer and the other people waiting for their money. It was very encouraging and it did help you, it

A view of Douglas beach and prom from the Hydro Hotel, 1950s.

gave you confidence. So they were happy days.[25]

Mrs Barlow found that as a boarding house keeper she gained a sense of freedom and independence despite the long hours. Letty Edgar also found that keeping a boarding house was a much better life than working in the shipyards of the Clyde:

It was different completely from what I did in Clydebank where I worked in a shipyard, in a great big shed where I used to make the linings for the boilers of the ships with wire and glass woven inside. You worked with your coat and your gloves on there. So I thought, 'There must be something better to do', and that was

why I decided to come to the Isle of Man. I'd never been to the Isle of Man and it was amazing. Everything was new, everything was different, a different way of life all together. It's hard to explain but I loved it. At that period of time the summers were wonderful, you were getting letters in January to get booked up for the busy time, and then of course people booked as they were leaving for the following year and they booked the same room. I used to have a very good clientele from Belfast, and from Glasgow. They'd book up because at that period of time there wasn't enough accommodation for all the people that wanted holidays so they wanted to make sure they got booked in.[26]

Letty Edgar worked in her own establishment during the post-war boom. The high demand for holidays made the business lively and profitable, and visitors remained regular in their holiday habits. The landladies who were happiest in their work at this time were those who were sociable by nature and for whom creating a homely atmosphere came most easily. Mrs Ivy Kaneen of Peel, for example, chose to cook home-made food even when frozen food would have been cheaper and easier. She felt that it gave added value to her business and kept visitors happy who would come

again. Such decisions were hers alone to make, and the power to choose how they ran their own businesses gave many people like Mrs Kaneen a lot of satisfaction.

Remembering the bad times

Proprietors worried a lot about their staff. Some family-run establishments managed to hire the same people every season, but this was never entirely possible. The larger the house, the larger the staff turnover. This meant that for many, the season usually began with some untrained staff which made many landladies very anxious. As the weeks passed, new staff grew more confident and useful, but if the pressure of work grew too great, or discontent bubbled, by the middle of the season there was always the threat of staff walking out. Another seasonal pressure was the temptation to move staff or children out of their rooms so that extra paying visitors could be brought in. Mrs June Hope, who was brought up in a boarding house and went on to run one of her own, remembers the problem when she was a young girl:

Well I hated it, to be honest. You would come home and you'd end up sleeping in an armchair — I've slept in the bath, and I've slept on the landing. When [it was so busy] of course, when you came home from school you had to help with the dishes . . . and children didn't expect to be taken out on the beach on summer afternoons because the parents were

or two. Troubled people sought the anonymity of a crowded resort to kill themselves in boarding houses or hotels. Even the genteel Fort Anne saw horror in July 1927 when a 'determined suicide', called William Pickup, cut his throat before jumping from a high window.[28] Dramatic deaths in season were as old as the season itself. As early as 1869 the boarding house keeper and butcher, Thomas Burden of Strand Street, cut his throat with one of his own knives in his busy shop, to the 'intense horror of all his customers'. A visitor staying in the boarding house part of Burden's business reported that the butcher had been depressed, downcast, and 'put about, with all the number of people in the house'. The overcrowding had tipped him into what the coroner judged as temporary insanity.[29] Fortunately, few boarding house keepers suffered so severely, but the pressures of the season affected all areas of life, especially in Douglas. In 1902 the Reverend John Davidson of St Andrew's church, Finch Road, wrote:

Peggy Love and Letty Edgar outside the Alma, 1947.

busy. Being shunted from pillar to post as a child, I vowed when we first moved in [to Christian Road] that I would never ever let out [my children's] rooms, and I never did.[27]

Hoteliers with relatives or friends in the country sometimes sent children out of town in August, allowing the parents to both let their rooms and work even longer hours. July and August were months when the health of boarding house staff often suffered because of overwork. Some proprietors even slept with their clothes on in case of emergencies. Most seasons saw a tragedy

The month of August is always a time of strain and anxiety to the great majority of the congregation. The passing weeks have been no exception to this rule. On ship, in shop, and in boarding-house there has been grinding toil, fretting care, and excessive worry . . . I have been praying for you that your health and strength might not fail.[30]

A grocer who made daily deliveries to many Douglas boarding houses remembered that some

places ran to a strict system, with every item organised to keep up with the rush. At other establishments, however:

> You went in and they'd be playing hell with you, [saying] 'Oh, you would arrive now, you would arrive now', and I'd say 'Well, look, when do you want me to arrive?' 'Oh, I don't bloody well know.' You'd get all sorts of abuse. And you used to think, well, they're all frazzled . . . their nerves are all shot to pieces.[31]

Over the years the Tourist Board developed a system of inspection to keep things running as smoothly as possible. It was long established when in 1972 Frank Swinnerton joined the staff:

> When I started to do the job I discovered that 90 per cent of it was about sex and violence, which are my favourite things [laughter]. I couldn't wait to get down there to discover the dreadful things that people seemed to do to each other . . . The problems that arose for the industry fell into four distinct groups. There were complaints from the guests about the hotels; and there were also quite frequently guests who caused the

hotels to complain about them. So we had guests and hotels complaining about each other from time to time. But then we had guests complaining about the other guests, and hotels complaining about the other hotels, so you had this combination of four lots of problems and it did give rise to a marvellous selection of things. It was all about people, and the extraordinary things that people do when they're on holiday, and the people trying to look after them.[32]

The end of the season

When the season came to its end it meant unemployment for many. Workers from England and Ireland asked for their references, hoped for a bonus and packed their bags. Proprietors got busy closing up houses, with the assistance of one or two local staff. Clearing up the kitchens took a lot of time, as one cook recalls:

> Oh, it was a big do at the end of the year, stripping them all down and cleaning them . . . so that they would be ready to leave for the winter. All the machinery was stripped down and it was all oiled, or Vaselined, and all the tins, they

were all scrubbed and wrapped in papers. And the stoves — as I say — all stripped out and all the shelves too. Everything was absolutely clean. They got spring-cleaned at the end of the summer and of course it left no smell then. No matter when you went in, you never thought 'Oh dear this has been a fatty kitchen' or something, no, nothing like that. The floor was tiled too, you see, that was all tiled and it was all scrubbed out.[33]

The season ended rapidly on the Isle of Man. It didn't tail off slowly and facilities were shut quickly because they became uneconomic to run. Sheila Barlow explains:

I never took anybody after October 1st, because my husband had to have his holiday then, and another thing you see: everything is dearer in the winter, you're having lights on in every corridor and passage and you're having fires going, you must give people comfort if you have them, so after the 1st October that was it — I never took anybody.[34]

Winter

Once the final visitors had gone, the character of the Island underwent a change. Many facilities closed. Bustle gave way to silence, crowds to open spaces. Douglas promenade in the winter was memorably evoked by the writer Freida Standen. In the 1920s

TT race visitors outside the Beresford Hotel, late 1960s, or even early 1970s.

she spent her childhood on Palace Terrace, and remembers:

> How different was the winter! How quiet it was! The sound of the sea crashing onto, and dragging back through, the stones was so loud. When the horse-trams approached, the sound of the horses' hooves clip-clopping on the road could be heard a long way off. Stormy nights in the winter used to frighten me somewhat. In our cosy sitting-room we could hear the wind howling and the sea crashing onto the promenade. The passage from our door onto the semi-basement would be flooded . . . If, due to a bronchial attack, I was sleeping in the big front bedroom with its fire burning constantly, the noise outside seemed tremendous, and strangely, for one so young, I was always conscious of the intense emptiness of this huge house.[35]

The world of the boarding house in winter was also called to mind in a 1939 short story by Dora Broome, who made radio broadcasts and wrote for the *Manchester Guardian*. Her 'Sketch of Douglas Boarding House Life' starred a fictional landlady called Mrs Quaggin who was a long-suffering woman with a former sailor as a husband. The story begins . . .

> Mrs Quaggin mounted the stairs from the warm basement to the cold upper storeys. A faint aroma of baked and boiled still lingered in the oilclothed hall, but the visitors' book was closed like the Tome of Judgement. She went into the dining-room where piled-up chairs played leap-frog over one another and a wisp of palm waved forlornly from its pot. On the monumental sideboard gothic cruets were planted like miniature cathedrals. . . . Mrs Quaggin went to the window and peered across the empty promenade, where every post was topped by an immobile gull. A scud of rain drove across the greyness of the sea and sky . . . She saw the steamer at the pier [bringing] those letters from the outside world that meant milk and bread and meat, and money in the bank until the summer. Those were the letters that Mrs Quaggin liked to read. Letters with strange postmarks on them, beginning, 'Dear Madam, will you please reserve rooms for us on the –th,' and convenient dates to them, for it seemed to Mrs Quaggin that all the world wanted to come to the island when it was full and no-one at all when it was empty.[36]

Mrs Quaggin may have been fictional but the problem of surviving the winter on modest funds, of securing bookings and keeping a marriage going were big responsibilities for women who kept boarding houses. A 'good winter' when letters streamed in made life so much easier. A landlady knew by February whether she was set for a good season.[37] Sheilagh Barlow recalls:

> I came in [to the trade] about January. I prepared and I got ready. I had to advertise, of course, and once you advertised you were getting letters. You could really tell how the season was going to be even in February because people were writing early and booking in. There was such an overflow coming to Peel, you remember all the boarding houses were full on the prom in those days, right over as far as Stanley Road . . . it was very interesting.[38]

With the assurance of forward bookings, winter could be a time of rest and renewal for both people and property. With British resorts closed for the winter, by the early 1960s (over twenty years after Mrs Quaggin had hung up her duster and retired, no doubt, to the chintzy suburban bungalow of her dreams) some successful proprietors could afford foreign travel in the off-season. They were keen to enjoy it. There were even travel advertisements in the local press aimed specifically at those who had worked a good season and who wanted to head off in search of some sun. The situation was rather ironic, for most guest house proprietors still expected their customers to somehow remain immune to the temptations they had given into and keep travelling to British resorts.

The winter was also a time when local art and culture had time to flourish. The immensely popular Manx Music Festival – usually known as The Guild – has been held every April since 1892.[39] Another popular pastime was amateur dramatics. In Peel, one group of players got the dining-room of a promenade boarding house to rehearse in because the landlady was a member. Mrs Betty Deans remembers just after the war:

> She had great big rooms and there was one particular play, a lot of people in Peel were in it, called 'Making it Pay'. It was ideal really because it was set in a café and we had all the tables there already because it was a boarding house. They were allowed an allocation of sugar – the boarding houses – and extra rations, so they could keep the boarding house trade going. I loved it, because I would be pinching sugar lumps when rehearsing. It was really quite an experience rehearsing there because in the winter, if you know anything about Peel Promenade, we couldn't open the front doors, we had

Watterson's Souvenir Shop, Peel, in the 1970s.

to go in through the back and all the front doors would be covered in salt from the spray and the sea was really quite frightening. So every winter this went on. We used to go in the Guild — the Music Festival they call it now — and they had a whole week of plays, One-Act Plays, they'd have the seniors and the juniors. Oh you couldn't do it in the summer, you couldn't possibly do it. People used to say 'Does anything go on in the winter here?', well, everything did go on in the winter [for us].[40]

The winter was a time to relax for those who had money. But leisure could only truly be enjoyed by those who were free from poverty. Young seasonal workers with no assets hated the winter. As early as 1910 this problem was apparent, according to an angry letter

printed in the newspapers. An unhappy young man complained:

> What chance has a young fellow got in the Isle of Man? Why should he stay here? I see that once again it was suggested that one could earn enough money in the season to keep oneself all the winter. I wish it were so.[41]

Young or single men were almost expected to leave. It was easier for landladies, who, although they ran up debts, knew that these could be secured on the businesses. Local clubs and societies held dinners, meetings and dances in boarding houses. These were a handy source of pin-money for landladies but generated little employment.[42] In the late 1920s, a Tynwald Commission on Seasonal Unemployment recommended public works as a way of easing the problem.[43] The Government could see little development of other industries. Direct labour was used as a means of job creation and a cheap way to improve the towns; promenades were widened, roads improved and parks maintained. There was no surprise when one Member of the House of Keys railed in 1930 that the outlook for the nearly 2,000 men likely to be unemployed that winter was 'simply appalling'.[44] Many married men whose wives were landladies tried to find year-round employment in industries outside tourism. In Port Erin after the war, Arthur King and his wife did just this. Mr King remembers how the men found work elsewhere:

> Oh they were all doing it, well most of them, the smaller ones were all doing the same. They were all working in Church Road. I knew the husbands — next door to me was working; there were two ladies on the other side of us; then the man was working in the next one and in the next road up again there was husband and wife, they ran it between them. But for the most part, in those houses, the husbands were leading their own lives.[45]

This is the story of Alf Duggan, who was a driver of taxis and hire cars in summer. He went in search of winter work in the early 1950s:

> The summers were very short and the money at that time was short too. I've known the fares to be as low as half a crown (2s 6d.) for the taxi from the boat to the Villa Marina, then they went up to 3s from Broadway over to as far as the Esplanade . . . it wasn't a big lot of money. Regarding the winter [for] a self-employed person, especially in a taxi, or anything like that, well, work was not very good on the Island

in the '50s and '60s. So the only alternative you had would be — if you could — to go to England. I saw this advert in the paper, 'Wanted: bus drivers, Coventry Transport'. So I went along to Coventry Transport and passed the medical and driving tests and the what–have–you to be a driver, conductor and courier. But Coventry Transport had an agreement that you could only go there twice. So after that I went with the Midland Red in Birmingham for the following years. I put many hours in there, driving all over the place. I had to go . . . I couldn't get work.[46]

It was not until early May that Alf could return, take his taxi off its blocks, and prepare for another summer season. By this point the landladies of the Isle of Man had preparations well in hand, as Muriel Cottier explains:

We'd start at the top [of the house] and work down and clean and then we'd go back to the top again and start making up beds and things like that nearer to the time you know. We had a large lounge on the first floor and we used to air all our bedding in there because it was always nice and sunny, then take it up from there gradually as we worked down. We'd start . . . decorating and start cleaning by March because we used to open about May.[47]

It was a whole way of life which endured from the late nineteenth century until the 1970s. But the advent of foreign holidays brought a swift decline in the Island's fortunes which changed resort life for ever.

The season in recent years

By the late 1960s, even large and traditionally successful guest houses were feeling the effects of an ever leaner season. At the Metropole, Gordon and Joy Birnie turned to package-tours to fill their 108 bedrooms at reduced prices during the early and late months, but this was not without problems. The bargain prices only paid for the cheapest rooms and a lower standard of service. When tour customers saw how they fared in comparison to other guests, arguments ensued.[48] Despite these worries, package tour operators such as Wallace Arnold were a boon to many struggling hoteliers. Although the companies negotiated hard on price, they 'block-booked' rooms and paid for them all up front which took risk away from the hoteliers.

Many other long-established practices began to change in the 1960s.[49] One was that most boarding houses could no longer only take bookings from

Entertainment TT style. A motorbike stunt by The Purple Helmets on the prom, 1990s.

Saturday to Saturday to avoid empty beds. Once they had almost been able to dictate terms to enquirers. Later, as visitor numbers fell and cheap midweek sailings became popular, it was the end for rigid booking. Proprietors had to take what they could and juggle bookings to fill their rooms. The rate of decline accelerated in the 1980s and many went out of business. As the old boarding houses either closed down or were improved to become guest houses or small hotels, the old seasons and their habits went the same way as coal-fired steamers and Wakes Weeks, into history.

Susan Gowing, who now runs Port Erin Hotels and who trained as a management accountant, is one of the new breed of hotel managers. She reflects:

We're probably fairly unusual in this day and age that we do have some people who still come every year; that's largely a dying trait, as you know. But 27 per cent of our independent guests have been before,

and that's a percentage we're extremely proud of. We still get a little bit of the traditional Irish market, but it tends to be in the lower groups although that is changing rapidly. We are now seeing a new trend of well–heeled Irish guests who are extremely different from those we had before. We see a lot of the north–west market, the traditional market is still there, but I think that we certainly need to understand that our product is actually quite saleable. We are working very hard to extend the season . . . the Royal Hotel is open year–round for functions and trade, with accommodation closed only for December and January. One of my campaigns is to get an all–round product to tie in for March, April and through to November.[50]

At the beginning of the twenty-first century, businesses like Mrs Gowing's now rely on a mixture of customers which would have surprised Mrs Quaggin. There is no standard group of visitors: no Wakes Week crowds from the same towns. Stalwart 'regulars', TT motorcyclists, rail enthusiasts, walkers, families, and many others have to mix but all appreciate the unique character of the Isle of Man. They patronise modernised hotels and guest houses which were once boarding houses but which are now run very differently. There is a new cautious optimism after the pain and decline which scourged the industry throughout the 1980s. Those who survived find that custom is not as certain as it once was; but there are visitors to be found in the new market. The promenades still smarten up for the summer, though sandwich-nibbling office workers from the financial sector frequently outnumber tourists on benches and in their sunken gardens. The season is not the same, but it lives on.

7

Promote *and protect*

The companies and people who worked in tourism were always keen to promote and protect their industry. Resort communities were the first towns in the British Isles to advertise and market themselves with the object of becoming more successful. They created organisations such as the Isle of Man Board of Advertising to make sure that they got lots of good publicity. When resorts were thought of as happy, healthy and fun, visitors were more likely to come and the resort grew more prosperous.

Ways of advertising

The most popular advertising method was to use the Official Guide. It was a high-quality and well read publication which began in the 1890s. It was paid for by the government and enquirers anywhere in the world could receive it free by post. Every boarding house proprietor on the Isle of Man was entitled to a free single line advert and a description in the accommodation lists and this was very popular. There was also the option to pay for display adverts of varying size, from a small box to an entire page. As printing technology developed and the printing of photographs became cheaper, some very effective publicity was created. In the 1930s the guide book began to offer adverts of a new modern type which were brighter and bolder than ever and full of fun.

These adverts are great to look at and they made a holiday in the Isle of Man sound irresistible. Old adverts are still very popular and there was even a retro-style marketing campaign by the Department of Tourism in the late 1980s which used a 1930s style of graphic design alongside the slogan 'you'll look forward to going back'. However, old adverts do need to be viewed with care. They were created for just the same

The Balqueen Hydro, Port St Mary,
advertising its many attractions in the
late 1950s.

reasons as their counterparts today. They were designed to sell products or services and make money, so of course they glossed over bad points, exaggerated benefits and generally made everything seem better than it was. With this caution in mind we can ask some fascinating questions about how the Manx holiday industry – and boarding house proprietors in particular – used publicity to promote and protect the trade. Manx businesses could choose from a wide range of options. There were newspapers and magazines, or they could advertise with the Official Board, with the Steam Packet, with English railway companies or in commercial guide books.

Guide books

With so many almost identical boarding houses looking for customers it was hard for a proprietor to stand out from the crowd. In the very early days of the tourist boom, adverts were placed in the local press and only a few enterprising hotels used newspapers in the north-west of England. By the 1880s, a plethora of guide books, papers, posters and leaflets had developed for advertisers to choose from. They were part of a nation-wide boom in advertising and publicity, which was one of the great innovations of Victorian Britain. As the market grew more sophisticated and competitive, the question of how best to advertise the Island led the Manx Government into one of its wisest decisions. It created an innovative Board of Advertising as early as 1894 which was the envy of many other resorts. Until 1921 hardly any British towns except Blackpool could use the rates to run collective publicity campaigns, because the Local Government Board would not let them.[1] However they could rely on railway companies to advertise because the companies wished to boost excursion traffic. The railway companies of the north-west also publicised the Isle of Man because they served its feeder ports and some even owned steamers. The Midland Railway published *The Barrow Route to the Isle of Man*, whilst the L.N.E.R. and the Cheshire Lines produced similar works in which Manx companies and boarding houses bought space. The Isle of Man Steam Packet Company was also a great advertiser. It issued guide books and posters and maintained a London office. These sorts of guides were usually distributed free.

There was also a thriving commercial guide book trade selling souvenir books at resorts all over the British Isles. The purchase price of the guides was subsidised by advertising. The drive to sell space meant that agents were often sent to canvass boarding house keepers. With so many publicity outlets on offer, it was hard for a landlady to choose where to spend the money she had set aside for advertising. A trusted local firm was one possibility. *Brown's Isle of Man Guide* was printed by the company which ran the *Isle of Man Times*. The *Isle of Man Examiner* also offered a range of guides. However, these were mostly for people who had already made it to the Island. Landladies who wanted to reach new customers could use the many English firms which covered the Isle of Man. There was Thomas Cook Ltd, which included the Island in its tours of the Lake District area. Ward Lock and Co. printed its famous red guides. The publishers Mate and Sons of Bournemouth paid the Reverend John Quine to write a glossy souvenir guide to the Island in 1899. It ran to more than one hundred pages and cost a shilling. Other firms which we know catered for the Manx market were Blacks of Edinburgh, Booth of Oldham, Bent & Co. of Birmingham and Heywood of Manchester, and there were many others.

It was a potentially lucrative business, which was enough to tempt some fly-by-night operators or fraudsters. It was not unknown for 'agents' to call on proprietors and offer cheap advertising space in a new guide whilst making impressive-sounding claims about its circulation and quality. They were usually never heard from again.[2] There were even occasional frauds by canvassers pretending to be from well-known organisations. In August 1936 several hoteliers were caught out by a man pretending to represent the AA or RAC.[3]

Even when guide books were totally genuine, publishers were often reluctant to reveal circulation figures. This made it hard for advertisers to make a judgement about which guide book was best. No wonder so many proprietors with only a few rooms to let were cautious about advertising outside the Official Guide. Those running larger establishments were keener advertisers as the range of advertising in various commercial publications reveals. At first, a series of set phrases was usually used in their advertisements and they varied little from year to year until the 1920s. An impossible number of boarding houses, it seemed, were 'one minute from shore' or 'two minutes from the landing pier'. Where such a claim was blatantly impossible, 'trams pass door' was a good second best. A 'sea view' would be boasted even if only a strained peep could be glimpsed. And of course, every single house in the Island offered terms that were 'strictly moderate'. Some also tried to suggest sophistication and a high social tone. The slogan of the Hotel Belvedere, that 'mountains look on Belvedere, and Belvedere looks on the sea' took its inspiration from Byron's poem 'The Isles of Greece'[4] and tried to suggest not only a stunning location but also gentility.[5]

A few boarding houses were able to link general advertising of this sort with small publicity brochures of their own from the early twentieth century. The

RAMSEY HYDRO
RAMSEY

DANCING ★

TENNIS ★

BUS
SERVICE
TO
TOWN

BATHING
FROM
HOTEL

Fully Licensed.   *Accommodation 130 Guests.*
Reduced Terms Early and Late Season.

For Terms Apply :
Manageress.   Tel. Ramsey 2115.

Proprietors :
HYDRO, RAMSEY (1933) LTD.

BELVEDERE
PRIVATE HOTEL
Telephone: RAMSEY 3229

MOORAGH PROMENADE
RAMSEY, ISLE OF MAN

OPEN ALL YEAR

Fully Licensed for Residents and
their Guests

99

Ramsey Hydro and the Belvedere Hotel advertisements emphasising dancing, tennis and bathing, pleasures of the 1950s.

proprietress of the Greenwood, at 2 Loch Promenade, offered an illustrated booklet in the 1910s, but only those running large places could afford the cost of printing.[6] They were the same local houses which could take out large pictorial adverts in many different guides. Westlake's Sea Level, for example, boasted that it was modern and up-to-date with the latest technology – the

telephone. It also had a place for bicycles and claimed to be 'a comfortable and refined home for boarders and private families, highly recommended by Doctors, Ministers and many others'. The Savoy concentrated not on health but on social tone. Trading off its classy name and a select location right next to the Castle Mona, it filled an entire page of *Brown's Isle of Man Guide* with hints that a holiday at the Savoy was for those on the rise.[7]

The importance of names

With so much similarity between terraced rows of houses, proprietors thought up a wide variety of names to help sell their businesses. The name of the Belvedere came from an Italian palace and also meant a place with a beautiful view. Other names made a direct appeal to customers from certain districts, such as Clyde House, Keighley House, Nottingham House, Birmingham House and Trafford House. Even those who did not use regional names sometimes boasted of their UK links in publicity, such as Dodsworth's which said in its advertisements it was patronised by people from Warwickshire and Staffordshire.[8] An alternative was to emphasise a sense of Manxness and difference, as with Mona House or Snaefell. A few appealed to special interests, for example, The Colonial, or The Masonic, while others took names suggesting holiday fun such as The Blondin, The Rookery, and Friendship. In an age of empire, there were of course many Empires, Imperials and Albions. Also common were names which evoked the French and Alpine resorts patronised by the rich, or names of the homes of the wealthy. Finally, some landladies simply gave prominence to their surnames, and the guide book reader of the 1890s found many

An artist's view of the Westlake's Sea Level hotel, 1930s. Emphasising closeness to the beach was the most important advertising method, followed by 'homeliness' and good food.

Composite photographs to promote the Westlake's attractions, early twentieth century.

establishments run by the likes of Mrs Craine, Mrs Kaighin, Mrs Faragher, Mrs Cannell, Mrs Cubbon and Mrs Corlett. A number with Irish names were also evident, such as Mrs Daugherty, Mrs O'Hara and Mrs Caugherty.[9]

New and old styles

After a long time the standard Victorian phrases gave way to new styles. By the 1930s many (but by no means all) had snappier slogans and brighter graphics. Ducker's Trevelyan changed its advert to offer enquirers 'Four guarantees: good cooking, good food, perfect sanitation, and moderate tariff'. 'Don't take my word,' said Ducker, 'come and try it yourself.'[10] The Empress boasted about its new dance-hall. Fashionable young ladies learnt that they could stay glamorous with the Ladies' Hairdressing Salon at the Savoy. Some novelty publicity devices such as the giant Alexandra Hotel beach ball were a great success. In 1936 the ball even rolled its way into the pages of the *Sunday Dispatch*, which got admiration from other hoteliers in the trade press as an example of really innovative publicity.[11]

At the same time as the new developments made themselves felt, many of the old methods continued and establishments in the cheaper parts of the Island were slow to change. Adverts like those of Mrs Cregeen at 5 Laureston Terrace which said that her house was 'in the healthiest part of Douglas' and had a 'sitting room with use of piano' were seen until the 1950s.[12] The small businesses put a lot of emphasis on home cooking and a 'liberal table' in their adverts.

Full information on a Victorian handbill for the Railway Hotel – and all for 6d a day!

Making headlines

The best way to get in the papers was for proprietors to band together. The longest running co-operative advertising effort was the Official Board of Advertising which raised money through local taxes for its work.[13] The Douglas Advertising Committee was a second voluntary co-operative effort assisted by Douglas Corporation. Its guide book praised the town's boarding houses to the skies, saying:

Boarding-house keeping, and catering generally, is the sole and absorbing industry of all the people of Douglas. The magnificent rows of houses lining the sea-front were built for it and for nothing else. Roads parallel and at angles to these are entirely composed of boarding-houses, capable of accommodating 60,000 people. These establishments are always maintained in an irreproachable manner . . . and the cost of accommodation will be found most reasonable.

After all, the pleasures of sport, of entertainment, are of little real attraction if the visitor is not comfortably housed; and in this respect it may be modestly affirmed that Douglas stands unrivalled among watering places for the elegance of its boarding and lodging-houses and hotels, the sumptuousness of their appointments, the moderate tariffs and the excellence of the meals. In the Isle of Man, catering has become an art and a science, and the epicure will find his wants anticipated and his

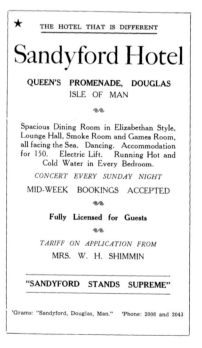

Happiness goes with electric lifts. The Rutland and Sandyford Hotels list their sporting and dancing facilities in these 1950s adverts.

appetite quickened by the seductive odour of savoury dishes — if it has not already been sharpened by his sojourn in this tone-giving climate.[14]

Other collective efforts organised by the Board of Advertising, local authorities and volunteers included stunts and carnivals which got the Island into the news. One observer joked that the advertisers would soon be using highly trained tail-less cats dancing the Hi-Kelly polka on Douglas promenade, 'with the natives in the background, in that warlike attitude known as "preparing to receive boarders!"'[15] 'Be co-operators, not competitive' warned another article, returning to a theme that the Boarding House Association repeatedly stressed.[16] To this end, the Douglas Boarding House & Hotels Association tried to maintain minimum prices, and tried to make sure that nobody advertised below the official price.

There was no stopping the publicity drive. Even in the late nineteenth century, magazines had devoted space to travel and holidays. The Albany Hotel got a write-up in the *Gentleman's Journal* of September 1887 and an enterprising proprietor quickly reprinted it alongside an enormous photo of Douglas Bay as an advertisement which declared:

'Pleasure is on parade' at the Douglas Bay Hotel, 1950s.

Prominent among the private hotels and boarding-houses for which Douglas is famous is the Albany, 60 and 61 Loch Promenade. It is in the centre of the parade, and commands grand views of the headlands and bay. It has 48 bedrooms, all clean and comfortable, most of them facing the sea; commodious drawing, dining, smoking-rooms &c, all stately and comfortably furnished. The charges are exceedingly reasonable — from 6s *a day inclusive. The proprietor and his wife, Captain and Mrs Morton, are not only good company, but thoroughly understand the value of good living, and we can heartily recommend the Albany to all intending visitors to the Island.*[17]

Publicity of this sort was very valuable. The Ridgeway Hotel under James Craig received free publicity in a new magazine, *The Tourist*, by running a competition in 1897 to win a free week at 'the newest and one of the most beautiful residential hotels on the Isle of Man'. To compete for the prize, readers had to write 500 words on 'why a man needs a holiday'.[18] The pleasures of holidaymaking were of course emphasised by boarding house proprietors. Many on the seafront had fake sailing boats painted on their souvenir postcards to suggest, as at The Alma on Loch Promenade, that visitors had fishing, bathing, boating and yachting at the door.[19]

Another Victorian virtue which boarding houses tried to emphasise was their modernity and sanitation. A good deal of guide book space was given over to talk about sandy soils, clean breezes and good drains. Resorts had to show themselves off as healthy places if they wanted to gain customers. New facilities built to the latest standards including indoor water closets on several floors were at first something to boast about. Many a landlady made sure that her advertisement contained the magic phrase 'perfect sanitation'. However, as facilities aged, it got harder to substantiate claims that the Island's boarding houses were 'modern and luxurious', as the Board of Advertising suggested

in 1920. In reality, most were showing their age and the effect of wartime neglect. Many were still filled with Victorian furniture and fittings. Their sanitation was no longer anywhere near perfect – expectations had moved on. This being so, the Island had to emphasise its cheap prices and friendliness instead, as this post-war advertising reveals:

Manx tariffs are much below those which obtain in connection with similar establishments in British, Irish and foreign seaside resorts. Moderate and slender purses need be no bar to visits to Manxland, for there is an abundance of good boarding-house accommodation at reasonable rates.[20]

The Island certainly needed to advertise and could not afford to be complacent about its position. For example, Ward Lock's 1928 guide to the Isle of Man contained a full page advert for Bournemouth, and small adverts for Manx boarding houses were listed alongside those from Aberystwyth to Weymouth. Another problem was that holidays by motor-car were becoming more popular. Whilst many mainland resorts were able to advertise their new garages and car parks, the cost of shipping cars to Douglas meant that the Isle of Man could not compete.[21]

The 1920s saw other changes. The UK railways were rationalised into four big companies and their publicity departments merged. Some became very good. The L.M.S., for example, produced a handsome guide to the Lancashire coast which included the Isle of Man. Yet few Manx establishments advertised in it; perhaps they thought that competing against Blackpool in the same guide was wasteful. The cost of advertising also grew to be an accepted part of doing business for some of the larger hotels, where advertising was estimated to take up about 8 per cent of income by 1935.[22]

Word of mouth advertising

Alongside all the printed advertising, guide books and stunts was another network. It was the oldest advertising method of all and was simply word of mouth. Most boarding house keepers got a steady flow of enquiries through personal recommendations. A few were so content with this approach that they never advertised at all. Even the larger establishments still prized personal recommendations. The McAdam family, who ran Silvercraigs on Loch Promenade in the 1930s, liked to quote personal recommendations in their advertisements. Mr McAdam had been a commercial traveller and as a result his adverts were better than most. His technique of reproducing letters from satisfied customers made Silvercraigs' advertisements not only successful but interesting to read for many years.[23]

The unrespectable end of word of mouth advertising was touting. This had a bad reputation. The authorities thought that it lowered the social tone, worried visitors, and undermined legitimate advertisers. People who were caught touting were punished. When Maria Kneale, a Douglas lodging house keeper, was heard on the Victoria Pier in 1891 asking two men if they wanted rooms, she was fined 10s, with fourteen days in prison if she failed to pay. As a result, the more canny touts on the promenade sometimes pretended to be visitors sitting out on the steps or benches. This way they could have protested if caught that they were merely making a personal recommendation. Blatant touting continued but the police did their best to stop it. In 1931 James Forester was caught touting for the Rothesay on Loch Promenade by a plain clothes policeman and both he and his employer were fined.[24] Touts followed the crowds and didn't just work for boarding houses. As the habit of booking in advance became almost universal, and an official bureau to clear empty rooms was established, the problem transferred itself to the charabanc trade. Almost sixty years after Maria Kneale's offence, visitors were complaining that 'rabid touters were almost tearing the people's clothes off' on the Queen's Promenade in efforts to persuade them to go on coach trips.[25]

Bad publicity

Every hotelier dreaded bad publicity or gossip. The death of a visitor, crime on the premises, infectious diseases, sex scandals, rumours of rats in the kitchen, the police turning up or bugs in the bedrooms could all harm trade. If a good reputation was lost, then a thriving business could become almost valueless.[26] Keeping trouble secret was thought to be the best way. Guests should never know that the undertaker, policeman or pest exterminator had paid a visit.

Sometimes a big scandal did occur which could not be hushed up. As the popular press grew more scandal-hungry in the 1930s, boarding house keepers grew more wary of the papers. The *Sunday Pictorial* and the *News of the World* led the rat-pack, and were even described as a 'formidable enemy to the hotel and boarding house industry' for perpetually seeking sleaze, adultery and crime which could put a boarding house in the headlines for all the wrong reasons.

Proprietors also hated the jokes about bad food, hard beds and terrifying landladies which covered so many seaside postcards. To almost everyone but themselves, alas, they seemed rather funny and not wholly untrue!

Was advertising necessary?

Many landladies spent their entire working lives – except the war years – watching visitors come and go every year with gratifying regularity. No wonder it seemed as if things would always be that way. Was advertising then necessary? On a visit to the Isle of Man in 1950, John Betjeman wrote that propaganda for the Isle of Man was hardly necessary, because 'the lodging-houses are stuffed to capacity, the bathing suits hang from the sixth floor downwards'.[27] But this trade was in fact built up in part through sixty years of constant and careful advertising. Decades of persistent effort by the Government, the Isle of Man Steam Packet Company and hundreds of boarding house proprietors placed the Isle of Man Guide free in 130,000 houses every year by the 1930s. It was a valuable tool. Those in the tourist industry could purchase space for only 1.4 pence per square inch per 1,000 copies, far more cheaply than their counterparts in Brighton, Cromer or Hastings.[28] The Island could not afford to mount huge poster campaigns like Blackpool, but it carried out good work on what it could afford. Its head-start of 1894 far outstripped the local councils of many UK resorts, which did not gain official powers to advertise until 1921. Advertising for the community as a whole was carried out consistently and competently, and was vital

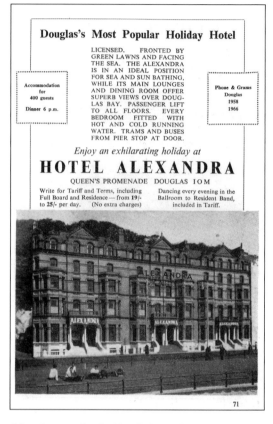

Advertisement for the Hotel Alexandra, 1950s.

in underpinning the success of a fairly hard-to-reach offshore island. Success was all the more remarkable given that the Island enjoyed far fewer of the subsidised posters which the railway companies offered her competitors. Boarding house keepers may often have been poor advertisers as individuals. Yet they supported collective action by bodies acting on their behalf, and paid for it by their taxes and voluntary contributions.

This consensus started to break down in the 1960s when decline began to bite and the industry turned to the Tourist Board to find solutions. As it began

By the mid-1950s, the Tourist Board had developed theme weeks in an effort to attract and retain visitors. This display, somewhere in the UK, advertises Dance Week.

Promotional material used to market the Isle of Man in Hull during 1953.

Example of Tourist Board publicity material at a rather old-fashioned tourist office in England in 1954.

to modernise its marketing strategies and conduct market research there seemed no easy answer. Large sums were belatedly spent by the Government; but £150,000 on publicity and £300,000 on a new sea terminal in the late 1960s were not enough to offset the decline caused by foreign competition.[29] Some people began to think that advertising was useless. This was not true, but it clearly had its limits, and these were becoming yearly more obvious. By the 1970s, instead of just competing with resorts in the UK, the Isle of Man

had to woo visitors from its rivals abroad. All the advertising in the world could not make its climate sunnier or warmer than that of the seductive Mediterranean.

The Trade Association

If promotion was desirable, so was the protection of commercial interests. From an early date, boarding house keepers created trade associations to defend

Selling the Isle of Man in Leeds in 1953 at a travelling stall operated by the Tourist Board, probably with its own representatives.

themselves against threats and to influence decisions in their favour.[30] However, they never gained the political strength of trade unions and left much less of a mark on history. Membership and activity levels tended to rise at times of crisis, such as during the First World War, but to decline once the trouble had passed.

The largest association was in Douglas. The Association did its best to advance a political programme which would make the visiting industry more popular and profitable. It tried to get Tynwald to spend more money on advertising the Island but also wanted the rates to be kept low as so many of its members had big boarding houses. One of its early presidents was James Ducker, a Scot who had moved to the Island to do business in tourism. At an official committee he

admitted (and even symbolised) the tensions which the rapid pace of development had caused. He claimed that the boarding house industry had been resented at first and that it took a long time to be assimilated into Manx life and culture.[31] He, like many proprietors, also resented the common gossip that boarding house keeping was a way to get rich quick.[32]

The nature of the industry did not lend itself to close organisation or union-style action and so the Association did not grow very strong. People came and left the industry at speed. They competed against one another. Some were part-timers with more than one job. The unity of the wartime Boarding House Women's League was unusual and by 1919 cut-throat competition was dissolving the coalition again. Wartime bankruptcy and a high turnover of tenants contributed to the small size of the post-war Douglas Boarding House Association, with only a committed core of proprietors remaining members. This was regretted by some in the local press who called for a strong Association to set an Island-wide scale of charges which would fund the new investments needed to sustain growth and prosperity.[33] Yet nothing was done and it was not until after the Second World War that the Isle of Man Visiting Industry & Catering Association resolved even to demand a deposit of £1 per person on all reservations.[34]

During campaigns in the 1950s, low levels of membership hindered the efforts of the Douglas Residential Hotel & Boarding House Association to speak authoritatively. The President lamented that only 350 houses were in the Association when more than 600 could have joined. As decline grew more obvious, the Association and the Government grew somewhat more critical of each other as both wondered what best to do.[35]

MOST COCKTAILS
MADE TO ORDER

FACTS ABOUT THE ISLE OF MAN

The Island has:—

No death duties.
No surtax.
Income tax at 4/3 in the £.
Car road tax at £5.
The oldest Parliament in the World.
430 miles of first-class motoring roads.
The largest dance hall in Europe.
Six golf courses.
The gulf stream to warm its waters.

THE ISLAND WELCOMES
NEW RESIDENTS

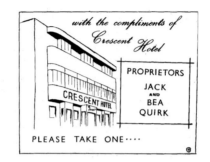

Nine facts about the Isle of Man to appeal to visitors.

Unfortunately, there is a great lack of records from the Association during the 1960s and 1970s and nothing seems to have survived until a new magazine called *The Link* started in 1977. The magazine's first issue in November recorded a disastrous drop of 78,000 visitors on the previous year. By the 1980s it was reflecting deep discouragement among the membership. President Bert Quirk, like his predecessors, had to urge members to keep coming to meetings which often became occasions dominated by the latest bad news.[36] It was even hard to stimulate enthusiasm for regular meetings of the Executive Committee.[37] Nevertheless some old principles for protecting the good name of the trade died hard. When a certain hotelier applied for membership of the Association, he was turned down because his hotel was 'a known disorderly house'.[38] In that same year, the Association's committee on staff conduct recommended that sleeping with guests should remain an example of gross misconduct punishable by instant dismissal.[39]

By the late 1980s the Association hoped desperately for a real upturn in bookings.[40] This period was the darkest yet for the hoteliers and any sign of improvement was eagerly sought. The introduction of jet-planes by Manx Airlines was welcomed and the idea of new hotels and motels was suggested from time

to time as it had been since the 1960s. But as had so often been the case, little action or investment was forthcoming. The Island had a huge surplus of existing accommodation and nobody had the confidence to build when a large number of hotels stood half empty, some literally falling apart.

The Association continued to lobby politicians in an effort to improve the trade. Some elected members, it hoped, might be 'easily led' into the policies it wanted.[41] In 1984 it even petitioned Tynwald with its grievances. It received a sympathetic hearing but little cash or policy change from the government, which knew only too well that traditional resorts across the British Isles were struggling with the same problem of decline to which nobody had an easy answer. The government continued to underwrite the 'Everyman' inclusive holiday scheme which placed the Isle of Man guide as a channel to bookings in nearly every travel agency in the UK, and the Minister of Tourism, Allan Bell, wrote to the hoteliers emphasising his 'total commitment' to the tourist industry.[42] He urged those in other businesses to realise the impact that its decline had made on the Island and pointed out that a healthy tourist industry was essential for the health of the rest of the economy.[43] In May 1987 the Department of Tourism and Transport stepped up its drive to improve standards of service and accommodation by threatening to take action against hoteliers and guest house operators who did not measure up by removing them from its lists. Once registration had become obligatory, this was more than an empty threat. 'The Department', wrote a member of the grading staff in 1987, 'looks to further improvements.'[44] It also tried to respond to one of the hoteliers' bitterest criticisms: the problem of government departments working against each other.

The harsh 1980s came as something of a shock to an industry which had grown used to stability and which had for so long provided a homely family-run product through little more than hard work, gut instinct and native intelligence. History has shown that aggressive marketing was not one of its strengths. However, when modern marketing methods were brought together with the strongest assets of the Isle of Man it was amazing what could be done. New campaigns centring on its natural beauty, heritage attractions and suggesting short breaks have shown the way forward, and the Island's hoteliers have risen to the challenge.

Donkey rides on the beach outside Castle Mona, Douglas, 1890s.

8

Buildings and architecture

If stones could speak . . .

We usually assume that buildings are solid, silent things, but stones can speak, and they have a lot to say if we can only understand their language. For example, the way society operates and does business can always be seen in the built environment. Victorian towns dominated by cotton-spinning contained many mills and streets of workers' houses. Resort towns such as Douglas, where leisure was an important business, had their own appropriate types of buildings. Dance-halls, refreshment rooms, and of course a huge amount of accommodation, were constructed and re-constructed all over the Isle of Man to suit the needs of the visiting industry. Times of growth were marked by waves of new building, while in slower times existing structures were repaired, or even demolished.

The tall, thin shape of many Victorian seafront boarding houses, and their many stairs, reminds us that

a lot of modestly sized businesses were competing for prime seafront land. These awkward buildings were practical when they were new, because domestic labour was cheap and plentiful and employees could be found to run up and down stairs all day.[1]

Early days

Some of the earliest structures built specifically for visitors to the Isle of Man were 'self-catering' cottages erected in the 1820s by the Duke of Atholl on Strathallan Crescent. The Island's elite needed places for their friends to stay, and these *cottages ornés* were summer retreats not far from the Duke's residence of Castle Mona. Their architecture allowed the occupants to indulge in the romantic fantasy of being peasants, and proximity to the sea shore made it easy for them

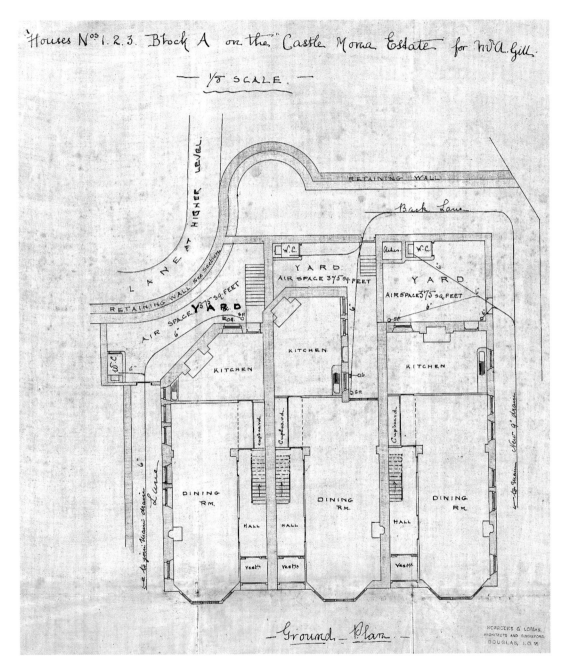

Castle Mona Estate, ground plan of development for three houses for Alexander Gill, 1896.

to take a newly fashionable daily dip. When in the 1830s the Atholls sold the Castle Mona estate, much of their land passed to a local consortium of businessmen. The castle itself was sold off quickly, and in 1836 was opened as a hotel by a Mr Heron of Dublin. The ground floor of the south wing was converted into a suite of baths, where hot, cold, fresh and salt water were all available to cater for the new fashion in therapeutic bathing.[2] An alternative in the early nineteenth century was Fort Anne, overlooking Douglas harbour. Converted from a private residence into an hotel in 1846, it was architecturally fine, retaining many fittings from its days as a private house. Sheraton woodwork and Carrera marble fireplaces made it a desirable place to stay,

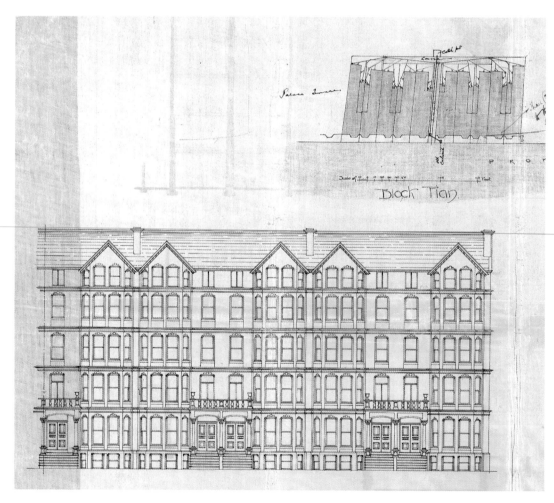

Cliff Estate, elevation plans for houses on Palace Terrace for Alexander Gill, 1909.

though it seems not to have been constantly profitable, for the hotel changed hands surprisingly often. Perhaps its owners had to work hard to compete with the more accessible Castle Mona.[3]

As the number of visitors increased, both public and private development showed how the Isle of Man was changing. Improvements in Douglas included oil street-lighting from 1829, and a waterworks from 1834. By the 1840s, new streets were built with houses designed to be let out, such as Clarence Terrace and the Esplanade. They were much praised as modern and desirable structures.[4] They used the Regency style – John Betjeman later called them 'stately stucco terraces, Brighton fashion' – and they were followed by Falcon Cliff and Derby Castle.[5] Some of the new building was backed by new sources of money: many of the landowners and speculators operating at this time were men from Lancashire and Merseyside who had made money in the booming industries of the industrial north, and were now looking to make more investments. They realised that holidaymaking was becoming a profitable industry.

As the Island became increasingly affordable for the middle classes, they too needed places to stay. When the traveller, linguist and writer George Borrow visited the Island in 1855, he first stayed at Hill's Royal Hotel, but found the cost of £3 7s 0d per week too great and soon moved to cheaper apartments in Albert Terrace. That same summer, *The Manx Sun* recorded:

. . . there could not be less than 4,500 visitors in Douglas. Large as this number of visitors may appear to be, added to our own population,

there is ample accommodation, as new buildings continue to be raised and lodging–houses increase fully in proportion to the demand.[6]

This report refers to 'lodging houses' because there were very few purpose-built hotels for the middle market (as opposed to those designed as public houses) until the mid-nineteenth century. A landmark was the Imperial, built on Douglas harbour in 1861. It was erected for High Bailiff Samuel Harris, a businessman with many interests. He co-founded the Isle of Man Bank and led the appeal to construct the first modern promenade in Douglas, which was named after him.[7] His Imperial Hotel was an early sign of the boom to come in Douglas, which gathered pace with a brand new pier and new thoroughfares in Duke Street and Strand Street.

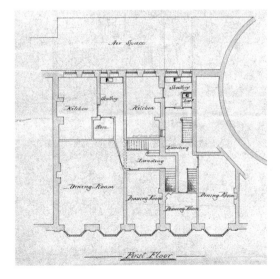

First floor plans, 1900, showing interior layout.

Boom time

As the pace of tourism development increased, so did speculative building, for which fresh land was required. Old estates began to be broken up into building plots. The Finch Hill Estate in Douglas, which included Buck's Road, Christian Road, Athol Street and Mount Havelock, began slowly to be sold off in the 1850s. Early sales were for private residences, but many later plots were used for tourist accommodation. The remainder of the once extensive Castle Mona grounds were sold off in the 1880s and partially developed for entertainment palaces and accommodation. The developers were a group of men who came to be known as the Manx Syndicate, a set which included many prominent names.

Although the members of the Syndicate became rich through development, they did not first come together for this reason. Their initial project was a controversial attempt to secure a near-monopoly on wholesale drink and grocery supply on the Island. They planned to achieve this goal by buying up independent pubs and boarding houses, which would then be supplied only through their own stores, which could become so large as to command the market.[8] This plan was bitterly and publicly opposed, so several members moved on to search for profit from the Island's building boom by purchasing and developing land.

The Syndicate was formed on 24th October 1888, with limited liability.[9] The key syndicalists were: John Archibald Brown, who came to be a director of twenty-six Manx companies including the Palace Company and was editor of the *Isle of Man Times*; Alexander Gill, who came to be the Island's leading developer; and Richard Maltby Broadbent, iron merchant and Commissioner for Onchan.[10] Other members were Thomas Mylchreest, James Sutherland, William Todhunter, John Parkes, Charles William Coole, and Herbert Kidson of Manchester.[11]

When they first acquired the Castle Mona, the syndicate tried to sell it to the Isle of Man Government as a residence for the Governor. When the Government declined, they offered it to Douglas Corporation, for use as a museum and park. When the Corporation rejected the offer, they promptly put 24 acres of land up for sale in several lots, with a total sea frontage of 1,500 ft. This was an enormous block of valuable land, and the speed of its development was accelerated by the condition of sale that houses had to be built on the lots by May 1890.[12] Much of the land which the Syndicate sold was bought by companies directed by the Syndicate members themselves.[13] Their single largest deal of this kind was the construction by the Syndicate of the Palace Ballroom, which they built and then sold to the Palace Company on 25th August 1890. Unsurprisingly, Brown, Broadbent and Gill were directors of that very company. There was a lot of money to be made by this sort of work, but not everyone was pleased. Some thought that the speculators cared little for town planning or public health. One critic, Dr Alfred De Haviland, wrote:

Many popular watering places . . . show a brave frontage of palatial houses and hotels, and have in their rear networks of squalid streets, and still more squalid houses, reeking with overcrowded rooms and tainted with the pestilential emanations of unemptied middens . . . during the last few years, since seaside resorts have been so much the rage, these

places have become the victim of
speculators of all kinds. The building
speculator is the one, however, who
does the most mischief . . . he runs
up houses in any fashion he likes . . .
[They] care only to cover the ground
they can lay their hands on with as
much rentable material as they can
pack upon it, knowing well they can
let their houses well before they are
finished, and that they will be
occupied before they are dry.[14]

At this time, the construction of most boarding houses was not commissioned by those who were to occupy and run them. On all but the most prestigious sites, a typical pattern was for builders – generally fairly small businessmen – to purchase plots on land laid out by an estate company. This was often financed by a mortgage. The builder then ran up a few houses and sold them on, paying off his mortgage and returning a profit. If nearby land was still available, he would then start the process all over again. For example, land plots 19 and 20 on the Loch Promenade were sold on by their first purchaser to a builder after just one day. After the builder had done his work, the next owner was the Douglas ironmonger J.T. Cowell, who bought the building as an investment to let.[15] His temperance principles meant that it was run as a temperance hotel. Other typical owners might be widows, or women of 'private means', or middle-class professionals who wanted to invest their capital and get back monthly rents as a steady income. Corporate investment in

property was far less significant in the past than it is today, but by the early twentieth century a little capital from insurance companies and similar undertakings was coming to the seaside. Builders were still developing boarding houses on their own account, but many were also executing contracts for others. There were few years late in the nineteenth century when Manx boarding house proprietors who had done well in the 1880s and 1890s could have new, larger premises built for them. A.F. MacAdam, a former commercial traveller who married a landlady's daughter, worked on the Loch Promenade for ten years before commissioning Silvercraigs on Queen's Promenade, which opened in 1908.[16] Those who moved to the Queen's Promenade when it was being built had the freedom to plan their buildings. One notably successful proprietor, Peter Milne, spent a considerable sum on the mock-baronial interior of the Waverley, which was much talked about.

The Queen's Promenade buildings were later and larger than those on Loch Promenade. One of the largest was Westlake's Sea Level, which has now been demolished.

How the promenades were built

The land on which many of the new boarding houses and hotels were built, especially in Douglas, Peel and Ramsey, was not easy to use. It had to be made secure from the sea by the construction of new promenades and sea walls, and building these was a costly exercise which did not begin in earnest until the third quarter of the nineteenth century. For this reason, most mid-century development, apart from the Esplanade in the centre of Douglas Bay, was in the upper parts of town. A guide book of 1848 recorded this, noting that:

The more elevated localities have in late years been seized upon by the better classes and for the lodging-houses of strangers, and a new town has thus rapidly grown up of a more respectable character, and this from its position being more conspicuous than the more ancient one, happily impresses the visitor with a very favourable opinion of the spot.[17]

The first public promenade to be completed in Douglas was the Harris Promenade, and it ran on the route of what was once Colonel's Road. The work was paid for by public subscription. It was presented to the town by Alderman Samuel Harris in 1868, and in his honour renamed the Harris Promenade.[18] The next big development was the combined Loch Parade and Victoria Street. The scale of this work necessitated an Act of Tynwald, to create and confer powers upon a New Street Board. After an unfortunate series of stormy and very public arguments between the Board, their architect and the construction engineer, work began in 1874, and proceeded quickly. An account written a few years later by the journalist J.A. Brown, who reported on the developments as they occurred, captured the atmosphere of the boom years:

On the 6th March 1876, a number of building plots in Victoria Street and Loch Parade were sold by auction, the land sold . . . amounting to £21,000. The prices obtained greatly exceeded what had been expected . . . Building commenced as soon as possession of the land was obtained; and in a short time there began to rise along the line of the new street and of the promenade a series of shops and boarding-houses of a size and character previously undreamed-of in Douglas. The remaining plots were rapidly sold at enhanced prices, and so great has been the success of this scheme, and so important its effects upon the progress and prosperity of the Island, that the same policy was subsequently adopted with regard to the other parts of the bay of Douglas, as well as upon a very large scale at Ramsey, and also on a smaller scale at Peel. On the 26th February 1877, the Loch Parade was formally declared completed by the New Street Board, and handed over by them to the Town Commissioners . . . the total cost had been £24,860. The total expenditure upon the new street and the shore enclosure had been £47,496; of which £21,000 had been paid for properties purchased by the improvement, while the total amount

A joyous classical style entrance at the Loch Hotel, Loch Promenade, showing how stucco was used with much skill to overcome the lack of suitable soft local stone for decoration.

realised by land sale had been about £40,000.[19]

A central figure in the development negotiations was Governor Loch. He had no doubt that the Isle of Man should equip itself as a forward-looking holiday resort and was heavily involved in the tortuous negotiations between Douglas Town Commissioners and Tynwald over how money was to be raised for the promenade project.[20] Once the difficulties were overcome, it was clear that his energy and progressive policies had been important in facilitating the new prosperity. Loch wrote to the Home Secretary in 1879, reporting that:

These works have been carried out in a most satisfactory manner, and have been the means of attracting a large amount of capital for building purposes into the Island; the value of building land instead of being reduced by the large quantity suddenly brought into the market, has risen very considerably, especially in the immediate vicinity of the improvements, building lots having sold for as high as forty-nine shillings a square foot, but the general average has ranged from 3s 2d to 9s 6d per square foot.[21]

Of the several competing schemes put forward for laying out the land, the winner was that of C.O. Ellison.[22]

He initially exercised control over what was built, and contractors had to send their plans to him for approval, but the Douglas Town Commissioners soon took this power away from him. The first boarding house to be built on the new promenade was Seaforth House, erected by R.A. Robertson, father of the influential Douglas Town Clerk, Alexander Robertson.[23] Other parts of the town were developed with rather less municipal involvement. The area of Demesne Road and Kensington Road was laid out by Philip Christian, who had inherited the land, and who produced plans and elevations for buildings upon it with Ellison's assistance.[24] Because Christian was president of the Douglas Temperance League, he prohibited the sale of alcohol on all his plots, a rare Manx example of the sort of covenant that was imposed in a few English resorts and estates by influential landowners with temperance principles.

By the 1880s, boarding houses were sweeping along the bay and into the upper town. Gaps in Christian Road were filled in, and existing buildings modified and extended. A common tactic was to increase the length of 'outlets' [long, tall, thin blocks] at the rear, to fit in as many bedrooms as possible. Some hotels, such as the Hazelwood and the Grosvenor, had additional floors added under the supervision of local architect John Robinson, who later designed Prospect Terrace.[25]

While the Loch Promenade needed sea walls and reclamation of the sandy foreshore, the north end of the bay presented different engineering problems. The slate cliffs which ran steeply down to the beach left little room for building. The ingenious answer was to cut them back, thus providing an *in situ* source of freestone for building houses and strong sea walls for the promenade.

The promenades were not just for walking on; they served a vital function in protecting property from the vicissitudes of angry winter waves. The lack of a sea wall in the Crescent and Castle Mona area of the promenade led to flooding in the winter of 1891. Many of the buildings in this area were affected, and there were allegations that 'narrow sectional jealousy' in the Town Commissioners had prevented the sea wall being extended further than the Iron Pier at the foot of Broadway. Many householders felt this was especially disgraceful because they already paid a heavy rate.[26]

The high rateable value of these houses was based on their large number of bedrooms. To fit these into the small plots of land, their outlets were thrown out at the rear, sometimes very nearly touching the cliff wall. Their unadorned and rather dark architecture and warren of small bedrooms was quite a contrast to airy front rooms faced with exuberant stucco work which looked on to the promenades.

The Drives

An area with an interesting history is that known generally as 'the Drives', standing close to Castle Mona. The land on which the Drives were built was once part of a carriage drive for the aristocratic guests at Castle Mona, which ran between lawns from the foot of Broadway.[27] On the death of the Duke of Atholl in 1830 the land was sold to an alliance of developers led by Hutchinson.[28] Thus began the slow dismantling of the Castle Mona estate, which was broken up in lots for development, starting with Clarence Terrace and the Esplanade in the 1840s, and finishing with the building of the Drives in the late 1880s and through the 1890s.

The development of the 1890s was spearheaded by the actions of the Manx Syndicate. The Syndicate bought land on the Drives for £80,000 in the late 1880s and laid it out for building plots.[29] When they sold it at auction in 1888, most of the forty-five lots were sold for a total of £13,210. But the Syndicate was running into trouble, and had borrowed heavily from the secretly unstable Dumbell's bank, which later crashed in 1900. Indeed, the Syndicate's hidden debts were a crucial factor behind the bank's later failure. After the liquidation of the Syndicate, some of the land on the Drives passed into the personal possession of R.M. Broadbent, one of the syndicalists. Broadbent was heavily committed to the development of tourist-related projects. He was behind the Groudle Glen and the Douglas Head railways, and also owned property in Victoria Street.[30] When Dumbell's Bank collapsed, he was ruined. Alexander Gill, on the other hand, managed to emerge virtually unscathed.

Other landowners on the Drives area were the Douglas Recreation Ground Limited, which ran the Olympia sports ground in the 1890s, and the Palace Company of which Gill was a director. Samuel Harris, High Bailiff and later Mayor of Douglas, also owned property there.

Building on the Drives started in earnest around the 1890s, and Alexander Gill was once again an important figure.[31] For example, he bought land on which to build the Welbeck Hotel block from Broadbent in March 1896, and a side plot on which the smaller Glenville Hotel was built cost him £2,360. At the time of this building, the Drives were a busier thoroughfare than they are today. A Gothic gateway to the popular Olympia pleasure grounds lay at the head of Mona Drive, and drew pedestrians up through the surrounding streets. Nevertheless, development often proceeded in fits and starts and land on the Drives and in the surrounding area was not always snapped up. Boarding house plots at Little Switzerland and on Queen's Promenade proved impossible to sell in the summer of 1893. This was because development had run ahead of itself. The industry was suffering from over-capacity – boarding houses proved hard to sell and Olympia and the Marina Pavilion went into liquidation that autumn.[32]

Other towns

For quite some years, Douglas was at the forefront of Manx growth. Although other towns were keen to develop, the Island's poor transport system held some of them back. Ramsey did not gain a rail link until 1899 and for thirteen years had to rely for its inbound traffic largely on steamers calling at the Queen's Pier. The 2,300ft pier was opened with high hopes that it would propel the town into an era such as Douglas was enjoying. Existing boarding houses close to the pier added extra floors and longer outlets to benefit from their newly favourable position, and development plans for the Mooragh – an area of swampy land reclaimed from the sea – went ahead. This scheme made parkland and new building plots available, but there were problems. It cost a great deal of money, and the Town Commissioners were late in completing a vital swing-bridge across the harbour to allow easy access. However, this did not stop entrepreneurs from building on the Mooragh Promenade. One was George Kaye, an architect and builder who also had an interest in Ramsey Brickworks. Ramsey developed slowly, and as rival boarding house keepers in Douglas were keen not to lose any business to the northern resort they fought tooth and nail against plans to electrify the Douglas promenade tramway, fearing that it would whisk potential customers straight past their doors and out of town.[33]

In Peel, a group of local merchants realised that the visiting industry was something that they could profit from and planned a new hotel, the grandest the town had yet seen. The Creg Malin was built on newly-stabilised land behind the sea wall at the northern end of the promenade.

In Port Erin, which remained a small fishing village until late in the nineteenth century, tourist premises also sprang up. This quiet resort came to specialise in families, and its streetscape was also heavily influenced by the work of Kaye and the builder McArd, who with his wife not only built boarding houses but also ran one of his own. McArd also worked with the popular architectural practice of Horrocks and Lomas, for example on Atholl Park.[34]

Architecture

All the deeds of sale for the Loch Promenade plots stated that:

> Any house or building which shall be erected on the said premises hereby conveyed shall be built and continue to be kept up with a front elevation facing the Loch Promenade, which shall be in accordance with an elevation plan to be approved by the [New Street] Board.[35]

As a result, one of the most striking elements in the promenade architecture of Douglas was its harmonious mixture of decoration and uniformity. Control of the appearance of the seafront was achieved through formal and informal means. There were clauses in the deeds of the houses which controlled usage, modifications, and colour schemes.[36] At first, the promenade boarding houses went unpainted as early photographs show. By the 1940s, painting façades became more common, but as everyone chose slightly different shades this led to something of an eyesore and the Corporation introduced a standard palette. Colour control sometimes lapsed, but was revived in the 1950s, in 1971, and again in the late 1990s under the Douglas 2000 initiative.[37]

The size of promenade boarding houses was generally dictated by the date of their construction. Early development was usually no higher than four storeys in Douglas, and three in the other resorts. The historical pattern can be seen in a sample of boarding houses in the 1920 guide to Douglas.[38] On the seafront, Loch Promenade buildings would comprise around twenty-five bedrooms and one or two sitting-rooms, usually accommodating a total of around sixty guests. Thirty bedrooms could be squeezed into a rambling above-the-shop facility such as the Oban in Peveril Buildings, near the Victoria Pier. On Central Promenade large establishments such as the Shaftesbury and Manningham offered up to fifty bedrooms. Double-fronted Loch Promenade units, such as the Belvedere, Windermere or Modwena, managed about fifty rooms and 100 guests. This was closer to the size of newer buildings like the Trevelyan on Queen's Promenade which could accommodate 160 people.

The Queen's and Central Promenades were the areas of the highest density. Here were gigantic boarding houses which could boast up to 150 bedrooms, such as Westlake's Sea Level with its huge outlet to

the rear. Here too were the splendid Metropole Mansions, built in 1896 by W.J. Faragher of Douglas to the design of W.J. Rennison for Robert Stott, who was heavily involved in the Palace Company. They were demolished in 1999. However, for more expensive hotels such as the Waverley which accommodated their visitors at lower densities, fifty rooms were sufficient.[39] Construction methods developed as the years went on; while the Loch Parade houses were nearly all stuccoed slate rubble, on the later Queen's Promenade much more brick and timber were used.

Off the promenades, shapes and sizes were more varied. Proximity to the promenades determined the price and size of boarding houses. Large places generally had about twenty to thirty rooms, while in upper Douglas the houses of Christian Road let sixteen to eighteen bedrooms. Their counterparts in Finch Road and Mount Havelock areas offered ten, or maybe fifteen. By Murray's Road, letting rooms were down to nine or ten, and Derby Square houses maintained around eight.

Architectural 'messages'

The Victorians left their mark on the Isle of Man. Most of its urban areas were either new or redeveloped by 1900, and it was with the typical confidence of the period that a leading local businessman of the era wrote:

> During this period great advances were made by the country in every department of moral and material progress. Stimulated by the new

Elevation plans for Windermere House, later the Windsor, Loch Promenade, 1889.

The Parade, Douglas c.1890.

facilities . . . by the new and improved accommodation provided for summer visitors, in the new streets and handsome terraces which were springing up along the margin of the bay.[40]

There was a tangible sense of progress and change. In 1872, the *Isle of Man Times* recalled the days 'when fishermen spread their nets to dry on spots where magnificent structures now rear their heads, in attestation of the advancement which Douglas has made'.[41] Older buildings were soon eclipsed by a new era of construction, beginning with Loch Parade.

The message which these buildings gave out was bold and confident, and the architectural unity and grand scale of the development once gave Douglas a unique and attractive appearance amongst seaside resorts.[42]

Out of the jumble of modest buildings scattered ad hoc around the Island's waterfronts, a new architecture had arisen, especially in Douglas and Port Erin. The fact that most of the Island's boarding houses were built within thirty years resulted in a remarkable uniformity of architecture, giving rise by 1890 to a townscape with a pleasing sense of harmony, in which nearly all the buildings seemed to complement each other, no matter whether they were large or small. The overall effect was not unlike Bath's stately Georgian terraces, in the sense that unity created strength.[43] This architectural treatment was pleasing to the eye, and the clauses in land sale deeds which forced builders to keep certain lines of height and proportion in many terraces were helpful.

Where the Island differed from Bath was that this grandeur was tempered by a seaside sense of fun and whimsy, as ever allied to business purposes. The Island was in the business of selling pleasure, and it made sense for the architecture of its resorts to reflect this. The trend was at its most obvious in buildings wholly dedicated to leisure. For the Victorians, decoration was used as an expression of purpose and status. Gothic architecture, implying seriousness, a celebration of British heritage, and often morality, was used a lot for churches and universities. Classical styles were usually secular, rational, and much used by seats of power, in banks, government premises, and similar institutions. By the end of the century, however, a new and highly ornamental style came to be used to attract attention. After all:

The Victorians had become more adventurous, and they had grown tired of [classical uniformity]. They wanted novelty, buildings that were going to vaunt themselves and catch the eye of the public . . . one of the primary functions of decoration in commercial buildings was to capture the attention of a potential customer.[44]

This was especially true at the seaside, a place where novelty was prized. Although Brighton boasted restrained Georgian terraces, it was also the home of Nash's exuberant Pavilion of 1827, the forerunner of many fantastic seaside designs. Curves were preferred to straight lines, openings were arched, columns fluted, everything that could be topped with mouldings, urns or globes was duly graced. The profuse decoration – both in advertising and architecture – that characterised the promenade hotels appealed to the social aspirations of visitors. They might live in a modest house in Burslem or Barnsley for most of the year, but for a week or two they could reside in something that looked (at least from the outside) like a palace. 'Aspirational' was once the appropriate term for much of the hotel architecture of the Isle of Man. The resort in its heyday did not attract a wealthy clientele, but visitors could daydream of being lairds in the Scottish-country-house style entrance hall of Milne's Waverley for a reasonable price. Cheap local stone walls were converted by skilled labour to great effect by a glorious outpouring of stuccoed detail, stained-glass and elaborate ironwork. This could all be done quite quickly by

*Changing fashions at the Douglas Hydro Hotel.
Top: Basement room in the 1930s, complete with the latest entertainment.
Middle: The modernised lounge in the 1950s.
Bottom: The same room in the 1960s as a bar.*

the Victorians, because the typical boarding house used a mixture of ready-made materials – especially iron-work and joinery – in combination with hand-worked decoration. The Island did not have much clay for brick making, and coal was expensive, so decorated terracotta bricks made few appearances. Clay was reserved for hard-wearing but sometimes highly elaborate floor and wall tiles, for example in Palace Terrace. Cheap Welsh slate from across the water did, however, enable builders to 'go to town' with Mansard roof turrets and gables, often hung with geometrically cut slates to enhance their effect.

Much skill went into the creation of stucco façades, which, at one quarter of the cost of dressed stone, offered elegance at a modest price. Skilled local craftsmen, about whom almost nothing is now known, developed a glorious repertoire of mouldings which can still be seen all over Douglas. Simple or shallow ornamentation was run or pressed in whilst wet; more elaborate features were cast elsewhere before being added to the scheme.

The overall impression of the promenade façades was one of respectable jollity. Other leisure buildings gave out the same message, such as the heavily rusticated 'fairyland' style of many Manx Electric Railway booking offices and stations. The Douglas and Ramsey piers, constructed in 1869 and 1882, fitted neatly into the two peak periods of pier construction in the UK. Though Douglas lost its pier in 1896, Ramsey's survived. Edwardian piers remained a relatively genteel social space, offering middle-class pleasures of the sort Ramsey set out to provide.[45] A pier was always a good advertisement, and offered a useful transport link in its capacity to berth large steamers. The architecture of the piers, with their slim cast-iron supports and often ornate buildings, was a real architecture of amusement,

bright with bunting by day and romantically gas-lit by night.[46] The appeal of 'watching the boats sailing or the nymphs bathing', as one Victorian put it, was also considerable.[47]

Inevitably, as time went on, the Victorian style fell out of fashion. The modern movement led many people to prefer simpler, sleeker styles of architecture and design. The grand promenade of Douglas, once showered with praise for its architectural delights, started to seem old-fashioned and out of step with the times. One critic even said: 'I saw the two-mile crescent of imposing hotels and boarding-houses, and fled in favour of something less imposing'.[48]

Architects and master builders

Who were the men who built these imposing terraces? Comparatively little is known about the Victorian architects and master builders who created so many streets, often so well. Names which shaped the Victorian streetscape, such as George Kaye, or the partnership of Horrocks and Lomas, are largely forgotten. One boarding house architect about whom we do know is William John Rennison, who came to the Island from Stockport. His most notable achievement was to design the Villiers Hotel in 1876. This was the largest and grandest hotel yet built on the Island, borrowing the family name of the wife of Governor Loch.[49] The Villiers boasted 200 bedrooms, later extended to 300, and at three guineas per week only the well-off could afford it. Local money alone could not raise the finance for such a large building, so of the first five directors, two were Liverpool merchants. Another was the hotelier Charles Udall, whilst the timber merchant Edward T. Quiggin brought his influence and useful contacts in the building trade.[50]

The success of the Villiers earned Rennison the contract to design the Grand on Victoria Street, a large hotel, boarding house and theatre complex close to the busy sea terminal. The development began in 1875 with the interest of a Manchester investor, John Robinson, in a site newly laid out by the New Street Board. The first architect to work on the scheme was Pons of Manchester, and several other Manchester and Salford architects served the company for short periods as it struggled to begin operations. These began in 1877 with a swimming-bath – which was only part of a planned complex of baths, hotel, shops and boarding houses. But the baths cost £15,031, consuming most of the £17,500 which had been budgeted for the entire set of buildings. The company was wound up and the concern auctioned to tramway entrepreneur Thomas Lightfoot for £5,000. Lightfoot went on to finish the development, but he had to sell up in 1891 to avoid bankruptcy.[51] These difficulties notwithstanding, Rennison went on to design numerous other buildings, including the Metropole block at the northern end of Douglas promenade in 1896. This represented a high point for boarding house architecture on the Isle of Man. Constructed close to a cliff edge, the Metropole's cramped site made height essential, but it also offered the opportunity to create a large and elegant facade, a task which Rennison handled ably, to create a building which was well-mannered despite its size.

Another prolific figure was John Robinson, a self-taught Manxman who designed a variety of buildings around Douglas up to the 1880s. His tourist premises included the Peveril Hotel, Falcon Cliff, the Douglas Head Hotel and the elegant classical Esplanade, as well as the pavilion on the Iron Pier.[52] During his working life, like many of his contemporaries, he would have submitted plans to competitions created by developers. Plans for the layout of the Castle Mona Estate, where the Drives were built, were commissioned in this way. In 1898 the property company offered prizes of £25 and £10 for the winning layout.[53] Land companies such as the Falcon Cliff rarely constructed buildings themselves. Although the same businessmen might, in reality, have been behind both sides of the development, in public and in law construction went on separately. In some resorts powerful aristocratic landowners controlled the process, which resulted in neat and orderly terraces and squares. In others, a free-for-all ensued. Douglas seems to have followed a middle path, with the most important areas being controlled either by the Corporation or estate development companies.

Alexander Gill

Once built, most boarding houses were let out to tenants who operated them as businesses. A typical landlord was Isaac Corlett, who owned numbers 8, 10 and 12 Demesne Road.[54] A larger type of landlord was Henry Bloom Noble, prominent Douglas businessman and philanthropist.[55] But there was one man who dominated and surpassed them all: Alexander Gill. Large numbers of properties were financed and built by him in the 1890s, and he was also able to use his own firm to undertake maintenance. Gill was commonly said to 'own half of Douglas'. His role was similar to that which aristocratic landowners took in some English resorts. His great period of buying was during the 1890s, when he covered most of the northern end of Douglas Bay with monumental boarding houses far larger than their predecessors of the 1870s and 1880s. Even fourteen years after his death the trust which he created still owned an amazing 124 boarding houses, plus a few dozen shops and diverse commercial premises, all over Douglas and Onchan (see the following selective list).[56]

Between 1894 and 1906 Gill bought and built on Palace Terrace, which had been part of the Castle Mona Estate. The boarding houses here included Palace View, the Grasmere, the Compton, Avondale, Clifton, Swindon, Friendship, Ravenscliffe, Iona, Crawford, Beresford, Ashfield, Santa Rosa, Hadfield, Excelsior and Caledonia. Numbers 1 to 11 Empress Drive were easily bought in September 1889 from the Manx Syndicate, of which Gill was a member. In December 1890 he bought the Shaftesbury, the Warrington and the Brookwood in Empress Terrace, again from the Syndicate. Palace View Terrace was bought in 1898. Property on what was called the Cliff Estate was acquired in 1907, on which Gill owned the Trevelyan, the Rosslyn, the Rutland, the Lancaster, the Almeda, and the Paragon. He built the Hydro in December 1910 and let it to Thomas Aylen, who had worked his way up from a substantial boarding house at 4 Metropole Mansions to this new and even larger place.[57]

In Empress Drive, Gill built and owned the Wavecrest, Fernlea, the Ratcliffe, Rustlier, Welbeck, Roseberry and Glenville, on land bought from Samuel Harris, who had in turn bought it from the dissolved Syndicate. In Empire Terrace he erected the Somerset, Ainsdale, Rosemeath, Castle Mount, Merridale, Fairhaven, Soho House, Richmond House, Gladsmuir, Sea Nook, Aston Ville, Mereside, Craig Villa, Ravenswood, Wood View and Seafield. The Empress Hotel itself was built by Gill, and bought in 1901. In Church Road, he bought up several properties. He was active in many other areas, and was the contractor for the celebrated theatre architect Frank Matcham during the reconstruction of the Gaiety Theatre.

Gill's last big venture was the construction of entire streets of medium-sized boarding houses in Onchan, some for sale and some for lease. He did not live to see the scheme completed. But the trust carried on his work, and twenty-nine out of the thirty-three plots in Royal Avenue West were built up to 1926, and development was pushing out onto Falkland Terrace and Belgravia Road, all of which had substantial Gill holdings. By 1933 his trust held fifty-eight boarding houses on the Onchan brows, and another two dozen shops and houses.[58]

During the First World War, Alexander Gill became known as a model landlord. He created a wartime 'barometer scale' for setting his rents, which protected his tenants by varying payments according to the number of visitors.[59] He died in January 1919, and in his will he left a substantial amount of property. His house, Lucerne Villa in Little Switzerland, went to his son Charles, as did the job of managing his real estate and a wage of £100 per year for the job.[60] But the remainder of his property was left in trust until the death of his longest-lived child. He hoped to create a stable source of income for his children and to avoid causing a slump in the Douglas property market by selling all his vast holdings at once at a vulnerable time just after the First World War. His assets were divided in half. One part went to the children; the other was used to pay off the mortgages and debts that he had incurred in his years of building and buying property. Most ordinary people in those days would never have aspired to own a mortgaged property, for mortgages for the middle classes only became freely available during the late 1920s. Gill also wanted to clear the debts before distributing his assets to the children, and gave the trustees plenty of power to do this, his 'desire being that at some time my real estate . . . may be free and

Alexander Gill, owner of a huge array of around 160 properties in the 1900s.

unencumbered'.[61] The trust ensured that rents from tenants kept rolling in.

Controversy followed the will, as it often does when a wealthy person dies. Notwithstanding the stress of a court case over its exact distribution, the solid wealth that the trust provided undoubtedly helped his son Charles set up as an architect with some success. He ran for the House of Keys and secured the seat for Middle in 1919. He settled his place in the top drawer of Manx society by marrying the daughter of the popular novelist Hall Caine, thereby coming into possession of Greeba Castle. He was elevated to the Legislative Council in 1935.[62]

Not until the death of Charles, the longest-lived of the four children, in April 1951, was it time for the trust to be dissolved. The first tranche of property sold included Palace Terrace and much of the Drives.

Charles Henry Gill, the son of Charles, took charge. The price of property in the 1950s was modest by today's standards, and a reasonably sized boarding house such as the Glenville (later the Granada) at 17 Mona Drive sold for £5,000.[63]

Buying, selling and renting

Boarding house proprietors were not unusual in renting their places of business until the 1950s. In the early twentieth century, 90 per cent of all houses in Britain were rented from private landlords, many of quite modest status. People such as builders, shopkeepers and professional men viewed property as an investment and a good source of income for retirement.[64] Therefore the businesses which operated in the buildings were valued separately from the building itself. When passed from tenant to tenant, as a going concern, they were sold for a sum known as 'the ingoing'.

There was an incredible variety of property for investors to choose from. In 1906, a boarding house with a dozen rooms in Ramsey was worth around £500.[65] But prime seafront property in Douglas could fetch considerably more, and so groups of shareholders would invest together. When the Belvedere Hotel Company failed, the shareholders auctioned its premises for £6,600.[66] Such prices represented a real high point. A medium-sized Gill-built boarding house in a good but not superb location such as Mona Drive was still only fetching around £5,000 in the 1950s (visitors at the time paid just over £5 per week).[67] But by the late 1970s property prices had increased many times. The boarding house which sold for £5,000 in the 1950s could sell for £23,000 – almost five times as much. By the late 1980s the same

The impressive Hydro Hotel at Ramsey, c.1920, with its palm-fringed stone steps down to the lawns and sea, and to where the salt baths once stood.

building might fetch £60,000. The increase sounds respectable, but compared with the general inflation in property prices over the 1980s such large and ageing buildings were not doing particularly well. By the late 1990s, with most of the redundant hotels demolished and the Island booming the possibility of converting such a property into flats would result in it selling for around £200,000.[68]

Making an impression

Newly built boarding houses often boasted about their architectural merits in their advertising. Size and grandeur were the ideal, but a good situation was also important. The Ramsey Hydropathic Establishment, usually known as the Ramsey Hydro, struggled to make a profit in its early years despite its pleasant facilities. Its publicity emphasised its four acres of grounds set with tennis courts and croquet lawns, as well as the brine piped from the sea to its private baths.[69] It may have been that although private leisure and health facilities combined with a secluded position gave a higher 'social tone', this was not enough to compete with hotels on the busy Douglas promenade, which could emphasise their position at the very heart of things, topped off with a sea view. The Claremont, for example, could boast that it was 'beautifully situated in the centre of the

Splendid stucco greets the visitor to the Salisbury House Hotel. The elaborate tympanum shows the narrative of Helios in his chariot.

Elaborate tympanum and filigree balconies at the Salisbury House Hotel, now converted into offices.

famous Loch Promenade . . . commanding Magnificent Sea Views with a fine sweep of Douglas Head, and the whole of the Bay'. Just in case visitors had missed the point, the manageress reminded them that from the house one could view 'the full length of the absolutely unrivalled Loch Promenade'. The emphasis reminds us that there was a real commercial advantage to being clustered together with similar businesses on the promenade. Its stuccoed terraces were, in the 1890s, a busy cluster of modern buildings expressly designed for the task of accommodating large numbers of visitors. The outsides of these buildings normally formed the main images on advertisements. The nature of photography at the time partially dictated this, because interior shots in under-lit parlours were somewhat hard to obtain. But a photo of the outside of a building also allowed visitors to 'size it up' and to feel informed about its nature, amenities and location.

Size remained an important selling point for the boarding houses constructed at the turn of the century. In Douglas, Aylen's Hydro boasted of its 'one hundred apartments', before going on to elaborate on the 'spacious dining hall, magnificent drawing-room, billiard-room, smoke-room and lounges' easily accessed on the ground floor. A special feature was the entrance, which 'affords a unique private promenade commanding the most beautiful views'.[70] This rather overstated the size of what was basically a porch, but in holiday-land, reality was never allowed to get in the way of good publicity!

The smaller Ramsey Hydro based its 1899 advertising on its amenities. Its 'elegantly furnished' interior was said to contain 'spacious dining, recreation, drawing, writing, smoke and billiard rooms'. The larger the building, the more public rooms and facilities it could offer. With size came smoke-rooms, billiard-

rooms, and other recreational areas. Smaller houses might offer only a dining-room plus lounge. The entrepreneurial J.W. Turner at 3 Mona Drive turned the loss of a room for his hobby to advantage by offering a dark-room to visiting photographers.[71]

Many such buildings retained their Victorian look and feel well into the twentieth century. The landlady Letty Edgar was doing well in the 1950s and wanted to take on a bigger boarding house. She remembers her first impressions of the house she took on Buck's Road:

When I went in to see about it, it was run by two sisters who had inherited it from their father and they were showing me around. It was beautifully clean and fresh, if a wee bit old-fashioned. The woodwork on the stairs was brown and they apologised to me for the chips that had been done during the war when they had the army in . . . I thought that was funny. I was quite excited going in. When you walked into the hall it had lovely coloured ceramic tiles and on the right was a big large room, you closed it up in the winter. You had your front room, and the back room as a dining-room at the back, but it was opened out for space for the visitors. Then straight through was a living-room and off that was a kitchen. It seemed massive to me,

of course, with the bigger rooms.
There was a beautiful room above the
dining-room and the ladies told me
it was a drawing-room at one time.
Beautiful it was, big, all beautifully
coved around, and it had a big white
marble fireplace, that room above,
which had to be made into a
bedroom, of course, but that was
a lovely part of the house, that
drawing-room above with the bay
window. We really decorated it from
top to bottom, staircase, carpets, I
think we put the modern fireplaces
in the front dining-room. In that
day it was all candlewick bedspreads
too! We made it brighter and
lighter.[72]

Bedrooms

Although bedrooms took up most of the space in every boarding house, they received little attention in publicity, and were rarely photographed until after the Second World War. All that Peter Milne had to say about his fifty rooms in the Waverley in 1899, apart from their number, was that they were 'large, lofty and well aired'. 'Spacious' was the sole adjective applied to bedrooms in most advertisements. Away from the choicest apartments at the front of the property, most boarding house bedrooms were situated in long outlets to the rear and tended to be small, crowded, and dark.

Those buildings on corner sites, such as the Hydro and the Savoy, made the most of architectural advantages which allowed many more rooms to boast a sea view.

Although the more expensive hotels offered well-furnished bedrooms as part of a suite, in a boarding house the bedrooms would be spartan. Iron bedstead, flock mattress, bentwood chair, mirror, wash-stand and wardrobe were the standard furnishings, with a print on the wall and lino or a square of carpet on bare, polished boards. The cheapest rooms might do away with the wardrobe to save space, substituting a row of

Milne's Waverley, Queen's Promenade, Douglas, 1890s.

A street level view of the Savoy, 1920s.

hooks screened by a curtain. Until the 1920s, many bedrooms in the less fashionable parts of the Isle of Man's resort towns were still lit by candlelight.

Kitchens

The kitchen was the working heart of the boarding house, but despite its vital importance to the efficiency of the business, this room rarely received much architectural consideration. To gain as many letting bedrooms as possible, there was no question of putting a kitchen where guests might be accommodated. It

was usually put in the back basement. As a result, such kitchens were often cramped, airless and prone to damp. Dominated by an immense range – often made by the local foundry – when first built, these rooms were lit by gas which often had to burn all day for lack of natural light.

As time went on, proprietors did what they could to improve their kitchens. Little could be done about the position of the room within the building, short of building an extension. Change was therefore restricted to adapting and improving. The biggest change was the switch from coal and coke to gas and electricity for cooking, and the introduction of refrigeration. Electric hot cupboards, toasters, mixers and even extractor fans also helped to make kitchens better places. The story of the cooks who worked in them and the food they made is told in Chapter 2.

Plumbing

One architectural element which Victorian and Edwardian boarding house advertisers took pains to stress was plumbing. A standard boast for all but the smallest boarding house was that its 'sanitary arrangements [were] perfect'. This phrase remained in regular use until the 1930s. The McAdams, proprietors of the Silvercraigs, went to even greater lengths. They proclaimed the presence of a Sanitary Certificate, of foundation on a sandy gravel bed, and that:

> All the fittings in the baths, lavatories, etc, are the best and most modern of their kinds. The drainage work was most carefully carried out, properly trapped and ventilated, we have since tested the drains and found them perfect. From a health point of view we have no hesitation in saying that the house is in a thoroughly efficient sanitary condition.

Drainage was taken seriously by the Island's commissioners, and Douglas Corporation was prepared to fail building plans on the grounds of inadequate drainage. Yet the very ubiquity of the advertising slogans suggests that the sanitation of many establishments was rather basic. 'Perfect sanitation' at least gave the assurance of indoor water closets, but these were not installed in large numbers. Even the larger promenade boarding houses might only have a couple of indoor WCs. Other plumbing was straightforward; if water ran to upper floors, it was not to bedrooms but to the landings. Here, often in a small cupboard, was installed a tap over a lead-lined sink where used water could be disposed of and fresh cold water drawn. Running hot water was confined to the kitchens, where a boiler would heat water for use in the kitchen and still-room, mainly for washing up in long teak or earthenware sinks. Some boarding houses managed to fit a small laundry into the back yard, where a coal-fired boiler heated water for washing sheets and clothes. Many small family-run places with only a few guests managed with facilities no better than the average house. Drying bedding in the yards was difficult, and led to the popular practice of laying sheets out on the beach to dry. By the early twentieth century, advances in industrial steam laundering had made the process cheap enough for all but the smallest business to afford, and the firm of Clucas grew large by catering for the needs of the Island's many boarding houses, cafés and hotels.

The demand for hot and cold running water in all rooms was being felt as early as the 1930s, although plenty of smaller houses were still installing pipe-work thirty years later. The statement by the organisers of the 1934 Rotary Club conference on the Isle of Man – that an hotel not equipped with hot and cold water in all its bedrooms no longer counted with the better-class visitor – sent shudders across the industry and made headlines in the local press.[73] Some enterprising local plumbers were quick to spot opportunities for work. The plumber J.H. Cubbon of Finch Road preyed on hoteliers' fears, telling them that hot water was already installed in all up-to-date hotels and boarding houses. With his system, they too could have:

> . . . not just a trickle of tepid, discoloured water (with a promise of more to come) but GALLONS GALORE of hot, steaming water on each floor. From all taps, a full bore of sparkling hot water. No waiting until next year — do it now! Don't delay![74]

But such a system was out of reach for many small proprietors in the 1930s; only hotels like the Majestic could boast hot and cold water in all bedrooms, and their prices started at 16s 6d per day.[75] For most people, a hot-water boiler was a valuable item, and if installed at a tenant's expense, it would be sold or taken with her when she left.[76] Almost all the larger boarding houses, at least in Douglas, had hot and cold water in their rooms by the outbreak of war, but many premises in the upper town with around fifteen to twenty bedrooms still lacked the facility. Bathrooms were also in short supply for many years. Increased expectations began to create a problem by the 1930s in many middle-market hotels and boarding houses. In the 1950s, most of the family-run boarding houses (up to fifteen rooms) being advertised for sale had only a couple of toilets and the same number of baths. As private bathing became ever more firmly desired by guests, proprietors scrambled to make their buildings match the demands of a more affluent society.

Heat and light

For most boarding houses, right up until the 1950s, heat meant coal. Central heating was used in a few large buildings, but the cost of installing systems in summer holiday premises was prohibitive. Fireplaces were, however, installed from the start in all but the smallest rooms; innumerable flues were built into party walls between properties, with fireplaces growing smaller the higher the floor. Although those in the bedrooms were rarely used, because visitors had to pay for a fire, they would never have been omitted. Furthermore, the open fire had a central place in the British idea of homeliness which still survives today. Even when not in use, the chimney was valued as a provider of ventilation and healthy fresh air. Of course, it also encouraged draughts, and one despairing Continental traveller observed of British heating that it had five priorities, in descending order[77]:

> One: safety
> Two: economy
> Three: ventilation
> Four: looks
> Five: heat!

The chilliness of an early or late season bedroom can easily be guessed at, but gas or electric fires were late in coming. Mains gas was available in Douglas from 1835, but it was used for light, not heat, and gas lighting was installed in most of the new boarding house premises built in the 1880s.[78] A network of small-bore pipes ran throughout larger buildings, and through the main rooms alone in smaller ones. Public spaces such as dining-rooms and lounges sometimes boasted gasoliers, with sparkling glass and elaborate metalwork.

Other parts of the houses received simpler treatment, being fitted with simple wall brackets, a good many of which can still be seen in service areas even today.

Gas was not widely employed for cooking or water heating until many decades later because it cost a lot more than coal. To heat 1,000 gallons of water per week with gas would have cost around £1 16s 0d in 1949 – a substantial sum. Coal ranges were dominant in most kitchens until after the First World War. In the 1920s, large premises began to convert, and inventions such as the 'Regulo' oven thermostat interested the more technically minded, but in most kitchens coal remained king. Many solid fuel ranges were still working in the 1940s, and coke boilers for hot water were also normal.[79] Tenants in rented boarding houses hesitated to install an expensive gas appliance that would become a fixture, owned by the landlord at the end of their tenancy. Finally, it is an astonishing fact to note that there was not, and is not, any Clean Air Act on the Isle of Man. Environmental pressures have never been brought to bear on the Island against this most filthy of fuels.

Coal was used for making gas at gasworks and for generating electricity. In the late nineteenth century, electricity was taken up enthusiastically by the more forward-looking boarding house proprietors, especially those with many bedrooms. Before the coming of mains current, some large houses generated their own. New hotels such as the Grand had had electric light since their construction.[80] So did the Douglas Bay Hotel, which drew current from the nearby electric tramway system. It was the first hotel on the Island to do so, and boasted two hundred and fifty incandescent lamps.[81] The large size of the Queen's Promenade houses made individual electric plants feasible. But no technology is without its downside, and the engines used to make the current were far from silent in the echoing spaces between outlets. Many neighbours must have been glad when in 1923 Douglas Corporation began belatedly to offer a public electricity supply.[82] This was a popular service, although it took some years for the larger users of power in the town to stop generating their own current on the premises, and use a mixture of gas and electricity.[83] However, the end of these arrangements was nigh and the full provision of mains electricity, at least in Douglas, rendered such apparatus unnecessary. The new source of power made a noticeable difference to life in the tourist and entertainment industry. The Manx Electric Railway allowed millions to enjoy the countryside, whilst hundreds of brilliant bulbs sparkled in the Gaiety Theatre and the dance-halls. Equally significantly, electricity powered the cinema boom of the 1920s and '30s, as well as domestic wireless sets. Women were targeted by the electrical industry and urged to consider electrifying their homes. Douglas even boasted its own branch of the Women's Electrical Development Association.[84] Sales publicity such as a 1930 poem cooed to harassed cooks that:

> There are cookers large and small,
> Such a benefit to all!
> Cakes and pastries bound to rise,
> Consider – and electrogize![85]

The electric building was said to have 'no flue, no smell, no dirty fumes, no matches, no waste of time, no dirty, hot, stuffy kitchen'. Unfortunately for the makers of electric cookers, the gas industry put up a spirited fight, and most who moved away from coal in commercial kitchens tended to go for gas. Electricity was also marketed as a solution to the 'staff problem'. It was claimed that although staff were 'more difficult to get every day – not often the right sort when you get them – ELECTRICITY is the cleanest, hardest working, most willing and cheapest servant under the sun. Always on duty, ready for instant service, day and night, at the flick of a switch'.[86] Lighting was the area in which most of the early inroads were made, yet the cost of electrification remained a big problem. How should the new installation be paid for: by landlord or tenant? Was it even necessary? After all, the Electrical Development Association itself admitted in 1930 that 'many people still visualise even electric lighting as a luxury and an expense'.[87] The more penny pinching boarding house keepers of the Isle of Man refused to invest at all in electricity in the inter-war period. In many industrial areas, including the Island's main catchments, the working classes still had gas light in their homes and so did not object to it on holiday. Some early installations took in only the ground floor, whilst gas lit the bedrooms above. The cost of current remained a worry to frugal proprietors, as the electrician Cyril Mulhern, who worked for Douglas Corporation, recalls:

> We used to put a supply into the bedrooms there [on the promenade] but most of them also had a master switch down below, in the hall. You might have a master switch for the various landings; say, one for the second floor, one for the third floor, and those controlling the bedrooms. The toilets and the landings and staircases were separate. Once it got to a certain hour the owners used to knock off the lights in the bedrooms!

> Another thing was, when you put lamps in there, they'd say 'Oh, 15 watts is big enough for them, because the visitors will leave it on all night'. Even the smaller boarding houses, they wanted some control over it. I did used to think that the cost of the supply to Douglas was, you know, rather on the expensive side.[88]

The added cost of shipping fuel to the Island's generating stations did make electricity more expensive than in many English cities and was a valid factor to consider when wiring up tourist premises. Nevertheless, by the end of the Second World War electrification, at least for lighting, was the norm in Manx towns. Over the next thirty years, its use became more widespread with new appliances from refrigerators to televisions and vacuum cleaners making their mark.

Obsolete boarding houses?

Most of the Island's boarding houses were designed to cater for the needs of the 1870s, '80s and '90s. As time passed they grew out of date. As early as 1920, one of the leading hoteliers of the UK, Sir Francis Towle, frankly admitted that the great bulk of Britain's hotels were obsolete. H.D. Henderson, the British Government's Chief Industrial Adviser, looked into the question in the 1930s, with some unease contrasting British neglect with French campaigns. France had created a special hotel improvement fund, the Crédit Hotelier. This gave grants and loans to French hoteliers for building works, and between 1930 and 1936 it spent over 55 million francs to modernise hotels, of which 40 million was grant aid, not loans.[89] By 1942, the fund had stimulated the construction of 12,000 new rooms, and improved a further 40,000. Back home, Henderson had to admit the 'poor standard of small English hotels', and suggested an enquiry into what could be done. But prospects for immediate action were bleak; as he had to admit, 'the question is not one which lends itself to any successful emergency policy . . . this is discouraging'.[90] Proprietors might want to improve their buildings, but as one wrote, 'the idea of modernising the furniture and equipment may seem very nice on paper . . . in reality it is an item which is controlled by the amount of money the residents will pay'.[91] Equally discouraging was this description of a downmarket British boarding house interior, as seen by the Mass Observation Bureau in the 1930s:

Bedrooms are eight feet by eight feet, the floor covered with oilcloth, the ceiling with leafy wallpaper, the walls with pictures of Dolores Costello[92], crosses and scrolls . . . Visitors come down to breakfast in a room whose most compelling decoration is its card of rules.[93]

Only a few hotels could afford to redevelop in the inter-war years; a time when the average set of improvements might run to new plumbing, full instead of partial electrification, and a general refurbishment of public rooms. Modern wallpaper, carpets, light fittings and Lloyd-Loom or square-bodied armchairs gave a contemporary look. This was invariably capped by a modern fireplace, replacing the now despised Victorian cast iron and mahogany with sleek, square tiles. The issue of how to create modern styles on a budget was a recurring one in *British Boarding-House*, a leading newspaper for the trade. One modernising tactic was to combine previously separate units to achieve economies of scale and allow at least some modernisation of public rooms. In the Metropole block in Douglas, several small boarding houses were amalgamated to become the Alexandra.[94] The public rooms were extensively modernised in the very latest style but this was unusual.

The Majestic, in Onchan, was another one of the few to spend heavily on improvements that were more than just cosmetic. In 1936 its new owners – a limited company – spent £14,000 on a steel-framed extension to the original Baillie Scott building, which doubled the hotel's capacity from 150 to more than 300 guests. Of the fifty new bedrooms, thirty had private bathrooms. The Majestic company was able to do this on the basis of its large size and dominance of the higher end of the Manx market, for it also owned Fort Anne.[95] Another encouraging sign was the invitation by Douglas Corporation in 1929 to E. Prentice Mason, an eminent town planner, to lecture at the Villa Marina on the improvement of seaside towns.[96] Two years later, they sent out a deputation to study town planning and development in English resorts.[97] The Villa Marina Colonnade was the main outcome of these enquiries. The Boarding-House Association supported this much-needed improvement, but there were many ratepayers who thought it a waste of money.[98] The modern styles of the inter-war period, 'the impact of the jazz age and of chromium plate, reinforced concrete and plate glass, made less impression on hotel design than on cinemas, teashops and dance halls'.[99] Those who could afford such things were not much given to taking seaside holidays. Such development plans as were in hand in the late 1930s were shelved under the stress of war. A shortage of money, labour and raw materials in the post-war years meant that little new building or even restoration was possible. It was not until 1948 that restrictions on the sale of utility furniture to commercial premises were lifted: until then, hoteliers had to buy expensive non-utility items as the government gave priority to families.[100] And as if worries over chairs, tables and beds were not enough, structural problems were also beginning to make themselves felt. Many Victorian speculative buildings, though not flimsy, lacked foundations to modern standards. Because much of Douglas promenade was reclaimed land, a degree of subsidence was only to be expected. In the Loch Promenade, bay windows started to detach themselves from their surrounding walls. In the Drives, dry rot and damp affected timbers, and buildings showed signs of slipping on the sloping ground.[101]

Government and improvement

It had become clear by the 1950s that many boarding house tenants wanted to improve their premises, but were unable to do so. Some landlords were unwilling, others unable, to help. Banks and building societies, aware of its limited profitability, were reluctant to lend to the holiday industry. Lack of access to capital frustrated those who wished to change this 'Catch 22' situation; the first major government enquiry into the visiting industry for many years made this clear. The 1955 Visiting Industry Commission Report recommended a traditional carrot-and-stick approach:

a government scheme of assistance to hotels and boarding houses should be introduced 'on a large scale', alongside registration and grading of premises. As the report noted, many of the amenities and attractions of the Island had fallen into 'an exceedingly bad state of repair' and the Commissioners felt 'bound to record a certain air of apathy and great lack of any sense of urgency within the industry'. Traffic had declined by 3 per cent in only four years, whilst continental visiting had increased by 10 per cent. Many recommendations for better entertainments, passenger transport, and leisure facilities were made.[102] The problem of accommodation had begun to be addressed with the Hotel and Boarding-House Improvement Act (1954), which broadly resembled schemes of state aid which had been proposed in England ten years earlier. Loans were offered at a low rate of interest with repayments over twenty years. But the scheme was not widely taken up. Only eighty-two loans were approved in four years. Seventy of these were for hot water in bedrooms, and thirty-three for extra toilets. Only six new bathrooms were applied for.[103] In Tynwald, the chairman of the Local Government Board stated that the board was 'definitely putting pressure on people', whilst admitting that many applicants were working with old and heavily mortgaged properties, which made bold improvements difficult.[104]

By 1960 alarm was growing, and the government had appointed several more commissions – a sure sign that something was going wrong. The Executive Council Sub-Committee on Hotels and Motels reported in 1961 that the Island had already fallen behind in the market, and warned that:

> Tourists have become more selective
> . . . the whole question of improved

tourist accommodation should be treated as a matter of grave urgency, which cannot admit of further delay.[105]

The demand from visitors was now for en suite rooms and central heating – yet only ten years earlier, many premises had still to install hot and cold water in all rooms. There was also a shortage of single rooms. The Island's eighty-year-old boarding houses had been constructed for families and group visitors. Hoteliers told anyone who would listen that the inadequacy of their buildings was mostly due to the short season, which did not return enough profit to improve them. The Government recommended that inefficient blocks of smaller boarding houses should be converted to more efficient single units. The most economic unit for an hotel was thought to be between 75 and 100 rooms. This, of course, condemned half the industry. But it proved difficult to persuade owners and occupiers to agree to such amalgamations. There were only two examples of major new hotels: the Viking Aparthotel in Ramsey, and the Palace Hotel in Douglas. The latter was jokingly referred to by a popular local columnist as 'the only new hotel to be built in Douglas since the dawn of time', and in many ways he was correct.

As the years went by, comparatively little resulted from the government schemes. The Kerruish Committee of 1967 noted that the 1962 scheme had proved 'totally ineffective . . . private enterprise has not responded, nor has the Government itself taken any steps to ensure action'.[106] Government was only prepared to put up 20 per cent of costs. Tenants remained unwilling to improve premises which they did not own, and to invest time and risk in efforts which

they might easily lose. Equally, landlords were not always happy to allow loans taken out by tenants to be secured on their real estate. Market research into visitors' opinions, carried out by the 1960s, did not throw any immediate light onto the problem. In 1969 it was declared that there was no single thing which visitors overwhelmingly wanted to see improved in their accommodation. Surprisingly, only 12 per cent wanted more bathroom and toilet facilities, while another 8 per cent wanted general modernisation. The survey noted that 'there seems little dissatisfaction with the accommodation that our respondents used during their stay and the suggestions for improvements are not extensive'.[107] The nub lay, as ever, in what questions were asked, and to whom. Market researchers found that the bulk of tourists holidaying on the Island in 1969 were 'mostly those who are prepared to return . . . this loyalty appears to be the most important finding of this survey'. So, the problem was not in keeping existing visitors, who were mostly of social class C1 and C2, but in recruiting new ones. Once again, attention was turned to the question of where the more demanding visitor might stay. Once again, the Island's Victorian boarding houses were under the spotlight. The 1969 Tourist Industry Development Commission recommended gravely that:

Notwithstanding the considerable and commendable efforts of recent years to improve the standard of hotels and guest houses [by this time 'boarding house' had gone out of fashion] . . . urgent and energetic action is still required in this field.

The Isle of Man is competing with other tourist areas where tremendous developments in new hotel construction, and in the complete modernisation of older premises, has occurred in recent years — e.g. the Channel Islands, Ireland and many Continental countries. The Isle of Man must . . . compete on equal terms. For holiday accommodation, the holidaymaker demands standards which are certainly not inferior and preferably superior to those which are enjoyed at home.[108]

The Commission also urged a programme of action that would replace old buildings with new, whilst recognising that this would not happen straight away. New developments radically different from the old town-centre boarding houses were called for, to include 500 self-catering chalets and 125 motel-type rooms, to be built on the edge of towns and in country areas. These were seen as the modern way forward, in contrast to the 'intractable' problems posed by the many small boarding houses which formed the majority of the Island's tourist accommodation. But the larger seafront boarding houses were also under threat, and proposals for the demolition of the Esplanade, Clarence Terrace and Castle Mona Avenue were put forward in the late 1960s, although like many other schemes they came to nothing. As for the chalet plan, only a few were ever constructed. A 1972 report on season extension explained that 'the tourist season in the Isle of Man

. . . limited to the three months of June, July and August . . . is too short to provide adequate utilisation of facilities and accommodation, and thus investment on the Island, particularly in new hotels, has been inhibited. The short season discourages expansion or improvement of facilities'.[109]

The Manx holiday accommodation sector was certainly more traditional than its UK counterpart. In 1976, 11 per cent of UK holidaymakers stayed in hotels, and 7 per cent in guest houses; on the Island, the figures were around 33 per cent and 25 per cent respectively. The old boarding house habit died hard.[110]

The Island's hoteliers became the subject of ever more attacks. In 1974 a director of British Airways went on the record to complain about the lack of en suite bedrooms in the resort.[111] Many smaller or less profitable businesses started to close down. Douglas Corporation became 'gravely concerned' at the number of applications to convert hotels and boarding houses to other uses. The town was losing its tourist heart. Over the previous decade, the number of beds available had dropped from 20,000 to 16,000. The authorities sought to manage the decline through the planning system, zoning some boarding houses for tourism and allowing others to be converted into flats.

As the Island's financial services economy grew, the demand for cheap, open-plan office space could not be satisfied by simply converting old boarding houses. Multinational businesses moving to the Island had little interest in what were seen as run-down Victorian buildings; they wanted purpose-built offices, quickly. The Isle of Man Victorian Society, formed in 1976, was sometimes almost a lone voice in the campaign against indiscriminate demolition.[112]

It was not until the late 1980s and early '90s that the fine Victorian buildings of the promenades began

The full grandeur of the newly completed Central Hotel, 1890s.

to receive the attention that they deserved. Economic development had made urban regeneration a possibility, and the Douglas 2000 initiative worked with the Department of Local Government and the Environment to make a study of the promenade in Douglas. 'Even with the current decline', it noted, 'the promenade is still an important, historic and exceptional example of Victorian seaside architecture.' But much architectural heritage was under threat. The empty Douglas Bay Hotel, already scheduled for demolition, was destroyed by fire.[113] The Villiers Hotel had closed and was under threat of demolition. The landmark Central Hotel had closed, and the Queen's Promenade had suffered major demolition, with a large amount of vacant property awaiting its seemingly inevitable fate.

The Douglas 2000 partnership responded with a number of suggestions. Schemes for the restoration of façades and fiscal incentives to promote the refurbishment of promenade buildings were suggested, as was some controlled redevelopment 'where this would not be detrimental to the character of the seafront'.[114] But

there was not sufficient political will, and economic and social factors militated against an extensive preservation or restoration programme. Hoteliers who were attempting to stay in business surrounded by derelict buildings were often only too pleased to see them go.[115] Indeed, in 1987 the Guest House Association railed against the collapse of the industry, asking publicly how the Government could explain its constant refusal to permit change of use from hotels to offices on the seafront, when offices were going up everywhere else in the town.

Planning policies were violently and repeatedly attacked in the local press, which showed a habit of

Window ornamentation at the Paparazzi Pizza Parlour, Loch Promenade, in 2000.

nostalgically printing old photographs whilst doing little to encourage the preservation of historic buildings. (For example, its reporting of the complaints of those who wished to insert unsuitable PVC windows into historic structures was nearly always supportive). With conversion rarely an option, developers saw demolition as the way ahead. The case of the Villiers demonstrated all too clearly how the land lay. This once-grand hotel had been allowed to fall into disrepair. Its fate followed a well-trodden path, almost a textbook lesson in how to demolish a listed or important building. Various options were discussed for its future whilst the structure became ever more dilapidated as agreement could not be reached. It was a far cry from its centenary in 1986, when manager Steven Dawson had presided over an hotel which was still busy and active, and which had optimistically reported its plans for the future.[116] Hoteliers at many levels found themselves in increasingly impossible positions.[117]

By the summer of 1994, AXA Equity & Law had purchased the Villiers site for £3.8 million, and planned to spend £20 million on its redevelopment.[118] The first section of offices constructed was an airy glass and steel structure that was inoffensive, even pleasant, but which made a poor replacement for that which had gone before. Compared to many new buildings which replaced Victorian boarding houses around this time, the AXA building was a model of quality. Wholesale destruction of the island's astonishing architectural heritage took place at many other sites, especially in the capital. The silence of Tynwald was eloquent. Many elected members were interested in heritage in a general way, but few were prepared to put in place the controls that would have forced developers to stay their hands or create buildings of real distinction. The argument for quality redevelopment was lost in the rush for jobs and prosperity. Not until the late 1990s did the process stabilise sufficiently for hopeful signs to be observed, such as the retention of the façade of the Grand Hotel. But further along Douglas promenade, demolition and unsuitable redevelopment continued. What some might term a risible pastiche of the Victorian style was used for new blocks of flats on the Queen's Promenade, the front being decorated with a peculiar series of balconies borne on oddly tapering pillars. A new shopping centre tried harder, with a slightly better result.

In 1929 it was commonplace to remark, as Ward Lock did, that buildings on Douglas promenade, 'are of uniform design, and have a way of looking always spick and span – a characteristic which, by the way, applies to the whole line of the front.'[119]

Now, this treasure of our patrimony has been thoughtlessly discarded. The architectural unity of the promenade – only a little frayed in the 1960s by the new Methodist church and the boxy Palace Hotel – has been fatally undermined by demolition and a rush for new buildings. These have, for the most part, proved to be an unholy mixture of bland modernism and pastiche Victorian. Prosperity has arrived, but at a price which was low for the developers but high for the architectural quality of Manx towns.

9

Decline *and* change

Decline and change in perspective

Most traditional seaside resorts throughout the British Isles suffered a great decline during the last quarter of the twentieth century and the Isle of Man was no exception. The waning seasons caused deep pain in the Island, and the suffering of those who worked in the visiting industry was no less real than that felt by people who lost their jobs in cotton, steel, or coal. The years of decline scarred Manx society. Many individuals suffered cruelly as their livelihoods seemed to wither away however hard they worked. This makes the experience a sad but important part of the Island's past. The need to escape it profoundly shaped government policy and led the Island away from tourism to become a centre for offshore finance, prompting further big changes to many lives.

Many experts who advise the modern tourist industry think that resorts have a life cycle. They pass through phases of creation, expansion, maturity and failure. The Isle of Man has been used as a prime example of this notion. Its history appears to support the idea that little could have been done by local people to solve the root causes of decline. This was particularly true in the 1970s and 1980s when the root causes were competition from cheap foreign holidays combined with the high cost of reaching the Island. These two factors seriously undermined the profitability of the small hotels. It was hard for the industry to reinvent itself because it had specialised in a certain type of holiday for so many years.[1] Yet despite all the gloomiest predictions, many seaside resorts including the Isle of Man have continued to attract visitors and have begun to reinvent themselves and have not died.

Tracing the roots of decline

Although the decline in Manx tourism became impossible to ignore during the 1970s, there were signs of problems for a long while before that. Business at seaside resorts was often slightly risky but returns had grown less sure long before visitor numbers fell away. The heyday of private investment, when hundreds of boarding houses, a complete rail system and the great dance-halls were built, was almost over by the First World War. By the inter-war period, very few new investments were being made and local authorities found that they had to take on more of the burden of maintaining and improving core public facilities. The returns on investment were no longer high enough to interest the private sector. Public money, therefore, paid for the Villa Marina Colonnade and the Loch Promenade Gardens because the attractions were important to keep many small businesses viable.

By the 1930s, the respectability and orderliness demanded of Victorian holidaymakers was being criticised as old-fashioned and off-putting. Not only

A Victorian trade card advertising the Bowling Green Hotel.

THE IMPERIAL. CENTRAL PROMENADE, DOUGLAS, ISLE OF MAN
Tel. 1656

A woodcut advertising the Imperial Hotel, Douglas, 1930s.

ments.[2] Some blamed the temperance campaigners and other moralisers for making the Island too staid.

Some boarding houses and facilities did begin to change. The more forward-looking proprietors tried to refurbish in contemporary styles, to bring in electric light and running hot water in all rooms and to make their houses friendlier with fewer rules. However, there were other forces at work to which the Isle of Man found it harder to adjust. One was motorisation. As the middle classes began to buy cars and take holidays in them resorts which had grown popular in the heyday of steam felt threatened. It was expensive and difficult to bring cars to the Isle of Man. Yet even resorts on the UK mainland, such as Scarborough and Blackpool, were worried. As early as 1929 they blamed the motor car for taking their high-class patrons away to country holidays, whilst charabanc trips seduced the middle classes. Cars enabled tastes to change. More and more people began to holiday in the countryside and to visit heritage attractions to which the car made access easy. Fortunately for the Isle of Man there were many who were able to take holidays for the first time in these years. Trade lost from the high end of the market was replaced by new customers coming up from below.

attitudes were criticised as outdated – so were the buildings. The boarding houses of Loch Promenade were compared to a 'faded beauty who obtains no effect from her diamonds'. It was reported that some put their lights out as early as half past ten and that this made the Isle of Man seem dull and boring. Ramsey was also called 'melancholy' and lacking in holiday spirit. Its boarding houses had become very old-fashioned and their proprietors had failed to back plans by the local commissioners for illuminations and other improve-

Indian summer

Neglect during the Second World War saw already elderly facilities become even more run down. Some, such as the Douglas Head electric tramway, had struggled to stay profitable for a while and never re-opened.[3] The post-war holiday boom did not bring universal sustained prosperity to resort economies. Problems began to show up in many of the smaller northern centres after the post-war rush had passed.[4]

Although boarding and apartment houses still accommodated 78 per cent of holiday demand, they faced growing difficulties and competition. These included the rising cost of labour, higher taxes, a decline in the average length of stay and also in the social status of seaside holidaymakers. The rise of alternative holidays such as camping, caravanning and holiday camps also took away potential customers.[5] As a result, the 1950s were not so much a golden age as an Indian summer for resorts which seemed in full flower but were increasingly troubled by social change and a hint of decay.[6] The talk in the industry was that seasons were getting worse.[7] Although visitors were still coming to the Isle of Man and their numbers had not declined too much, the buildings and machinery used to run the visiting industry were getting very old. Many motor-coaches bought in the 1930s were still on the roads after twenty years of use.[8] However, some people persisted in denying the problem. When an Action Group was formed in Douglas to try to fight decline, the MHK J. Lindsay Quine railed that:

> We hear of action groups, or pressure groups as they are called, loudly proclaiming that a serious decline has set in and that our national economy is in jeopardy. I do not accept this view, and I affirm most strongly that our Island is getting (everything considered) a good deal . . . there is, and always has been, a hard core of visitors who come to our Island anyway.[9]

The Group was successful in prompting government action. The first major government report into the state of the tourist industry for decades was published in 1955 and it offered a wide range of options for improvements. They included registration and grading for boarding houses and hotels; government grants on a large scale, and the introduction of new leisure facilities.[10] Some facilities could also serve as winter works, it suggested, and these were sorely needed. Though Manx summers were still generally busy, the winters of the 1950s were woeful. In an effort to bring new money in and to make the local economy more diverse the Government began a New Residents policy in the 1960s. It also encouraged light industry and began slowly to develop the Island as an offshore financial centre.[11]

The Government continued at the same time to devote a lot of attention to the problems facing tourism. Market research commissioned in 1969 revealed that existing visitors were indeed loyal, but new ones were not coming through to replace them. The sorts of holidays these loyal customers enjoyed were very traditional. This didn't fit in with the vision of a modernised Isle of Man. The political clout of the visiting industry had produced a weak grading system which was not delivering improvements – its standards were simply 'far too low' according to a Tourist Industry Development Commission report.[12] When some high-flying consultants were brought in by the Tourist Board in 1972 they pointed out problems that many people knew already: the season was too short, there was a loyal but ageing visitor base, and Continental holidays were a real threat.[13] The problem was so pressing because, as the Government's Economic Survey of 1974 revealed, tourism still employed 3,000 people and generated 24 per cent of the Island's total income – perhaps £8

The main lounge of the Savoy Hotel in the 1950s.

The Grasmere lounge, complete with wireless in 1951, though its decor owed much to the fashions of the 1930s.

million. It was, said the economists, simply too big and important a part of the economy to be allowed to atrophy.[14] The Manx Government began to offer loan and grant provisions which although criticised locally were still far more generous than those available in England, where no help was available for most hoteliers.[15] Many of the grants and loans were used to convert uneconomic small premises into self-catering flats, whilst larger boarding houses were modernised into private hotels. It was obvious however that traditional boarding houses were still in vast over-supply for the shrinking market and as a result their numbers fell by half between 1962 and 1975 to only 1,028. The new Palace Hotel was a solitary sign of modernisation, yet its construction on the Coliseum Theatre site only emphasised that there was a crisis not just in accommodation but also in formerly popular seaside entertainments which seemed to have lost their attraction for the public.

A lot of criticism was levelled at the Government, but during the 1970s it annually spent between one third and one quarter of its total revenue on tourism and even began to fund loss-making core tourist infrastructure such as buses and railways. What it could not do, however, was save the many hotels and boarding houses which continued to go out of business. Between 1980 and 1987 the Island lost 303 premises, almost one third of the remaining sector. From providing 12,856 bedrooms it dropped to 9,269.[16] Several of the greatest hotels which had once been solid investments fell into bankruptcy, closure and demolition.

By 1985, penury was staring the tourist industry in the face. An American visitor wrote that Douglas was a 'faded Victorian seaside resort, a relic' and that 'nothing has been added to the Victorian boarding houses but plumbing and, in some cases, neon signs'.[17]

Instructions to visitors, from Demesne Road in about 1971.

Ironically the stagnation had preserved some fine period architecture which began to attract attention from the discerning.[18]

The rise in government intervention

Government intervention became vital to the industry. One of the great ideas of the 1950s which came out of the war was market research. For the first time, companies and governments began to find out in detail

Waverley - *Port Erin* - *Isle of Man*

TARIFF 1968

	Front	Side	Single Rooms
MAY, JUNE	33/-	32/-	33/-
JULY, AUGUST, SEPT.	36/-	35/-	36/-

per person per day

BED & BREAKFAST   21/-   per person per day

BED, BREAKFAST, EVENING MEAL & SUPPER

CHILDREN 20/-   30/-   per person per day

Children under 12 years sharing parents room 25/- per day.   All other children full price.

Booking deposit £1 per adult.   Accommodation 34 visitors.

Cheques not accepted, unless presented four days before departure.

Waverley Hotel tariff, 1968.

Waverley   ★   Port Erin   ★   Isle of Man

TARIFF 1970

ROOM & BREAKFAST   25/- per person per day

ROOM, BREAKFAST
DINNER & SUPPER   35/- per person per day

Children under 12 years sharing room with two adults 25/- per day
All other children full price.
LUNCH or HIGH TEA 10/-
BOOKING DEPOSIT £1 PER ADULT
ACCOMMODATION 34 VISITORS

Cheques not accepted, unless presented 4 days before departure or presenting Bank Cheque card

---

Waverley Hotel tariff, 1970.

what their customers and citizens thought. Resort towns were quick to realise that this might help them. Resorts from Jersey to Southsea, from Weston-super-Mare to Blackpool all commissioned research from companies such as Gallup and the results were analysed by the British Tourist and Holidays Association. They revealed what many feared – there was a huge pent-up demand for holidays abroad. As soon as people could afford them they were determined to take them. Another problem which came into sharp focus was that the loyal core base of satisfied repeat visitors was ageing.[19] In all these areas the Isle of Man suffered more than its competitors. Whilst Jersey gained a 37 per cent increase in visitors between 1950 and 1954, and benefited from its warm climate and the prosperity of the south-east of England, the Island lost 3 per cent and suffered from the declining fortunes of the north-west.[20] The average amount spent by visitors per week – at £18 – showed that the well-to-do were not visiting the Isle of Man. A survey of 1955 suggested that poor standards of service and amenities dissuaded people who had lots to spend.[21]

The effort to make improvements reached a peak when important sites such as Summerland and

A happy crowd at the Waverley Hotel, 1960s.

The Dining Room Milne's "Waverley" Douglas, I. o. M.

The Waverley dining room at the height of its popularity in about 1910.

the Sea Terminal were redeveloped. The trouble was that government money was not matched by any large private work. Major attractions only continued to decline as investors fled from the resort. Facilities such as theatres and dance-halls fell into disrepair, then total dereliction. The promenade centrepiece, the Gaiety Theatre, was threatened with demolition by 1968, and had to be rescued by the state in 1971. With such core facilities going broke it was no wonder small businesses continued to struggle. Their fate was important because in 1969, over 90 per cent of the Island's tourist accommodation was provided in units with fewer than twenty-six bedrooms. The 1969 Tourist Industry Development Commission noted that under the conditions of the

day it could not see many of the small units surviving. There was no way that they could improve, invest in new facilities and afford to pay staff at the rates which would deliver high levels of service.[22]

It was a time when many proposals were made but few came to fruition. The construction of motels, chalet villages, and even the long-hated caravan parks were all discussed. Another suggestion was that the Tourist Board should buy two adjacent hotels on the Loch Promenade, knock them together, modernise them then operate them as a showpiece of the best architectural and furnishing practice.[23] This did not occur. However, by the late 1960s at least three schemes were available to help hoteliers to mod-

The Melrose Hotel TV room, 1969, with a fascinating mixture of furniture and decor from the 1930s, '40s and '60s.

ernise. They were the Tourist Premises Improvement Acts from 1961 to 1969, the Improvement of Tourist Accommodation schemes of 1962 and 1968, and the Housing Advances schemes of 1968 and 1969. The Tourist Premises Improvement Acts made loans of up to £10,000 per property available, but even the Government admitted that the system was complicated and involved, and only 282 loans were made in eight years.[24] The Improvement of Tourist Accommodation scheme, active from 1969, was weighted towards the construction of large, new premises and was created almost solely to make sure that the Palace Hotel got built. The Housing Advances scheme was essentially a government mortgage system covering guest houses

with up to eight bedrooms, and was tailored to the smallest properties which official studies had already shown to be in trouble.

By the late 1960s fewer young people were entering the boarding house and hotel business on the Isle of Man because it looked like such an uncertain career. This left an ageing population of boarding house keepers not only working hard to make a living but also unable to sell up so that they could retire. Cecil McFee MHK pointed out that:

> [Many] proprietors are growing old, many are past the age of retirement

— but their entire life savings have been ploughed back into their premises, and in some instances lost. They cannot afford to retire and some have been near bankruptcy after a lifetime of service to the tourist industry.[25]

Efforts to revive the flagging industry peaked with the very successful Millennium of Tynwald in 1979. This was a landmark event and it pointed to a marketing strategy based on heritage which would become increasingly important. Although numbers fell once Millennium Year was over, by the late 1980s the Department of Tourism could look back on the decade with a measure of optimism. In a memorandum designed to entice investment, it argued that the Island was moving up-market. It also alleged that the tourist sector had earned £2.6 million in 1982–83, but that this had risen to £4.2 million by 1984–85. Air arrivals – indicative of the better off type of customer – were also rising healthily. The problem for hoteliers was that the market was not evenly spread. Smaller businesses, or those unable to modernise, continued to fail. Some large well-modernised hotels were successful, as were some country B&Bs with low overheads and lots of rustic charm.[26]

Unfortunately the problem of attracting investment grew even worse. Many hoteliers found that banks were no longer prepared to lend to the Manx tourist industry, and prospective purchasers for hotels could not obtain mortgages.[27] The Department of Tourism tried to get the Island's banks to take a more positive view.[28] Money for improvements was desperately

needed because the newest Manx hotels – apart from the 1960s Palace – were by then 90 years old. The British fondness for preserving old steam trains, cars and other old machinery did not extend to boarding houses from the same era and they were not seen as loveable antiques.

Planning policies

As guest houses and hotels went under in the late 1970s and early '80s, it was initially the policy of the Hotel & Guest House Association to oppose planning applications to convert premises to other uses. However, in the late 1980s this changed and by 1987 the executive of the Association joined forces with the Manx branch of the British Hotels, Restaurants & Catering Association to change the rules of the Local Government Board. The two associations lobbied for carte blanche to convert any former boarding house to other uses, provided that those who remained in the industry did not object.[29] This goal was not achieved and a lot of tension arose between the planners and the hoteliers.

The row came about because of two different approaches to the same problem. In the past, there had been little tension between planners and the holiday industry. Planning controls were weak and the industry had shown no significant land hunger, changes or growth for a long time. Planning controls, by contrast, had been gradually extended in keeping with modern thinking. The crisis came with the application of these policies to a shrinking industry which was already in trouble and under stress.

During the arguments it was clear that everyone, the Government and the industry alike, was locked

into the troubles of decline. With no clear answers, each body was inclined to blame the other. But both were largely victims of the nationwide decline in traditional seaside holidays and of forces outside their control. It did not stop many bitter words being spoken. The hotel association thought that the Government was 'ignorant' and called its policies 'sinister'.[30] Guest House Association president Bert Quirk sharply questioned the Chief Minister at the 1987 members' meeting. How, he asked, when the Government was all too aware of the decline in tourism, could the minister explain the constant refusals of the planners and his ministry to grant permissions for change of use?[31] Bitterly he recalled the remarks of Walter Gilbey MHK, who told industry representatives earlier that year that Government would not change its policies just 'to save failed hoteliers'.[32]

The planners countered that the tourist industry was viable and that its heartland area needed to be preserved. Enough space, they argued, had already been zoned for office development in non-tourist areas. If a glut of converted hotels came onto the market at low prices, then they could undercut the rents developers needed to earn to finance new buildings elsewhere in Douglas. Other parts of the town, they pointed out, were also run-down and needed attention. Some were much more suitable for the erection of large office buildings than the promenades.

These were new problems for the Isle of Man and there were no precedents to draw upon. The Association's call for total freedom to convert was not met but a gradual increase in conversions and demolitions did begin. The Tourist Board lent its support to changes of use in the Drives area of Douglas and around the Castle Mona because it saw the risk of empty and derelict buildings becoming eyesores and the argument

was eventually won. Over time, this policy extended to the Queen's Promenade, where the giant boarding houses of the 1900s were falling empty. It was not long before demolition began. On a sad day in 1986 the once profitable Grasmere met its fate at the hands of the demolition men. Its past glories forgotten, the demolition was welcomed by neighbours who called it an eyesore.[33] By the 1990s, demolition was racing ahead as the demand for residential land in Douglas grew high enough to make the demolition of old boarding houses worthwhile. On their sites were erected blocks of flats, and even sites of high architectural significance such as the Villiers were sacrificed in the rush for development.

Registration and grading

Some form of registration for boarding houses was mooted by the Chief Constable of the Island as early as 1875. Discussing the Common Lodging House Act with the Governor, he wrote:

> I do think it would be desirable that all lodging and boarding-houses in the towns and villages of the Island should be brought under the provisions of the Act. For I frequently receive during the season complaints of overcrowding, bad drainage, or defective water-closets and boarding house keepers selling liquor without a licence . . . If all boarding and lodging-houses were

Grasmere Hotel holidaymakers in 1953.

brought into the Act, and licensed, the Police would be able to see that they were kept in better order than they are at present.[34]

However little came of his plan and the idea was swept under the carpet for a hundred years. The Island's boarding houses remained free from all but basic taxes and sanitary regulation. Nor was there any scheme to differentiate between the services they offered, or how well these were carried out. The AA and RAC were grading hotels by the 1920s, but the Isle of Man Publicity Board held back from such a politically sensitive process. Even twenty years later, few hoteliers

on the Island thought it worth their while to get involved. Many proprietors argued that it was for the high end of the market and was an irrelevance to visitors who simply wanted a family holiday in homely comfort. The mandatory inspection of hotels and boarding houses was mooted in Tynwald in a 1950 Bill for the Publicity Board, and although it was rejected, over the next few years the topic was not forgotten.[35] Jersey ran a compulsory scheme administered by the States Committee for Tourism as early as the 1950s. By contrast, when the Ramsey MHK A.S. Kelly proposed similar plans for the Isle of Man, the Boarding House Association opposed them and called on all their political allies in the process.[36] In 1951 the Chairman of the Publicity Board and Speaker of the House of Keys

Joseph Qualtrough gave his opinion that although a great deal of talk had been heard on the subject of poor accommodation, a state run inspection scheme was not the answer. Nevertheless the 1955 Visiting Industry Commission made it a key recommendation. The suggestion was not well received by the industry but the report was too important to ignore so a compromise was reached. To ease the burden, the Commission recommended that it be voluntary for the first two years and compulsory thereafter. Opposition to the plan made it even later than expected. Compulsory registration guaranteeing minimum standards was not introduced until 1962.

Registration was a very basic scheme and as soon as it was introduced the Tourist Board had plans to develop a system of grading. Through grading the comforts and services offered by hotels and guest houses won them a certain rank which could be used in advertising and on the door. In the UK it was marked by stars. In the Isle of Man the symbols were keys. Claims were verified by inspectors. Many proprietors violently opposed the scheme at first so it was begun on a voluntary basis in 1963. The voluntary approach did not succeed very well, for only one in four registered premises were graded after five years. By 1970, the Tourist Board was frustrated and was keen to press ahead with compulsory grading. It pointed out that the Republic of Ireland, Northern Ireland, Jersey, Guernsey and most continental countries operated similar schemes. Its surveys showed that only 11 per cent of visitors considered their accommodation to be an 'attractive feature' of their holiday.[37] A team of consultants employed by the Board also thought that the standards were too low and said:

It is a travesty of the objectives of the [voluntary grading] scheme to give the seal of approval to an establishment which is not required to have a bathroom for the use of guests . . . we have been advised of numerous cases where tourists have complained that they had been misled by the fact that official approval had been awarded to premises of comparatively low standards.[38]

The protests of the boarding house lobby had, in fact, been so successful that they had created a nearly worthless scheme. The watering-down of regulations was no good in the long term however and it only delayed much-needed improvements and landed both government and hoteliers in a position from which they later struggled to escape. At the time, however, this did not stop hoteliers and the Tourist Board grumbling about each other. The new regulations led some to say that it seemed 'as if we were working for the Tourist Board rather than the other way round'.[39] The Board tried to soothe the industry's fears by describing a typical grading visit for the Guest House Association newsletter and explaining that the system was there to help not to punish.[40] It reminded hoteliers that the AA and RAC had been inspecting premises for decades and that this had been good for trade.[41] A real historical change had occurred. The freedom of Edwardian hoteliers to benefit from state-funded publicity without having to do anything for it had gone. Some accepted the pressure philosophically. Others did not.

The Summerland fire – a turning point

Another cause for intervention appeared almost over-night. After the terrible Summerland fire of 2nd August 1973 in which fifty people died, the Government acted swiftly and very publicly to improve fire precautions in all local buildings in a measure to restore public confidence.[42] Joy Birnie witnessed the fire from her nearby hotel, the Metropole, but she little realised the effect it would soon have on her own business. The Fire Precautions Act 1975 and the Hotels & Boarding Houses Fire Protection Order 1976 made it compulsory for premises to have a certificate of fire safety compliance without which they could not legally operate.[43] Government grants were available to help with fire precautions and escapes, although many boarding house owners (as ever) thought the scheme too bureaucratic.

Summerland was a symbolic turning point and stands as a symbol of the years of decline. The leisure complex built to revive the Island's fortunes was horribly lost and the hopes of many died with its victims. The cost of subsequent fire precautions combined with other necessary improvements and ever-falling numbers was enough to make many people feel that they did not want

Fire at Douglas Bay Hotel, 2 November 1988.

to continue in the business any more. Bert Quirk, then President of the Boarding House Association, remembers that the aftermath of the fire was:

> Literally the death knell for tourism on the Island; certainly the small ones. They didn't have enough money; grading and classification came in and that really was a lot of money . . . that was where we stuck and they [the small operators] were getting older then. On registration and grading, while we weren't at loggerheads with the Tourist Board, we were certainly worried about what was happening to the trade. Because no matter what happened the Tourist Board were going to make it compulsory and that was going to be it, you know. So we as an Association had to just try and ease it in as best we could.[44]

Although by the 1980s the Association still hoped to influence policy and negotiate a better position for its members, it was trapped between a decreasing customer base and an increasingly interventionist government which wanted to see its costly assistance to tourism bearing fruit. The years of decline were a painful time to wear the chain of office.

New hope

Since 1965, the number of foreign holidays taken by the British has risen from five million to twenty-seven million per year. Many of these were at the cost of older home resorts like the Isle of Man which were hit hard.[45] Fortunately, the Isle of Man was able to use its greatest asset, self-government, to turn its fortunes around. When it began a series of tax and financial reforms in 1985 the Island became attractive as an offshore business centre. This had implications for all areas of life including guest houses and hotels. Business people began to use its hotels. Many liked the Island very much but most thought that its accommodation was very old-fashioned and run down.[46] This was not surprising, for the sector had long catered for modestly priced family holidays and was not really adapted to corporate users. However, a new opportunity had arrived for those hoteliers who could find the money to redevelop. They could tap into a new and potentially lucrative market all year round. The bold refurbishment of the Empress Hotel in 1989 was the first sign of the changes and it was quickly followed by others.[47] It was a time of fresh hope, especially for the larger hotels which had barely survived. The efforts of many small family-run establishments to cater for modern tastes were also bearing fruit and the decline in the holiday market seemed to have slowed down.

There was a remarkable surge in prosperity. New jobs were created and average wages rose dramatically. The tourist industry was not saved by this alone but it certainly gained a lot more than it dared to hope. A journalist from the London *Independent* newspaper recently wrote:

If my grandmother (a regular Isle of Man visitor around 1910) was standing on the prom in Douglas, she would still recognise the place. But just a few streets away are the new office blocks that house the outposts of nearly every one of the UK's leading financial institutions . . . a mini City of London tucked away up the back streets.[48]

Within this brave new world, many hotels and bed and breakfast establishments still cater for holidaymakers. Some come for a traditional bucket and spade holiday. Others take short breaks, walking holidays, or explore the fascinating local heritage. The changes have brought prosperity but have also brought new tensions, just as the brand-new tourist industry did in the late nineteenth century. Then, as now, a time of great economic and social change saw the decay of old certainties, a rise in immigration and a faster pace of life. Then, the Victorian ideology of faith in progress and the value of modernity pushed aside doubts, as did the possibility of making lots of money. Yet the boomers of a century ago left all sorts of problems for their successors. Some people ask the same questions about the changes of today. Has the Island sold out? Has it lost even more of its sense of place? Where should it go from here? The debate is not just about money. Within it are issues of cultural identity, national pride, heritage and political power. The answers will only become clear with time.

Farewell Mona's Isle, c.1890s, from a Board of Advertising Official Guide.

Notes

Introduction

1 The classic work on the subject is Walton, J.K. (1983), *The English Seaside Resort: A Social History 1750–1914*, Leicester University Press. This detailed study and other works by Walton are essential reading for anyone who wants to take a deeper look at the subject, which this simplified account has no space to cover.

2 *Isle of Man Weekly Times*, evidence of Douglas Town Clerk, 29th March 1919, p. 7.

3 Loch to Home Department, November 1873, MNH Lib. 9845.

4 *Porter's Directory for the Isle of Man* (1889), p. 12.

5 Ibid.

6 'Public Companies in the Isle of Man', in *Brown's Isle of Man Directory* (1889), pp. 226–8.

7 *Isle of Man Examiner*, 20th July 1872, p. 3.

8 Robinson, V. and McCarroll, D. (eds.) (1980), *The Isle of Man, Celebrating a Sense of Place*, Liverpool University Press.

9 Walton, J.K. (2000), *The British Seaside: Holidays and Resorts in the Twentieth Century*, Manchester University Press, p. 154, citing V.S. Pritchett.

10 Caley, J.M. (1996), *Isle of Man Summer Passenger Arrivals 1887 to the Present*, Douglas, Isle of Man Treasury, Economic Affairs Division.

11 Kniveton, G., Forster, R., Kelly, R., Slack, S. and Cowin, F. (1995), *Centenary of the Borough of Douglas, Isle of Man, The Manx Experience*, pp. 144–5. There were many alterations and extensions as well as some conversion of other premises into hotels, most notably the Majestic on Onchan Head.

Chapter 1

1 Aylen, T., 'The Hydro Hotel and Boarding House' (c.1910), advertising broadsheet, Guard collection.

2 Interview with Violet Bridson.

3 Interview with Vanda Dudley.

4 Ibid.

5 Ibid.

6 Walton, J. (1978), *The Blackpool Landlady: A Social History*, Manchester University Press, p. 4.

7 Interview with Terry Cringle.

8 Interview with Vanda Dudley.

9 Ibid.

10 Interview with Muffett Tarrant.

11 Interviews with Jennifer Leece and Vanda Dudley.

12 Interview with Violet Bridson.

13 Interview with Bert Quirk.

14 Interview with Elsie Wegener.

15 Ibid.

16 Interview with June Hope.

17 Interview with Bert Quirk.

18 Interview with Maureen Quirk.

19 Interview with Sheilagh Barlow.

20 Advertisement for Imperial Machine Co., *Hotel Management*, January, 1955, (remnant in private collection) p. 82.

21 Interview with Rosalia Black.

22 Interview with Elsie Wegener.

23 *Hotel*, June 1936, p. 292.

24 The design historian Adrian Forty states: 'The manufacturers' illustrations of cookers, with ovens brimming with roasts, soufflés and other dishes, while smartly-dressed women stood idly by, suggested that these were magical cooking machines with the capacity to deliver ready-cooked meals by some process of immaculate conception', in Forty, A. (1986), *Objects of Desire*, London, Thames and Hudson, p. 209.

25 Interview with Elsie Wegener.

26 Schlosser, E. (2001), *Fast Food Nation*, London, Penguin.

27 Interview with Gordon Birnie.

28 Interview with Brian King.

29 Aylen, 'The Hydro Hotel and Boarding House' (above n. 1).

30 Interview with Joy Birnie.

31 Interview with Sheilagh Barlow.

32 Ephemera; collection of Mrs Megan Creer.

33 *Isle of Man Weekly Times*, 26th July 1930.

34 Interview with Terry Cringle.

35 Interview with Gordon Birnie.

36 Interview with Elsie Wegener.

37 Ibid.

38 Interview with Beatrice Quirk.

39 *Hotel Management*, January 1948, p. 10.

40 *Official List of Holiday Accommodation* (1948), Isle of Man Publicity Board, p. 1.

41 Interview with Sheilagh Barlow.

42 Interview with Hilary Guard.

43 Interview with Muriel Cottier.

44 Interview with Sheilagh Barlow.

45 *Hotel Management*, February 1948, p. 59.

46 Interview with Bert Quirk.

47 Interview with Hilary Guard.

48 Interview with Margaret Hodson.

49 Interview with Muriel Cottier.

50 *Hotel Management*, February 1948, p. 46.

51 Interview with Terry Cringle.

52 T.T. Thurman to parents, undated, c. 1890, MNH Lib. MS 9370/1/1.

53 *British Boarding House Proprietor*, May 1932, p. 13.

54 *Hotel Management*, March 1936, p. 113.

55 Interview with Elsie Wegener.

56 *Isle of Man Examiner*, 6th May 1899.

57 *Isle of Man Examiner*, 4th August 1933.

58 *Report of the Isle of Man Visiting Industry Commission* (1951), Isle of Man Government, p. 12.

59 Interview with Frank Swinnerton.

60 Dana, M. (1932), 'Cook Well and Do Well', *British Boarding House Proprietor*, July, p. 6.

61 Ibid.

62 *Report of the Isle of Man Visiting Industry Commission* (above n. 58), Appendix 8, p. 1.

63 Interview with June Hope.

64 Debate on Isle of Man Publicity Board estimates, Tynwald Court, March 21st 1951, p. 525.

65 Aylen, 'The Hydro Hotel and Boarding House' (above n. 1).

66 Interview with Sheilagh Barlow.

67 *Isle of Man Publicity Board Official Guide* (1930), p.78.

68 Interview with Elsie Wegener.

69 Interview with Muffett Tarrant.

70 Interview with Ivy Kaneen.

71 Interview with Shirley Birch and Jeanne Bell.

72 *Brown's Popular Guide to the Isle of Man* (1878), p. 32.

73 This was one of the reasons why the Manx Milk Marketing Board began to promote Manx cheese, as a way to use up excess milk production out of season.

74 Tynwald Commission of Enquiry into Local Industries (1898).

75 Interview with Breesha Maddrell.

76 Kelly, R. (1988), 'Wish You Were Here', *Manx Life*, vol. 17 no. 6, August, p. 15.

77 *Isle of Man Publicity Board Official Guide* (1930), p.50.

78 Testimonial, used in advertisement for Milne's Waverley, in Quine, J. (1899), *Isle of Man Illustrated*, Bournemouth, W. Mate and Sons.

79 *British Boarding House Proprietor*, May 1932, p. 13.

80 Advertisement for Cunningham's Camp, in Drower, J. (1982), *Good Clean Fun: The Story of Britain's First Holiday Camp*, London, Arcadia Books, p. 17.

81 *Report of the Isle of Man Visiting Industry Commission* (1955), Isle of Man Government, p. 12.

82 Interview with Elsie Wegener.

83 Interview with Bert Quirk.

84 Interview with Elsie Wegener.

85 Hilary Guard, private collection.

86 Interview with Frank Swinnerton.

87 MNH Lib. MSS MD911.

88 Ibid.

89 *Brown's Popular Guide to the Isle of Man* (1878), p. 33.

90 Interview with Letty Edgar.

91 Interview with Ivy Kaneen.

92 Wood, J.A. MHK, 'The Douglas of Yesterday and its Inhabitants', MNH Lib. class 9406, undated – thought to refer to the 1880s.

93 Interview with Violet Bridson.

94 Interview with Harry Watterson.

95 Interview with Terry Cringle.

96 Interview with Ivy Kaneen.

97 Ibid.

98 S.W.W. (1936), 'Furniture in the small guest house: behind the scenes', *Hotel*, January, p. 20.

99 Ibid.

100 Interview with Muriel Cottier.

101 Interview with Terry Cringle.

102 Ibid.

103 *Isle of Man Weekly Times*, 13th Jan 1967.

104 Ibid.

105 Interview with Ron Needham.

106 Interview with John and Carmel Sherlock.

107 Interview with Bert and Maureen Quirk.

108 Interview with Maureen Quirk.

109 Interview with Elsie Wegener.

110 *British Boarding House Proprietor*, 1948 various issues.

111 Interview with Terry Cringle.

Chapter 2

1 See for example the case of National Insurance evasion in Empire Terrace in *Isle of Man Examiner*, 22nd September 1933, p. 9.

2 *Hotel & Boarding House*, November 1936, p. 668.

3 *Isle of Man Guide* (1910), Isle of Man Board of Advertising.

4 S.W.W. (1935), *Hotel & Boarding House Management for Small Establishments*, London, Blandford Press, p. 27.

5 Ibid. p. 31.

6 *Hotel*, January 1935, p. 22.

7 S.W.W., *Hotel & Boarding House Management* (above n. 4), p. 29.

8 Shaw, G. and Williams, A. (1997), 'The private sector: tourism entrepreneurship – a constraint or resource?', in *The Rise and Fall of British Coastal Resorts: A Cultural and Economic Perspective*, London, Mansell (Cassell).

9 Interview with Terry Cringle.

10 Interview with Violet Bridson.

11 See interview with Muffett Tarrant for an excellent example of such a chain of recruitment.

12 Interview with Muriel Cottier.

13 *Guide to the Isle of Man* (1913), Douglas Advertising Committee, MNH Lib. B266/6.

14 Interview with Susan Gowing.
15 Interview with Violet Bridson.
16 Interview with Rosalia Black: 'It was just something you did, and I don't remember really learning anything. You knew it, you'd been brought up with it, so you knew it already.'
17 SWW *Hotel and Management*.
18 *Convincing Arguments for the UK Hospitality Industry* (1999), British Hospitality Association.
19 Interview with Bea Quirk.
20 *Hotel Management*, February 1956, p. 15.
21 IoMHGHA, Exec. minutes, 2nd Dec 1986.
22 Advertising poster (c.1987) for Guild Sound and Vision training videos: 'Are You Serving Yourself', Quirk papers.
23 Interview with Susan Gowing.
24 *Commission on Local Industries Report 2: Agriculture and Other Industries* (1900), Isle of Man Government, p. 6.
25 *Hotel*, February 1936, p 70.
26 Ibid.
27 Interview with Muriel Cottier.
28 Interview with Harry Watterson.
29 *Hotel*, August 1936, p. 466.
30 Interview with Muffett Tarrant.
31 Interview with Ivy Kaneen.
32 Interview with Ronnie and Mary Rigby.
33 Ibid.
34 Interview with J.H. Clague.
35 Interview with Muriel Cottier.
36 Interview with Margaret Hodson.
37 Interview with Sheilagh Barlow.
38 Interview with Hilary Guard.
39 Interview with Bert Quirk.
40 S.W.W. (1936), 'Furniture in the small guest house: behind the scenes', *Hotel*, January, p. 20.
41 Of which sixteen slept in. Interview with Beatrice Quirk.
42 Interview with Terry Cringle.
43 Interview with Frank Swinnerton.
44 Interview with Letty Edgar.
45 Interview with Violet Bridson.
46 Interview with Ronnie Rigby.
47 Ibid.
48 Interview with Rosalia Black (née Raineri).
49 Interview with Frank Swinnerton.
50 Interview with Hilary Guard.
51 Interview with Muffet Tarrant.
52 Ibid.
53 Interview with Ron Needham.
54 Ibid.
55 Interview with Muriel Cottier.
56 Interview with Rosalia Black.
57 Wilkinson, T.W. (1936), 'Slaves of the Seaside', *Tit Bits*, 25th July, p. 18.
58 Interview with Harry Watterson.
59 Interview with Violet Bridson.
60 Ibid.
61 Interview with J.H. Clague.
62 Interview with Sheilagh Barlow.
63 Interview with Muriel Cottier.
64 Interview with Violet Bridson.
65 Interview with Olive McFee.
66 Belvedere Hotel Papers, chef's contract, 25th February 1955, MNH Lib. box 9966.
67 *Monthly Report of the Hotels & Restaurants Association of Great Britain* (1926), December, vol. 13, no. 12, pp. 251–2.
68 Ibid.
69 *Hotel*, February 1936.
70 Interview with Rosalia Black.
71 *The Times*, March 1949, cited in *Journal of the British Hotels & Restaurants Association*, April 1954, vol. 1, no. 9, p. 547.
72 Interview with Terry Cringle.
73 *Hotel Management*, February 1956, p 37.
74 *Isle of Man Weekly Times*, 23rd August 1930, p. 9.
75 *Isle of Man Weekly Times*, 5th August 1939, p. 4.
76 *Isle of Man Weekly Times*, 26th August 1939, p. 13.
77 Interview with Muriel Cottier.
78 Ibid.
79 *Isle of Man Weekly Times*, 9th September 1927, p. 5.
80 Greenwood, W. (1933), *Love on the Dole*, cited in

Williams and Shaw (eds.) (1997), *The Rise and Fall of British Coastal Resorts*, Thomson Learning, p. 1.

81 Greenwood, W. (1933), *Love on the Dole*, 1993 Vintage edition, p. 121.

82 Interview with Letty Edgar.

83 Broome, D. (1939), 'Sketch of Douglas Boarding House Life', *Isle of Man Weekly Times*, 29th July, p. 13.

84 Interview with Margaret Hodson.

85 Interview with Maureen Quirk.

86 Interview with Shirley Birch and Jeanne Bell.

87 Interview with Carmel Sherlock.

88 Interview with Ron Needham.

Chapter 3

1 For a scholarly exposition of this subject, see Walton, J. (1978), *The Blackpool Landlady: A Social History*, Manchester University Press, ch. 6: 'Making ends meet'.

2 *Mona's Herald*, 26th December 1906, p. 1.

3 Ducker, James, President of Boarding House Association, in Minutes of Evidence given to the IoM Constitutional Committee (1912), vol. II, pp. 279–280, MNH Lib. D151/23x.

4 Taylor, D. and Bush, D. (1974), *The Golden Age of British Hotels*, London, Northwood, p. 29.

5 Walton, *The Blackpool Landlady* (above n. 1), p. 84.

6 See for example *Isle of Man Times*, 19th November 1890.

7 *Isle of Man Weekly Times*, 3rd March 1951, p. 2.

8 S.W.W. (1935), *Hotel and Boarding House Management for Small Establishments*, London, Blandford Press, p. 9.

9 *Hotel*, February 1935, p. 1.

10 Morgan, N. and Pritchard, A. (1999), *Power and Politics at the Seaside*, University of Exeter Press, p. 55. Morgan notes: 'This lack of a business culture, industry experience and an entrepreneurial base, however, holds severe implications.'

11 Walton, *The Blackpool Landlady* (above n. 1), p. 122.

12 *Isle of Man Weekly Times*, 24th February 1967, p. 5.

13 Ducker, Minutes of Evidence (above n. 3).

14 S.W.W. (1936), 'Combating the Insect Pest in Hotels', *Hotel*, February, p. 66.

15 Belvedere Hotel Papers, 25th February 1956, MNH Lib.

16 Bond to Jackson, 1st July 1955, Belvedere Papers, file 6.

17 Jackson to unnamed landlord (carbon copy letter), 20th November 1954, Belvedere Papers, file 7.

18 Various 1950s hotel trade advertising leaflets, Belvedere Papers.

19 See for example Mrs Watterson, *Guide to the Isle of Man* (1913), Douglas Advertising Committee, MNH Lib. B266/6, p. 66.

20 Interview with Letty Edgar.

21 Norris, S. (1938), *Manx Memories and Movements*, 1994 reprint of third edition, Douglas, Manx Heritage Foundation.

22 *Isle of Man Times*, 19th November 1910, p. 1.

23 Inglis, F. (2000), *The Delicious History of the Holiday*, London, Routledge, p. 52.

24 'Tariff' and 'Reservations' (trade jottings), *Hotel*, February 1936, p. 76.

25 Walton, *The Blackpool Landlady* (above n. 1), p. 93.

26 Herbert, A. (1909), *The Isle of Man*, London, John Lane, Bodley Head, p. 169.

27 *Isle of Man Times*, 8th June 1872, p. 4.

28 Advertising circular letter (1926), Kane's Falcon Cliff Hotel, MNH Lib. B240/11x.

29 *Isle of Man Official Guide, (1908)*.

30 Kniveton, G., Forster, R., Kelly, R., Slack, S. and Cowin, F. (1995), *Centenary of the Borough of Douglas*, Isle of Man, The Manx Experience, p. 23.

31 *Isle of Man Times*, 2nd January 1892, p. 4.

32 Ducker, James, Minutes of Evidence to Home Office Commission on Manx Reforms (1911), in scrapbook of W. Cubbon, p. 223, MNH Lib. D151/30x. Cubbon notes: 'this is a selfish and one-sided view by a Scottish boarding-house keeper'.

33 Interview with Frank Swinnerton.

34 *Isle of Man Examiner*, 21st December 1928, p. 4.

35 *Isle of Man Times*, 19th November 1910, p. 11.
36 'Bertie' (pseudonym) (1888), *Exit Care: The Sick Boarding House Keeper*, British Library, rare books 011652.de.4.
37 *Isle of Man Examiner*, 4th August 1933, p. 5.
38 *St Andrew's Signal*, No. 9, September 1902, single sheet, obverse, MNH Lib. MS 10302.
39 Interview with Violet Bridson.
40 Aylen family not present on Isle of Man in all-Island list of surnames in the 1881 census. First mentioned in 1891 census as resident at 31 Loch Promenade. Also listed in *Brown's Isle of Man Directory* (1894), p. 331.
41 Information regarding Metropole from Peter Kelly.
42 Schedule of property attached to the will of Alexander Gill (1919), Rolls Office, Douglas, Isle of Man.
43 The Hydro Limited (1922), company file, registry no. 404, MNH Lib.
44 Register of The Hydro Limited, created 1922, dissolved 1965.
45 The Hydro Limited (1922), company file, registry no. 404, MNH Lib.
46 Ibid.
47 Ibid.
48 The Hydro Limited (1959), company file, registry no. 1470.
49 Information from Hilary Guard.
50 Ibid.
51 The Hydro Limited (1959), company file, registry no. 1470.
52 Ibid.
53 Ibid. 18th November 1891, p. 3. *Advertising the Island*, Official Tynwald Report
54 *Isle of Man Times*, 14th August 1869, p. 6 and 1st September 1869.
55 *Isle of Man Times*, 8th June 1872, p. 4.
56 *Isle of Man Times*, 2nd January 1892, p. 3.
57 *Isle of Man Times*, 14th April 1900, licensing court.
58 Taylor and Bush, *The Golden Age of British Hotels* (above n. 4), p. 141.
59 *Isle of Man Guide* (1913), Isle of Man Board of Advertising.
60 *Isle of Man Times*, 15th March 1919, p. 4.
61 *Isle of Man Weekly Times*, 29th March 1919, p. 3.
62 Isle of Man Board of Advertising Accommodation List (1920).
63 S.W.W., *Hotel & Boarding House Management* (above n. 8), pp. 76–77.
64 Caley, J.M. (1996), *Isle of Man Summer Passenger Arrivals 1887 to the Present*, Douglas, Isle of Man Treasury, Economic Affairs Division.
65 *Isle of Man Weekly Times*, 25th March 1932, p. 8.
66 *Accommodation Guide* (1930), Isle of Man Publicity Board, MNH Lib. B266/4g.
67 *Isle of Man Examiner*, 12th May 1933, p. 3.
68 *Isle of Man Weekly Times*, 19th July 1930, p. 4.
69 *Hotel*, February 1935.
70 Brown, M. and Winyard, S. (1975), *Low Pay in Hotels and Catering*, London, Low Pay Unit, p. 2.
71 Ibid. p. 1.
72 Ibid. p. 9.
73 Ibid. p. 28.
74 *Isle of Man Examiner*, 18th January 1957, p. 1.

Chapter 4

1 Belchem, J. (1999), 'The Isle of Man 1830–1880', in *A New History of the Isle of Man*, Liverpool University Press, p. 70. With thanks to Prof. Belchem for his most helpful guidance.
2 *The Licensing Laws: Report of the Tynwald Court Committee* (1894), Tynwald, p. 3.
3 Ibid. p. 2.
4 Papers of the Isle of Man Temperance Association, 1845–1849, MNH Lib. MD17.
5 Harrison, J.F.C. (1990), *Late Victorian Britain*, London, Fontana, p. 156.
6 Cunningham, H. (1990), 'Leisure and Culture', in *The Cambridge Social History of Britain 1750–1950*, Cambridge University Press, p. 299.
7 Franklin, A.G.F., 'The Independent Order of Rechabites in the Isle of Man', Liverpool University MA dissertation 1999, p. 25.

8 Cited in Franklin, *Rechabites* (above n. 7), p. 26.

9 *Isle of Man Times*, 29th May 1894, p. 2.

10 Ibid.

11 Rev. J.S. Ayre even claimed that seven-eighths of the Manx revenues were obtained through taxing the liquor traffic in his 1894 broadside 'Liquor Traffic in the Isle of Man', MNH Lib. D36.

12 *The Licensing Laws* (above n. 2), p. 3.

13 Winterbottom, D. (1999), *Governors of the Isle of Man since 1765*, Douglas, Manx Heritage Foundation, p. 109.

14 *Isle of Man Times*, 29th May 1894, p. 2.

15 Franklin, *Rechabites* (above n. 7), p. 26; *The Times* [of London], 19th June 1894, p. 6 and 9th November 1894, p. 7.

16 Brandon, P. (1991), *Thomas Cook: 150 years of Popular Tourism*, London, Secker and Warburg, p. 26.

17 Ibid.

18 Drower, J. (1982), *Good Clean Fun: The Story of Britain's First Holiday Camp*, London, Arcadia Books, p. 35.

19 *Debates in the Isle of Man Legislature* (1888), vol. III, pp. 306–307.

20 'Return of the number of permits to boarding houses in Douglas for the sale of beer issued for the period commencing 1st May 1897' (December 1897), Douglas Constabulary, MNH Lib. D36/5x/6114.

21 Franklin, *Rechabites* (above n. 7), p. 27.

22 *Debates in the Isle of Man Legislature* (1897), vol. VIV, p. 140.

23 *Isle of Man Weekly Times*, 21st April 1900, p. 4; *Isle of Man Weekly Times*, 29th March 1919, p. 7; *Report of the Isle of Man Licensing Commission* (1959), p. 10.

24 *Isle of Man Examiner Annual* 1930, p. 79.

25 *Isle of Man Weekly Times*, 5th August 1939, p. 4.

26 *Isle of Man Weekly Times*, 12th August 1939, p. 5.

27 *Isle of Man Examiner Annual* 1930, p. 91.

28 *Isle of Man Weekly Times*, 1st July 1939, p. 4.

29 *Isle of Man Examiner Annual* 1952, p. 177.

30 Official list of holiday accommodation 1948, Isle of Man Publicity Board, p.1.

31 *Report of the Isle of Man Licensing Commission* (1959), p. 11.

32 Allegation of R.B. Moore, Attorney-General, in *Report of the Isle of Man Licensing Commission* (1959) p. 67.

33 'Advertising the Island' (1894), Tynwald Committee, MNH Lib. B266/2x, p.ii.

34 Annual Report 1894 p. 2; Annual Accounts 1894.

35 Bailey, P. (1978), *Leisure and Class in Victorian England: Rational Recreation and the Contest for Control*, London, Routledge; P. Bailey (1979), 'Will the real Bill Banks Please Stand Up?', *Journal of Social History*, XII; G. Steadman-Jones (1983), *Languages of Class: Studies in English Working Class History, 1832–1982*, Cambridge University Press.

36 Rippon, Rev. T. (1874), *The Morals of Douglas, What is the Remedy?*, Clucas & Fargher, privately printed p.19.

37 *Isle of Man Times*, 2nd September 1894.

38 'Libellous aspersions on Douglas', *Isle of Man Times*, 14th April 1900, p. 7.

39 Ibid.

40 Perkin, H.J. (1975–6), 'The Social Tone of Victorian Seaside Resorts of the North-West', *Northern History*, vol. 11, p. 180.

41 *Isle of Man Weekly Times*, 19th July 1930, p. 6.

42 Drower, *Good Clean Fun* (above n. 18), p. 12.

43 Ibid. p. 14.

44 Ward, D. and Hardy, C. (1984), *Arcadia for All*, London, Mansell.

45 Cited in Caley, J.M. (1996), *Isle of Man Summer Passenger Arrivals 1887 to the Present*, Douglas, Isle of Man Treasury, Economic Affairs Division, p. 2.

46 Evidence of Attorney-General, in minutes of meeting of Imperial Contributions Committee, Douglas, 8th July 1925, MNH Lib. 9982.

47 Norris, S. (1938), *Manx Memories and Movements*, 1994 reprint of third edition, Douglas, Manx Heritage Foundation, p. 147.

48 Shepherd, J. (1994), *The Life and Times of the Steam Packet*, Pentlepoir, Ferry Publications, p. 24.

49 Minutes of meeting of ICC (above n. 46).

50 Norris, *Manx Memories and Movements* (above n. 47), p. 161.

51 Cresswell, Y.M. (ed.) (1994), *Living With the Wire*, Douglas, Manx National Heritage, p. 3.

52 Ibid p. 11.

53 Norris, *Manx Memories and Movements* (above n. 47), p. 151.

54 Dyson and Thomas, circular letter dated 26th April 1915, MNH Lib. D151/29x.

55 Ibid.

56 Hargreaves, T., 'The Development of the Seaside Hotel in Great Britain from 1730 to the present day', Manchester University MA dissertation 1977, p. 78.

57 Resolution of Boarding and Lodging House Keepers Women's League, 12th May 1915, MNH Lib. D151/29x.

58 Minutes of meeting of ICC (above n. 46).

59 Norris, *Manx Memories and Movements* (above n. 47), p. 159.

60 Ibid p. 286.

61 Ibid p. 159.

62 Minutes of meeting of ICC (above n. 46).

63 Norris, *Manx Memories and Movements* (above n. 47), p. 167.

64 Ibid p. 168.

65 Ibid p. 174.

66 Ibid p. 179.

67 Circular letter to Members of Parliament by Samuel Norris, 10th October 1916, MNH Lib. D151/29x.

68 Memorandum to Lord Raglan, 'Redress, Retrenchment and Reform', 5th July 1916, MNH Lib. D151/29x.

69 Circular letter, 'Redress, Retrenchment and Reform', 10th October 1916, MNH Lib. D151/29x.

70 Kniveton, G., Forster, R., Kelly, R., Slack, S. and Cowin, F. (1995), *Centenary of the Borough of Douglas*, Isle of Man, The Manx Experience, p. 61.

71 Norris, *Manx Memories and Movements* (above n. 47), p. 192.

72 Ibid. p. 195.

73 Ibid. p. 227.

74 Ibid. p. 316.

75 *Isle of Man Times*, 15th March 1919.

76 Norris, *Manx Memories and Movements* (above n. 47), p. 326.

77 Ibid. p. 328.

78 Kniveton et al., *Douglas Centenary* (above n. 70), p. 62.

79 Caley, *Isle of Man Summer Passenger Arrivals* (above n. 45), p. 8.

80 Kniveton et al., *Douglas Centenary* (above n. 70), p. 65.

81 *Isle of Man Times*, 15th March 1919.

82 *Isle of Man Weekly Times*, 11th August 1923, p. 6.

83 *Monthly Report of the Hotels & Restaurants Association of Great Britain* (1926), December, vol. 13, no. 12, pp. 251–2.

98 For example, *Isle of Man Weekly Times*, 5th April 1919.

84 *Isle of Man Weekly Times*, 15th March 1919, p. 4, Editorial.

85 *Loch Promenade and Marine Gardens* (1934), opening souvenir notes, Douglas Corporation, p. 9.

86 Witham, G. (1994), *The De La Warr Pavilion*, Bexhill, Pavilion Trust; Hassan, J., 'Environmental revulsion and attractions in the making of the English Seaside Holiday, with special reference to the 1930s', paper given at a Conference on Environmental History, School of Environmental Studies, University of East Anglia, May 2000.

87 Cook, C.P. and Stevenson, J. (1977), *The Slump*, 1979 edition, London, Quartet Books, p. 3.

88 Ibid. p. 55.

89 Ibid. p. 3.

90 'Extension of UK tourist traffic', UK Public Record Office, memoranda, BT159/19.

91 Reprinted in *Isle of Man Weekly Times*, 15th July 1939, p. 8.

92 *Isle of Man Weekly Times*, 9th September 1939, p. 3.

93 Interview with Violet Bridson (edited excerpt).

94 *Isle of Man Weekly Times*, 9th September 1939, p. 4.

95 *Isle of Man Weekly Times*, 16th September 1939, p. 10.

96 Ibid. p. 2.

97 Chappell, C. (1984), *Island of Barbed Wire: Internment on the Isle of Man during World War Two*, 1986 edition, London, Corgi Press, p. 23.

98 *Isle of Man Weekly Times*, 7th October 1939, p. 6.

99 Interview with Violet Bridson.

100 *Isle of Man Weekly Times*, 28th October 1939, p. 10.

101 Stent, R.A. (1980), *A Bespattered Page*, London, Andre Deutsch.

102 Chappell, *Island of Barbed Wire* (above n. 97), p. 31.

103 Ibid. p. 45.

104 Cannell, H. (1996), 'Hardships Caused by the Internment Camps in the Isle of Man During the Second World War', typescript account of requisitioning and its subsequent effects, MNH Lib. 9555.

105 For exact dates, see Cresswell, *Living With the Wire* (above n. 51).

106 Chappell, *Island of Barbed Wire* (above n. 97), p. 89.

107 Hargreaves, 'The Development of the Seaside Hotel' (above n. 56), p. 102.

108 Chappell, *Island of Barbed Wire* (above n. 97), p. 39.

109 Winterbottom, *Governors of the Isle of Man* (above n. 13), p. 193.

110 In Cresswell, *Living With the Wire* (above n. 51), p. 52.

111 International Co-operative Women's Guild Report on Women's Internment Camp, in Cresswell, *Living With the Wire* (above n. 51), p. 51.

112 Interview with Olive McFee.

113 Cresswell, *Living With the Wire* (above n. 51), p. 44.

114 Chappell, *Island of Barbed Wire* (above n. 97), p. 47.

115 Cresswell, *Living With the Wire* (above n. 51), p. 67.

116 Ibid. chapter 11.

117 Chappell, *Island of Barbed Wire* (above n. 97), p. 90.

118 Interview with Mona Atkinson.

119 Interview with Terry Cringle.

120 Chappell, *Island of Barbed Wire* (above n. 97), p. 118.

121 Smith, M. (1998), *Station X: the Codebreakers of Bletchley Park*, London, Macmillan and Channel Four Books.

122 Interview with Pamela Clark.

123 Interview with Violet Bridson.

124 Chappell, *Island of Barbed Wire* (above n. 97), p. 193.

125 Ibid. p. 215.

126 Cannell, 'Hardships' (above n. 104).

127 Chappell, *Island of Barbed Wire* (above n. 97), p. 231.

128 Information from Charles Guard.

129 Shimmin, W.A. (1944), 'Inventory and Valuation of Damages to Furnishings by Alien Internees in Windsor House, Promenade, Port Erin', MNH Social History (Internment) Collection, 12pp typescript. Equivalent currency values from Bank of England historical series: £1 in 1944 equivalent to £19.43 in 1992, Munby, L. (1992), *How Much Was That Worth?*, Chichester, British Association for Local History, p. 39.

130 Munby, *How Much Was That Worth?* (above n. 129), p. 56.

131 Interview with Hilary Guard.

132 Interviews with Betty Kelly and Letty Edgar.

133 Interview with Betty Kelly.

134 Walton, J.K. (1998), *Blackpool*, Edinburgh University Press, p. 149.

135 Ibid. p. 135.

136 Phrase 'please bring ration books' struck out on pre-printed response card, Milne's Waverley, postmark 13th May 1947, Basil Wood Collection.

137 Davison, R. (1945), *Introduction to Holidays: A Study of the Post-war Problem and the Field of Non-commercial Enterprise made by the National Council of Social Services*, London, Oxford University Press, pp. vi–vii.

138 Interview with Bill Watson.

139 Walton, *Blackpool* (above n. 134), p. 138.

140 *Isle of Man Weekly Times*, 6th May 1966.

141 *Isle of Man Weekly Times*, 13th May 1966.

142 *Isle of Man Weekly Times*, 20th May 1966.

143 Ibid.

144 Ibid.

145 *Isle of Man Weekly Times*, 27th May 1966.

146 Ibid.

147 'Seamen's Strike', *Life International*, 11th July 1969, p. 18.

148 *Isle of Man Weekly Times*, 3rd June 1966.

149 *Isle of Man Weekly Times*, 10th June 1966.

150 Ibid.

151 Ibid.

152 *Isle of Man Weekly Times*, 1st July 1966.

Chapter 5

1 *Debates in the Isle of Man Legislature.*

2 Reach, A.B. (1852), 'The Sea Side, and the Summer Sea Siders', *The British Journal*, vol. 2, no. 9, September, p. 106.

3 Walton, J.K. (2000), *The British Seaside: Holidays and Resorts in the Twentieth Century*, Manchester University Press, p. 52.

4 Inglis, F. (2000), *The Delicious History of the Holiday*, London, Routledge, p. 51.

5 Leonard, T.A. (1935), *Adventures in Holiday Making*, London, Co-operative Holiday Fellowship, pp. 19–20.

6 Walton, *The British Seaside* (above n. 3), p. 53.

7 Inglis, *The Delicious History of the Holiday* (above n. 4), p. 53.

8 Caley, J.M. (1996), *Isle of Man Summer Passenger Arrivals, 1887 to the Present*, Douglas, Isle of Man Treasury, Economic Affairs Division.

9 Walton, *The British Seaside* (above n. 3), p. 59.

10 Brunner, E. (1945), *Holiday Making & the Holiday Trades*, Oxford University Press and London, Humphrey Milford.

11 Brunner, *Holiday Making & the Holiday Trades* (above n. 10), p. 17.

12 *A Guide to the Isle of Man* (1824).

13 Interview with Bill Watson.

14 *Isle of Man Times*, 19th November 1890, p. 4.

15 Thomas, V. (1972), 'The Manx and their Isle of Man', *National Geographic*, September, pp. 4–26.

16 *Porter's Directory for the Isle of Man* (1889), p. 10.

17 Kinvig, R.H. (1944), *A History of the Isle of Man*, Liverpool University Press, p. 144.

18 Interview with Bill Watson.

19 *Isle of Man Times*, 22nd May 1894, p. 2.

20 Inglis, *The Delicious History of the Holiday* (above n. 4), p. 43.

21 *Isle of Man Times*, 3rd July 1869, p. 3.

22 Norris, S. (1938), *Manx Memories and Movements*, 1994 reprint of third edition, Douglas, Manx Heritage Foundation, p. 22.

23 Brown, J.A. (1921), 'Amusements in Douglas', reprinted from the *Isle of Man Times*, MNH Lib. B240/17.

24 Interview with Bill Watson.

25 Letter, Braithwaite to Cropper, 8th September 1895, Wood collection.

26 *Hotel*, November 1936, p. 690.

27 *Isle of Man Weekly Times*, 12th August 1939, p. 3.

28 *Isle of Man Weekly Times*, 12th August 1939, p. 4.

29 *Isle of Man Examiner*, 7th December 1928.

30 *Isle of Man Weekly Times*, 16th August 1930, p. 6.

31 *Isle of Man Examiner*, 12th May 1933, p. 6.

32 Walton, J.K. (1998), *Blackpool*, Edinburgh University Press, p. 121.

33 *Isle of Man Weekly Times*, 9th August 1930, p. 11.

34 *Isle of Man Weekly Times*, 2nd August 1930, p. 5.

35 Leonard, *Adventures in Holiday Making* (above n. 5), p. 13.

36 Taylor, J. (1994), 'Kodak and the "English" market between the wars', *Journal of Design History*, vol. 7, no. 1, pp. 29–30.

37 Wood, S. (1999), 'Treasured Island', unpublished diary, courtesy of Mr Wood. Excerpts taken pp. 11–49.

38 *Picturesque Mona* (1913), Douglas, IoMBoA.

39 *Isle of Man Weekly Times*, 30th August 1930, p. 9.

40 *Isle of Man Examiner*, 6th September 1929, p. 2.

41 Interview with Harry Watterson.

42 Ibid.

Chapter 6

1 *Isle of Man Examiner*, 11th August 1933, p. 9 (truncated).

2 *Isle of Man Weekly Times*, 22nd July 1939, p. 3.

3 Belchem, J. (1999), 'The Isle of Man 1830–1880', in *A New History of the Isle of Man*, Liverpool University Press, p. 69.

4 *Mona's Herald*, 1st September 1869.

5 *Isle of Man Times*, 21st September 1872, p. 4.

6 *Isle of Man Times*, 27th May 1871.

7 Evidence of W.M. Kerruish MHK to 1911 Constitutional Commission of Enquiry, cutting in scrapbook at MNH Lib. D151/30x.

8 *Guide to the Isle of Man* (1913), Douglas Advertising Committee, MNH Lib. B266/6, p. 37.

9 'List of wakes . . . for the guidance of boarding-house and lodging-house keepers in the Island', in *Norris Meyer Press Year Book* (1911), published 1909–1924.

10 Annual Report Submitted to the Secretary for Overseas Trade (1947–1948), British Tourist & Holidays Board.

11 Pomfret, J. (1972), 'Wakes Week', in *The Old Peel Line: Poems of Lancashire and the Isle of Man*, Church (Accrington), Hacking, pp. 6–7, MNH Lib. J8/POM [pamphlets].

12 'Advertising the Island' (1894), Tynwald Committee, MNH Lib. B266/2x.

13 *Guide to the Isle of Man* (above n. 8), p. 37.

14 *Isle of Man Examiner Yearbook* (1925), p. 47.

15 Evidence of Attorney-General, in minutes of meeting of Imperial Contributions Committee, Douglas, 8th July 1925, MNH Lib. 9982. Reference courtesy of Kit Gawne.

16 *Isle of Man Weekly Times*, 15th July 1939, p. 5.

17 *Isle of Man Examiner*, 15th January 1932, p.2.

18 *Isle of Man Examiner Yearbook* (1950), p. 179.

19 Minutes of Imperial Contributions Committee (above n. 15).

20 *Isle of Man Weekly Times*, 30th August 1930, p. 6.

21 *Isle of Man Weekly Times*, 2nd August 1930, p. 7; *Isle of Man Examiner*, 4th August 1933, p. 4.

22 *Isle of Man Weekly Times*, 22nd July 1939, p. 3.

23 Interview with Bert and June Hope.

24 Interview with Dollin Kelly.

25 Interview with Sheilagh Barlow.

26 Interview with Letty Edgar.

27 Interview with Bert and June Hope (edited excerpt).

28 *Isle of Man Examiner Year Book* (1928), p. 53.

29 *Isle of Man Times*, 7th August 1869, p. 4.

30 *St Andrew's Signal*, No. 9 September 1902, single sheet, obverse, MNH Lib. MS 10302.

31 Interview with Harry Watterson.

32 Interview with Frank Swinnerton.

33 Interview with Elsie Wegener.

34 Interview with Sheilagh Barlow.

35 Standen, Freida (1992), *Those Were the Days*, Douglas, The Manx Experience, p. 7.

36 *Isle of Man Weekly Times*, 29th July 1939, p. 13.

37 Interview with Maureen Quirk.

38 Interview with Sheilagh Barlow.

39 Griffin, Amanda, 'Power through the People: The Manx Music Festival', paper given at Music & Power, British Forum for Ethnomusicology Annual Conference, London, Royal Holloway, 21st April 2001.

40 Interview with Betty Deans.

41 *Isle of Man Times*, 10th November 1910, p. 9.

42 For example, the dinner dance and whist drive of the Douglas Progressive Debating Society at the Windermere, Loch Promenade, *Isle of Man Times*, 19th November 1910, p. 7.

43 *Isle of Man Examiner Yearbook* (1929), p. 39.

44 Alcock, W.H. MHK for Ramsey, in *Isle of Man Weekly Times*, 5th July 1930, p. 6.

45 Interview with Arthur King.

46 Interview with Alf Duggan.

47 Interview with Muriel Cottier.

48 Interview with Gordon and Joy Birnie.

49 Information from Bert Quirk.

50 Interview with Susan Gowing.

Chapter 7

1 Beckerson, J. (2006), 'Marketing British Tourism 1914–1950' unpublished, PhD thesis, UEA, Norwich.

2 *Hotel & Catering Management*, January 1936, p. 40.

3 *Hotel & Catering Management*, August 1936, p. 489.

4 From the Belvedere Palace in Italy.

5 Quine, Rev. John (1899), *The Isle of Man Illustrated*, Bournemouth, W. Mate and Son. Lord Byron's poem 'The Isles of Greece' mentions the 'Islands of the Blest', a phrase to thrill any Manxman. The adapted stanzas were: 'The mountains look on Marathon / And Marathon looks on the sea / And musing there an hour alone, / I dream'd that Greece might still be free'.

6 *Guide to the Isle of Man* (1913), Douglas Advertising Committee, MNH Lib. B266/6, p. 57.

7 Brown, J.A. (1894), *Brown's Guide to the Isle of Man*, p. 10.

8 *Bent's Isle of Man Business Directory* (1899), advertising section, (no page nos), Birmingham, Bent and Co.

9 *Bent's Isle of Man Business Directory* (1892).

10 *The Isle of Man* (1930), London, Midland and Scottish Railway.

11 *British Boarding House Proprietor*, vol. 7 no. 5, May 1936, p. 233.

12 Quine, *The Isle of Man Illustrated* (above n. 5).

13 Beckerson, J. (1998) 'Advertising the Island', unpublished MA dissertation, UEA (copy in Manx National Heritage Library).

14 *Guide to the Isle of Man* (above n. 6), p. 34.

15 Quine, *The Isle of Man Illustrated* (above n. 5) and *Isle of Man Times*, 3rd June 1891, p. 2.

16 *Hotel*, January 1935, pp. 4–5.

17 Quine, *The Isle of Man Illustrated* (above n. 5).

18 *The Tourist*, vol. 1 no. 1, May 1897, MNH Lib. L6/T1/1.

19 *Bent's Isle of Man Business Directory* (1899).

20 *Guide to the Isle of Man* (1920), Isle of Man Board of Advertising, MNH Lib. B266/4e, p. 19.

21 *A Pictorial and Descriptive Guide to the Isle of Man* (1928), London, Ward Lock and Co.

22 Costing for the likely running costs of a medium-sized boarding house, open for four months in summer, *Hotel*, February 1935, p. 39.

23 *Isle of Man Publicity Board Official Guide* (1930), p. 55.

24 *Isle of Man Examiner*, 4th August 1933, p. 10.

25 *Isle of Man Weekly Times*, 1st July 1939, p. 14.

26 'Combating the insect pest in hotels', *Hotel*, February 1936, p. 66.

27 Betjeman, J. (1951), 'The Isle of Man', in *Portrait of the Islands*, London, Dennis Dobson, p. 16.

28 *Hotel*, October 1936, p. 573.

29 Article on Isle of Man seamen's strike, *Life International*, 11th July 1969, p. 18.

30 The tendency of the industry to leave few records is also manifest in the history of its associations. Neither at Manx nor UK level are there any substantial archives to reveal the history of such trade bodies.

31 Ducker, James, Minutes of Evidence to Home Office Commission on Manx Reforms (1911), in scrapbook of W. Cubbon, p. 223, MNH Lib. D151/30x. Cubbon notes: 'this is a selfish and one-sided view by a Scottish boarding-house keeper'.

32 Ibid.

33 *Isle of Man Weekly Times*, 15th March 1919, p. 4.

34 *Isle of Man Examiner Annual 1949*, review of the 1948.

35 Evidence of C.F. Faragher, Boarding House Association to 1955 Visiting Industry Commission, Appendix 16, p. 8, MNH Lib. 9482. Also evidence of Raymond Milne Barron and C.F. Faragher to Licensing Commission 1956, pp. 50–1.

36 Quirk, B., President's letter in *The Link*, Summer 1987, p.1.

37 IoMHGHA Exec. minutes, 5th Nov 1986.

38 IoMHGHA Exec. minutes, 7th Jan 1987.

39 Ibid.

40 *The Link*, Summer 1987, p. 1.

41 IoMHGHA Exec. minutes, 3rd Dec 1986.

42 *The Link*, Summer 1987, p.2.

43 Ibid p. 2.

44 Ibid p. 14.

Chapter 8

1 King, A.B. (1980), *Buildings and Society*, London, Routledge and Kegan Paul.

2 Craine, L. (1972), 'The Castle Mona Estate', *Proceedings of the Isle of Man Natural History & Antiquarian Society*, vol. VIII (1972–80), p. 21.

3 Forrester, M.T. (1905), *Fort Anne Hotel*, Douglas, Forrester, p. 17, MNH Lib. F71/13.

4 For parallels with Brighton terraces, see Muthesius, S. (1982), *The English Terraced House*, Yale University Press, p. 23.

5 Betjeman, J. (1951), 'The Isle of Man', in *Portrait of the Islands*, London, Dennis Dobson, p. 16.

6 Cited in Fraser, M. (1980), 'George Borrow's Wanderings in Quest of Manx Literature', *Proceedings of the Isle of Man Natural History & Antiquarian Society*, vol. VIII no. 3, p. 297.

7 Cringle, T., 'A Millennium Portrait: Samuel Harris', *Manx Millennium Supplement to Isle of Man Examiner*, January 1999.

8 Chappell, C. (1981), *The Dumbell Affair*, Merseyside, T. Stephenson, p. 93.

9 Ibid. p. 90.

10 Deed of 11th March 1896 between Broadbent and Gill for the conveyance of land for boarding houses (17 Mona Drive).

11 Faragher, M. (1988), 'The Hutchinsons Behind the Square', *Isle of Man Victorian Society Newsletter*, no. 22, p. 2.

12 Craine, *The Castle Mona Estate* (above n. 2), p. 24.

13 Faragher, M., 'The Browns of the Times', MS of paper given to Isle of Man Victorian Society members' evening, Manx Museum, 23rd April 1999, p. 5. With thanks to Martin Faragher.

14 Haviland, A. (1883), *The Essential Requisites of a Seaside Resort: and the Requirements of a Health Seeker; with the Physical Geography and Climate of the Isle of Man*, Douglas, Brown and Son, MNH Lib. B464/3 item 2.

15 Deeds of the Belvedere Hotel, notes from General Registry, Douglas.

16 Silvercraigs Ephemera (c. 1909), MNH Lib. F71/13.

17 Cummings, Rev. J.G. (1848), *The Isle of Man: its History, Physical, Ecclesiastical, Civil and Legendary*, London, John van Voorst, p. 13.

18 Kniveton, G., Forster, R., Kelly, R., Slack, S. and Cowin, F. (1995), *Centenary of the Borough of Douglas*, Isle of Man, The Manx Experience, p. 19.

19 *Brown's Isle of Man Directory* (1894), Douglas, Brown and Son, p. 43.

20 Winterbottom, D. (1999), *Governors of the Isle*

of Man since 1765, Douglas, Manx Heritage Foundation, p.84.

21 Loch to Home Secretary, printed letter bound in confidential correspondence book, 13th Sept 1879, MNH Lib. 9845/4/1.

22 Slack, S. (1996), *Streets of Douglas*, Douglas, The Manx Experience, p. 91.

23 *Loch Promenade and Marine Gardens* (1934), opening souvenir notes, Douglas Corporation, p. 7.

24 Information from Isle of Man Victorian Society secretary Peter Kelly, 18th March 1998.

25 Ibid.

26 *Isle of Man Times*, 30th December 1891, p. 2.

27 Slack, *Streets of Douglas* (above n. 22).

28 Ibid.

29 Ibid. p. 49.

30 Kelly, P. (1994), *Onchan Commissioners' Centenary Directory*, pp. 23 – 24; *Brown's Isle of Man Directory* (1894), p. 110.

31 See architectural plans held by Douglas Corporation.

32 Kelly, P. (1994), *Isle of Man Victorian Society Newsletter*, no. 37, p. 19.

33 St. Quintin, L. (1998), report of paper by Martin Faragher, 'Queen Victoria's Jubilee Year in the Isle of Man', *Isle of Man Victorian Society Newsletter*, May, no. 50, p. 5.

34 Information from Isle of Man Victorian Society secretary, Peter Kelly, 18th March 1998.

35 Deeds of the Belvedere Hotel, dated October 1882, Onchan Parish, number 49, p. 3, clause 2.

36 *Isle of Man Victorian Society Newsletter*, (1997) no. 47, p. 16

37 'Loch Promenade Colour Scheme', *Douglas 2000 Development Partnership Newsletter*, April 1998, p. 3.

38 For the purposes of this discussion, boarding houses and not hotels such as the Peveril or Grand are under consideration.

39 Figures taken from *Douglas Guide* (1920), Isle of Man Publicity Board, pp. 12 – 92.

40 *Brown's Isle of Man Directory* (1894), Douglas, Brown and Son, p. 43.

41 *Isle of Man Times*, 2nd July 1872, supplement issued on opening of Queen's Pier, p. 1.

42 Harrison, A. (1980), 'Richard Sherwood in Manx Politics', *Proceedings of the Isle of Man Natural History & Antiquarian Society*, vol. VIII, p. 335.

43 Robinson, V. and McCarroll, D. (eds.) (1980), *The Isle of Man, Celebrating a Sense of Place*, Liverpool University Press, p. 4.

44 Barnard, J. (1973), *The Decorative Tradition*, London, The Architectural Press, p. 33.

45 Fischer, R. and Walton, J.K. (1987), *British Piers*, London, Thames and Hudson, p. 8: 'Piers . . . were associated above all with a distinctive kind of Victorian seaside holiday, the bourgeois, family centred, sedate, conformist, culturally undemanding fortnight at the coast . . . upon which most resorts depended.'

46 Adamson, S. (1977), *Seaside Piers*, London, Batsford, for the Victorian Society.

47 *Isle of Man Times*, 21st August 1869, p. 5.

48 *Isle of Man Examiner*, 4th August 1933, p. 10.

49 Information from Peter Kelly, Martin Faragher and Victorian Society lectures.

50 Villiers Hotel Company Ltd, 1875 Prospectus, MNH Lib.

51 Kelly, P. (1981), 'The Grand Hotel Complex', *Isle of Man Courier*, 27th February 1981, p. 9.

52 Cowin, S. (1984), 'His Loved Name Will Not Perish',

report of a lecture on John Robinson by Peter Kelly, *Isle of Man Victorian Society Newsletter*, p. 16.

53 Handbill, MNH Lib. B60/3x (3).

54 *Isle of Man Times*, 15th November 1890.

55 Moore, T.M. (1973), 'Architectural and Social Aspects of Douglas', *Proceedings of the Isle of Man Natural History & Antiquarian Society*, vol. VIII, no. 2, p. 157.

56 Taken from a memorial for registration of the will of Alexander Gill, listing the trust's property at 24th May 1933. IoM Government Registry.

57 *Bent's Isle of Man Directory* (1907), Douglas.

58 A memorial for registration of the will of Alexander Gill, listing the trust's property at 24th May 1933.

59 *Isle of Man Weekly Times*, 15th March 1919, p. 4.

60 Will of Alexander Gill, original typescript, p.1.

61 Ibid.

62 With thanks to Trudi Overman, Tynwald Researcher, for this information given on 25th August 2000.

63 Deeds of 17 Mona Drive.

64 Muthesius, *The English Terraced House* (above n. 4), p. 17.

65 *Mona's Herald*, 26th December 1906, p. 8.

66 Ibid.

67 Official list of holiday accommodation 1948, Isle of Man Publicity Board, p.17: Mona Drive average rate.

68 Deeds of 17 Mona Drive.

69 *An Illustrated Encyclopaedia of the Isle of Man* (1997), Douglas, The Manx Experience.

70 Aylen, T., 'The Hydro Hotel and Boarding House' (c.1910), advertising broadsheet, Guard collection.

71 Quine, Rev. John (1899), *The Isle of Man Illustrated*, Bournemouth, W. Mate and Son.

72 Interview with Letty Edgar (quote truncated).

73 *Isle of Man Examiner*, 12th May 1933, p. 6.

74 *Isle of Man Weekly Times*, 2nd August 1930, p. 3.

75 *Isle of Man Weekly Times*, 30th August 1930, p. 1.

76 *Isle of Man Examiner*, auction news, e.g. 5th May 1933, p. 12.

77 Muthesius, *The English Terraced House* (above n. 4), p. 49.

78 Sidley, C.J. (1992), 'Douglas Gas Light Company', in Rodgers, K. (ed.), *Our Heritage: Did You Know?*, Isle of Man, privately printed, p. 23.

79 Barty-King, H. (1984), *New Flame: how gas changed the commercial, domestic and industrial life of Britain 1813–1984*, Tavistock, Graphmitre & Southern Gas, p. 233.

80 Inauguration of the Grand Hotel Electrical Installation, *Isle of Man Times*, 4th June 1892, p. 4.

81 Pearson, K. (1992), *One Hundred Years of the Manx Electric Railway*, Yorkshire, Leading Edge Press, p. 20.

82 Rodgers, *Our Heritage: Did You Know?* (above n. 78), p. 69.

83 Interview with Cyril Mulhern.

84 Their tablecloth is preserved in the Manx National Heritage reserve Social History collections along with other electrical development propaganda from the 1930s and '40s.

85 Luckin, B. (1990), *Questions of Power: Electricity and Environment in Inter-War Britain*, Manchester University Press, p. 12.

86 Ibid. p. 29.

87 Ibid. p. 24.

88 Interview with Cyril Mulhern.

89 Chief Industrial Advisers' papers, Board of Trade, ex. CIA 1941, PRO: BT 156/19.

90 Minute of 14th January 1931, PRO: BT 156/19.

91 S.W.W. (1935), *Hotel & Boarding House Management for Small Establishments*, London, Blandford Press, p. 77.

92 A 'goddess of the silent screen', b.1903–d.1979.

93 Walton, J.K. (1998), *Blackpool*, Edinburgh University Press, p. 131.

94 Kelly, P., Manx Millennium Supplement to *Isle of Man Examiner*, May 1999, p. 14.

95 'Isle of Man Hotel Extensions', *Resort Publicity*, March 1936, p. 160.

96 *Isle of Man Examiner Year Book* (1929), p. 61.

97 *Isle of Man Examiner Annual* (1930), p. 80.

98 Evidence of G.S. Johnson to Local Government Board Commission, in *Isle of Man Examiner Annual* (1930), p. 99.

99 Lindley, K. (1979), *Seaside Architecture*, London, Hugh Evelyn, p. 90.

100 *Hotel & Catering Management*, July 1948, p. 22.

101 Information from Frank Cowin, surveyor and architectural historian, 17th March 1999.

102 *Report of the Isle of Man Visiting Industry Commission* (Davies Report) (1955), MNH Lib. 9482, p. 2.

103 *Report of the Special Committee appointed to consider the Hotel and Boarding-house Improvement Bill, 1957*, IoM Government, MNH Lib. B266/10x.

104 *Debates in the Isle of Man Legislature*, Tynwald Court, 15th March 1955, p. 580.

105 *Report of the Sub-Committee of Executive Council on Hotels and Motels* (Kneale Committee) (1961), IoM Government, MNH Lib. B497/2.

106 Kerruish, H.C. (chair) (1967), *Interim Report of the Tourist Accommodation Committee*, IoM Government, MNH Lib. B266/10x, p. 4.

107 *Research Carried Out by the Isle of Man Tourist Board in the Summer of 1969 and Evaluated by Hobson, Snow & Associates* (1969), London, Hobson, Snow & Associates, British Tourist Authority Library, Hammersmith, old reports store, item Z1/13M, p. 11.

108 *Report of the Tourist Industry Development Commission* (1969), p.24, MNH Lib. B266/1969.

109 *Proposals for Extending the Season* (1972), London and Douglas, McLintock, Mann and Whinney Murray for IoM Tourist Board, p. 2.

110 *Manx Tourism 1977* (1977), Douglas, Isle of Man Tourist Board, p. 35.

111 *Isle of Man Examiner*, 4th October 1974, p. 4.

112 The Manx branch was established on 1st October 1976 by Peter and Ruth Kelly, Ian and Claire Faulds, Ann Harrison and Valerie Roach. Sir John Betjeman was the first patron. *Isle of Man Victorian Society Newsletter*, no. 48, November 1997.

113 *Manx Independent*, 5th November 1988, p. 1.

114 *The Douglas Promenade Study*, Douglas, DoLGE, Isle of Man Government, un-paginated insert (no date).

115 *Manx Independent*, 20th October 1988, p. 6.

116 'The Villiers Hotel: a hundred years on', *Manx Life*, Summer 1986, p. 15.

117 'Demoralised Hoteliers', *The Gazette*, 28th November 1985.

118 'New Future for Villiers Site', *Manx Life*, Summer 1994, p. 53.

119 *A Pictorial and Descriptive Guide to the Isle of Man* (1928), London, Ward Lock and Co., p. 40.

Chapter 9

1 Cooper, C. and Jackson, S. (1989), 'Destination Life Cycle: the Isle of Man Case Study', *Annals of Tourism Research*, vol. 16, p. 387.

2 *Isle of Man Times*, 19th August 1939, p. 11.

3 Goodwyn, A.M. (1978), *Douglas Head Marine Drive and Electric Tramway*, Douglas, MER Society.

4 Walton, J.K. (2000), *The British Seaside: Holidays and Resorts in the Twentieth Century*, Manchester University Press.

5 Ibid. p. 157. The 78 per cent figure is from *Survey of Holiday Accommodation in Great Britain* (1949), BTHB, Home Holidays Division, p. 12.

6 Walton, *The British Seaside* (above n. 4), p. 7.

7 Interview with Dollin Kelly.

8 Ibid.

9 J. Lindsay Quine papers, undated speeches for 1955, MNH Lib. MS 9857.

10 My thanks to Martin Caley of the Treasury for his generosity in providing information on registration and grading as well as many other matters over the last few years. His willingness to share information instead of hoarding it is an asset to the Island's government.

11 Stenning, E.H. (1958), 'A Portrait of the Isle of Man' (fourth edition 1978), MNH Lib. F64/168, p. 132.

12 *Report of the Tourist Industry Development Commission* (1969), IoM Government, MNH Lib. B266/1969.

13 *Proposals for Extending the Season* (1972), London and Douglas, McLintock, Mann and Whinney Murray for IoM Tourist Board.

14 Perrin, H.F.R. and Thomas, J.F. (1975), *Economic Survey of the Isle of Man*, London, P.A. International, Economic Studies Division, for Isle of Man Government, p. 93.

15 Perrin and Thomas, *Economic Survey* (above n. 14), p. 106.

16 Cooper, C., Latham, J. and Westlake, J. (1987), *A Five Year Strategy for Tourism on the Isle of Man*, University of Surrey, Appendix C.

17 Phillip, E.W. (1985), 'Georgian Houses, Green Fields, Great Prices', *Rare Earth*, unlabelled cutting, MNH Lib.

18 Stamp, G. (1985), *The Spectator*, 28th September.

19 Studies in BTA archive, BTA library, Hammersmith, London.

20 *Tourism in Jersey* (1955), London and Jersey, BHTA and British Institute of Public Opinion, for States Tourism Committee, pp. 8–9.

21 *The Importance of Tourism and the Holiday Traffic to the Isle of Man: Summary of a Gallup Poll Survey Held in June 1955* (1955), London, BHTA and Gallup, pp. 2–3.

22 *Report of the Tourist Industry Development Commission* (above n. 12), p.27.

23 Ibid.

24 Ibid. p. 29.

25 *Isle of Man Weekly Times*, 24th February 1967, p. 5.

26 Crellin Memorandum, *The Manx Tourist Industry* (c.1987), IoM Department of Tourism, private collection.

27 'Progress and the L.G.B.', *The Link*, Summer edition 1987, p.11.

28 Bell, A. (1987), 'Article by Mr Allan Bell', *The Link*, Summer edition, p.3.

29 'Progress and the L.G.B.' (above n. 27), p.11.

30 Ibid.

31 Quirk papers: questions for IoMHGHA meeting of 4th January 1987.

32 Quirk papers: speech at IoMHGHA meeting of 4th January 1987.

33 *Manx Independent*, 20th October 1988, p. 6.

34 Chief Constable to Lieutenant Governor, 12th May 1875, MNH Lib. GO 29/154.

35 *Debates in the Isle of Man Legislature*, 31st October 1950.

36 *Isle of Man Weekly Times*, 24th February 1951, p. 5.

37 *Research Carried Out by the Isle of Man Tourist Board in the Summer of 1969 and Evaluated by Hobson, Snow & Associates* (1969), London, Hobson, Snow & Associates, British Tourist Authority Library, Hammersmith, old reports store, item Z1/13M, p. 4.

38 Ibid.

39 'What happened to the season?', *The Link*, November 1977, p.2.

40 *The Link*, Summer 1987, p.14.

41 Ibid.

42 *Sunday Times*, 10th February 1974, p. 5.

43 Hinnigan, J. (1977), 'It always happens to somebody else – or does it?', *The Link*, November, p. 3.

44 Interview with Bert Quirk.

45 'Seaside resorts: the End of the Pier Show', *The Economist*, 28th August 1999.

46 Department of Transport 1986 Passenger Survey findings, cited in *The Manx Tourist Industry* (above n. 26), p. 4.

47 Date given in interview with Empress Staff.

48 Salter, M., in *The Independent*, undated press cutting given to author circa 1999.

All interviews mentioned in the Notes were carried out as part of the Manx Heritage Foundation Boarding House Project, managed by Charles Guard and undertaken by John Beckerson in 1998–9. They may be consulted in both written and recorded form at the Manx National Heritage Library, Douglas, Isle of Man, where the project is deposited under classmark MNHL MS 10422.

Further reading

Barnard, J. (1973), *The Decorative Tradition*, London, The Architectural Press.

Barty-King, H. (1984), *New Flame: How Gas Changed the Commercial, Domestic and Industrial Life of Britain 1813–1984*, Tavistock, Graphmitre & Southern Gas.

Belchem, J. (1999), 'The Isle of Man 1830–1880', in *A New History of the Isle of Man*, Liverpool University Press.

Betjeman, J. (1951), 'The Isle of Man', in *Portrait of the Islands*, London, Dennis Dobson.

Chappell, C. (1984), *Island of Barbed Wire: Internment on the Isle of Man during World War Two*, 1986 edition, London, Corgi Press.

Cunningham, H. (1990), 'Leisure and Culture', in *The Cambridge Social History of Britain 1750–1950*, Cambridge University Press.

Drower, J. (1982), *Good Clean Fun: The Story of Britain's First Holiday Camp*, London, Arcadia Books.

Harrison, J.F.C. (1990), *Late Victorian Britain*, London, Fontana.

King, A.B. (1980), *Buildings and Society*, London, Routledge and Kegan Paul.

Kinvig, R.H. (1944), *A History of the Isle of Man*, Liverpool University Press.

Slack, S. (1996), *Streets of Douglas*, Douglas, The Manx Experience.

Standen, Frieda (1992), *Those Were the Days*, Douglas, The Manx Experience.

Walton, J.K. (1983), *The English Seaside Resort: A Social History 1750–1914*, Leicester University Press.

Walton, J.K. (1998), *Blackpool*, Edinburgh University Press.

Walton, J.K. (2000), *The British Seaside: Holidays and Resorts in the Twentieth Century*, Manchester University Press.

Ward, D. and Hardy, C. (1984), *Arcadia for All*, London, Mansell.

Image sources

Images for the Boarding House Project were collected from a wide variety of sources. These are given below. Images lent by individuals are identified by surname of the collector, except in the case of collectors who wished to remain anonymous. Full details of these loans may be found in the project archive and its detailed image index, deposited at the Manx National Heritage Library (MNH Library). Copyright is acknowledged where this is known. Since many images are of considerable age, the photographers who took them are now unknown. Please contact the Manx Heritage Foundation (MHF) regarding any copyright issues.

Introduction

3: Running a Business and Keeping a Family

4: Hard Times

5: The Visitors

8: Buildings and Architecture

9: Decline and Change

Index